Python Data Analysis

Learn how to apply powerful data analysis techniques
with popular open source Python modules

Ivan Idris

BIRMINGHAM - MUMBAI

Python Data Analysis

First published: October 2014

Production reference: 1211014

Published by Packt Publishing Ltd.
Livery Place
35 Livery Street
Birmingham B3 2PB, UK.

ISBN 978-1-78355-335-8

www.packtpub.com

Cover image by Amy-Lee Winfield (abjure@outlook.com)

Credits

Author
Ivan Idris

Reviewers
Amanda Casari
Thomas A. Dyar
Dr. Hari Shanker Gupta
Puneet Narula
Alan J. Salmoni

Commissioning Editor
Akram Hussain

Acquisition Editor
Owen Roberts

Content Development Editor
Prachi Bisht

Technical Editor
Pankaj Kadam

Copy Editors
Roshni Banerjee
Sarang Chari
Adithi Shetty

Project Coordinator
Shipra Chawhan

Proofreaders
Simran Bhogal
Maria Gould
Ameesha Green

Indexers
Hemangini Bari
Mariammal Chettiyar
Rekha Nair
Tejal Soni

Graphics
Sheetal Aute

Production Coordinators
Adonia Jones
Manu Joseph
Komal Ramchandani

Cover Work
Manu Joseph

About the Author

Ivan Idris has an MSc degree in Experimental Physics. His graduation thesis had a strong emphasis on Applied Computer Science. After graduating, he worked for several companies as Java developer, data warehouse developer, and QA analyst. His main professional interests are Business Intelligence, Big Data, and Cloud Computing.

Ivan Idris enjoys writing clean, testable code and interesting technical articles. He is the author of *NumPy Beginner's Guide - Second Edition*, *NumPy Cookbook*, and *Learning NumPy Array*, all by Packt Publishing. You can find more information and a blog with a few NumPy examples at `ivanidris.net`.

I would like to take this opportunity to thank the reviewers and the team at Packt Publishing for making this book possible. Also, my thanks go to my teachers, professors, and colleagues, who taught me about science and programming. Last but not least, I would like to acknowledge my parents, family, and friends for their support.

About the Reviewers

Amanda Casari is currently a data scientist and engineer in the Seattle area. Amanda received her MSEE degree and Certificate of Study in Complex Systems from the University of Vermont and a BS degree in Systems Engineering from the United States Naval Academy. She has more than 10 years of professional experience, ranging from naval officer, analyst, conservation trip leader to integration engineer. Her research interests focus on discovering attributes of natural systems to update and optimize man-made complex networks. Amanda is passionate about making Mathematics and Science approachable to everyone.

> I would like to thank my family for supporting our journey and inspiring me during this effort, N. Manukyan for all of her data enthusiasm, C. Stone for creative breakfasts, the Carnation Climbing Club, and P. Nathan for kindly encouraging my myriad interests.

Thomas A. Dyar (Tom) is a senior data scientist in the Genomic Sciences group at BD Technologies (www.bd.com), Research Triangle Park, North Carolina, where he develops algorithms to process genomic data in a variety of contexts—from targeted panels to whole genomes—for infectious disease and oncology diagnostics applications. His areas of expertise are scientific programming in Java, Python, and R; machine learning, including neural networks and kernel methods; and data analysis and visualization. His primary interests are in conceptualizing and developing large-scale data-driven solutions using Cloud resources.

Tom started his career in software, developing neural networks and expert systems tools for process control in the aerospace and petrochemical industries. He has also worked on distributed virtual environments for stroke rehabilitation at MIT and automated image processing for high-throughput cell biology experiments at BD.

Tom earned his BA degree in Pure & Applied Mathematics from Boston University and is a member of the ACM and IEEE associations.

Dr. Hari Shanker Gupta is a senior quantitative research analyst working in the area of algorithmic trading system development. Prior to this, he was a post-doctoral fellow at the Indian Institute of Science (IISc), Bangalore, India. He obtained his PhD in Applied Mathematics and Scientific Computation from IISc. He completed his MSc in Mathematics from Banaras Hindu University (BHU), Varanasi, India. During his MSc, he was awarded four gold medals for outstanding performance at BHU.

Hari has published five research papers in reputed journals in the field of Mathematics and Scientific Computation. He has experience working in the areas of Mathematics, Statistics, and Computation. His experience includes working in numerical methods, partial differential equations, mathematical finance, stochastic calculus, data analysis, finite difference, and finite element methods. He is very comfortable with the mathematics software, MATLAB; the statistics programming language, R; Python; and the programming language, C.

He has reviewed the book *Introduction to R for Quantitative Finance, Packt Publishing*.

Puneet Narula has over 8 years of experience in the Banking and Finance industry, but his aptitude and passion for the technology sector has brought him back into the world of data and analytics. Leaving behind a stable career in banking was a very tough decision, but following his dreams was even more important to him. He completed his MSc degree in Data Analytics from Dublin Institute of Technology in 2013 to enter the world of analytics and data science. Currently, Puneet is working with Web Reservations International as a PPC data analyst.

At Web Reservations International (WRI), Puneet works with massive clickstream data from both direct and affiliate sources. The technologies used for the analysis is a combination of RapidMiner, R, and Python.

I want to thank Silviu Preoteasa for all his support and motivation at all times.

Alan J. Salmoni enjoys making sense of data and is the author of Salstat (`http://www.salstat.com`). He has been using Python for data analysis since 2001 and has taught statistics to undergraduates and postgraduates. When not with his family, he spends time generating large statistical models of text for natural language processing.

Alan owns a company, Thought Into Design, which specializes in data analysis and user experience.

I would like to thank my wife, Jell, and my daughter, Louise, for their patience.

www.PacktPub.com

Support files, eBooks, discount offers, and more

You might want to visit www.PacktPub.com for support files and downloads related to your book.

Did you know that Packt offers eBook versions of every book published, with PDF and ePub files available? You can upgrade to the eBook version at www.PacktPub.com and as a print book customer, you are entitled to a discount on the eBook copy. Get in touch with us at service@packtpub.com for more details.

At www.PacktPub.com, you can also read a collection of free technical articles, sign up for a range of free newsletters and receive exclusive discounts and offers on Packt books and eBooks.

http://PacktLib.PacktPub.com

Do you need instant solutions to your IT questions? PacktLib is Packt's online digital book library. Here, you can access, read and search across Packt's entire library of books.

Why subscribe?

- Fully searchable across every book published by Packt
- Copy and paste, print and bookmark content
- On demand and accessible via web browser

Free access for Packt account holders

If you have an account with Packt at www.PacktPub.com, you can use this to access PacktLib today and view nine entirely free books. Simply use your login credentials for immediate access.

Table of Contents

Preface

"Data analysis is Python's killer app."

– Unknown

Data analysis has a rich history in the natural, biomedical, and social sciences. You may have heard of *Big Data*. Although, it's hard to give a precise definition of Big Data, we should be aware of its impact on data analysis efforts. Currently, we have the following trends associated with Big Data:

- The world's population continues to grow
- More and more data is collected and stored
- The number of transistors that can be put on a computer chip cannot grow indefinitely
- Governments, scientists, industry, and individuals have a growing need to learn from data

Data analysis has gained popularity lately due to the hype around *Data Science*. Data analysis and Data Science attempt to extract information from data. For that purpose, we use techniques from statistics, machine learning, signal processing, natural language processing, and computer science.

A mind map visualizing Python software that can be used for data analysis can be found at http://www.xmind.net/m/WvfC/. The first thing that we should notice is that the Python ecosystem is very mature. It includes famous packages such as NumPy, SciPy, and matplotlib. This should not come as a surprise since Python has been around since 1989. Python is easy to learn and use, less verbose than other programming languages, and very readable. Even if you don't know Python, you can pick up the basics within days, especially if you have experience in another programming language. To enjoy this book, you don't need more than the basics. There are plenty of books, courses, and online tutorials that teach Python.

What this book covers

This book starts as a tutorial on NumPy, SciPy, matplotlib, and pandas. These are open source Python packages useful for numerical work, data wrangling, and visualization. Combined, they can compete with MATLAB, Mathematica, and R. The second half of the book teaches more advanced topics such as signal processing, databases, text analysis, machine learning, interoperability, and performance tuning.

Chapter 1, *Getting Started with Python Libraries*, guides us to achieve a successful installation of the numerical Python software and set it up step by step. Also, we will create a small application.

Chapter 2, *NumPy Arrays*, introduces us to NumPy fundamentals and arrays. By the end of this chapter, we will have basic understanding of NumPy arrays and the associated functions.

Chapter 3, *Statistics and Linear Algebra*, gives a quick overview of linear algebra and statistical functions.

Chapter 4, *pandas Primer*, provides a tutorial on basic pandas functionality where we learn about pandas data structures and operations.

Chapter 5, *Retrieving, Processing, and Storing Data*, explains how to acquire data in various formats and how to clean raw data and store it.

Chapter 6, *Data Visualization*, teaches how to plot data with matplotlib.

Chapter 7, *Signal Processing and Time Series*, contains time series and signal processing examples using sunspot cycles data. The examples mostly use NumPy/SciPy, along with statsmodels in at least one example.

Chapter 8, *Working with Databases*, provides information about various databases (relational and NoSQL) and related APIs.

Chapter 9, *Analyzing Textual Data and Social Media*, analyzes texts for sentiment analysis and topics extraction. A small example is also given of network analysis.

Chapter 10, *Predictive Analytics and Machine Learning*, explains artificial intelligence with weather prediction as a running example and mostly uses scikit-learn. However, some machine learning algorithms are not covered by scikit-learn, so for those, we use other APIs.

Chapter 11, *Environments Outside the Python Ecosystem and Cloud Computing*, gives various examples on how to integrate existing code not written in Python. Also, setup in the Cloud will be demonstrated.

Chapter 12, Performance Tuning, Profiling, and Concurrency, gives hints on improving performance with profiling and Cythoning as key techniques. For multicore, distributed systems, we discuss the relevant frameworks too.

Appendix A, Key Concepts, serves as a glossary containing short descriptions of key concepts found throughout the book.

Appendix B, Useful Functions, gives an overview of functions used in the book.

Appendix C, Online Resources, lists links to documentation, forums, articles, and other important information.

What you need for this book

The code examples in this book should work on most modern operating systems. For all chapters, Python 2 and pip is required. To install Python, go to `https://wiki.python.org/moin/BeginnersGuide/Download`. To install pip, go to `http://pip.readthedocs.org/en/latest/installing.html`. Instructions to install software are given throughout the chapters. Most of the time, we need to run the following command with admin privileges:

```
$ pip install <some software>
```

The following is a list of software used for the examples and versions used for testing purposes:

- NumPy 1.8.1
- SciPy 0.14.0
- matplotlib 1.3.1
- IPython 2.0.0
- pandas Version 0.13.1
- tables 3.1.1
- numexpr 2.4
- openpyxl 2.0.3
- XlsxWriter 0.5.5
- xlrd 0.9.3
- feedparser 5.1.3
- Beautiful Soup 4.3.2
- StatsModels 0.6.0
- SQLAlchemy 0.9.6

- Pony 0.5.1
- dataset 0.5.4
- MongoDB 2.6.3
- PyMongo 2.7.1
- Redis server 2.8.12
- Redis 2.10.1
- Cassandra 2.0.9
- Java 7
- NLTK 2.0.4
- scikit-learn 0.15.0
- NetworkX 1.9
- DEAP 1.0.1
- theanets 0.2.0
- Graphviz 2.36.0
- pydot2 1.0.33
- Octave 3.8.0
- R 3.1.1
- rpy2 2.4.2
- JPype 0.5.5.2
- Java 7
- SWIG 3.02
- PCRE 8.35
- Boost 1.56.0
- gfortran 4.9.0
- GAE for Python 2.7
- gprof2dot 2014.08.05
- line_profiler beta
- Cython 0.20.0
- cytoolz 0.7.0
- Joblib 0.8.2
- Bottleneck 0.8.0
- Jug 0.9.3
- MPI 1.8.1
- mpi4py 1.3.1

Of course, it's not necessary for you to have the same version of the software. Usually, the latest version available should work.

 Some of the software listed are used for a single example; therefore, please check first whether the example is relevant for you before installing the software.

To uninstall Python packages installed with pip, use the following command:

```
$ pip uninstall <some software>
```

Who this book is for

This book is for people with basic knowledge of Python and Mathematics who want to learn how to use Python software to analyze data. We try to keep things simple, but it's not possible to cover all the topics in great detail. It may be useful for you to refresh your knowledge of Mathematics via Khan Academy, Coursera, or Wikipedia.

I would recommend the following books by Packt Publishing for further reading:

- *Building Machine Learning Systems with Python, Willi Richert and Luis Pedro Coelho* (2013)
- *Learning Cython Programming, Philip Herron* (2013)
- *Learning NumPy Array, Ivan Idris* (2014)
- *Learning scikit-learn: Machine Learning in Python, Raúl Garreta and Guillermo Moncecchi* (2013)
- *Learning SciPy for Numerical and Scientific Computing, Francisco J. Blanco-Silva* (2013)
- *Matplotlib for Python Developers, Sandro Tosi* (2009)
- *NumPy Beginner's Guide - Second Edition, Ivan Idris* (2013)
- *NumPy Cookbook, Ivan Idris* (2012)
- *Parallel Programming with Python, Jan Palach* (2014)
- *Python Data Visualization Cookbook, Igor Milovanović* (2013)
- *Python for Finance, Yuxing Yan* (2014)
- *Python Text Processing with NLTK 2.0 Cookbook, Jacob Perkins* (2010)

Conventions

In this book, you will find a number of styles of text that distinguish between different kinds of information. Here are some examples of these styles, and an explanation of their meaning.

Code words in text, database table names, folder names, filenames, file extensions, pathnames, dummy URLs, user input, and Twitter handles are shown as follows: "Notice that `numpysum()` does not need a `for` loop."

A block of code is set as follows:

```
def pythonsum(n):
    a = range(n)
    b = range(n)
    c = []

    for i in range(len(a)):
        a[i] = i ** 2
        b[i] = i ** 3
        c.append(a[i] + b[i])

    return c
```

Any command-line input or output is written as follows:

```
$ yum install python-numpy
```

New terms and **important words** are shown in bold. Words that you see on the screen, in menus or dialog boxes for example, appear in the text like this: "Click on the **Next** button."

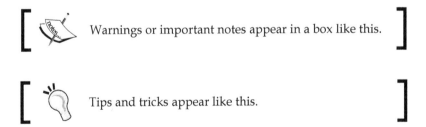

Warnings or important notes appear in a box like this.

Tips and tricks appear like this.

Reader feedback

Feedback from our readers is always welcome. Let us know what you think about this book—what you liked or may have disliked. Reader feedback is important for us to develop titles that you really get the most out of.

To send us general feedback, simply send an e-mail to feedback@packtpub.com, and mention the book title via the subject of your message.

If there is a topic that you have expertise in and you are interested in either writing or contributing to a book, see our author guide on www.packtpub.com/authors.

Customer support

Now that you are the proud owner of a Packt book, we have a number of things to help you to get the most from your purchase.

Downloading the example code

You can download the example code files for all Packt books you have purchased from your account at http://www.packtpub.com. If you purchased this book elsewhere, you can visit http://www.packtpub.com/support and register to have the files e-mailed directly to you.

Errata

Although we have taken every care to ensure the accuracy of our content, mistakes do happen. If you find a mistake in one of our books—maybe a mistake in the text or the code—we would be grateful if you would report this to us. By doing so, you can save other readers from frustration and help us improve subsequent versions of this book. If you find any errata, please report them by visiting http://www.packtpub.com/submit-errata, selecting your book, clicking on the **errata submission form** link, and entering the details of your errata. Once your errata are verified, your submission will be accepted and the errata will be uploaded on our website, or added to any list of existing errata, under the Errata section of that title. Any existing errata can be viewed by selecting your title from http://www.packtpub.com/support.

Piracy

Piracy of copyright material on the Internet is an ongoing problem across all media. At Packt, we take the protection of our copyright and licenses very seriously. If you come across any illegal copies of our works, in any form, on the Internet, please provide us with the location address or website name immediately so that we can pursue a remedy.

Please contact us at copyright@packtpub.com with a link to the suspected pirated material.

We appreciate your help in protecting our authors, and our ability to bring you valuable content.

Questions

You can contact us at questions@packtpub.com if you are having a problem with any aspect of the book, and we will do our best to address it.

1
Getting Started with Python Libraries

Let's get started. We can find a mind map describing software that can be used for data analysis at `http://www.xmind.net/m/WvfC/`. Obviously, we can't install all of this software in this chapter. We will install NumPy, SciPy, matplotlib, and IPython on different operating systems and have a look at some simple code that uses NumPy.

NumPy is a fundamental Python library that provides numerical arrays and functions.

SciPy is a scientific Python library, which supplements and slightly overlaps NumPy. NumPy and SciPy historically shared their code base but were later separated.

matplotlib is a plotting library based on NumPy. You can read more about matplotlib in *Chapter 6, Data Visualization*.

IPython provides an architecture for interactive computing. The most notable part of this project is the IPython shell. We will cover the IPython shell later in this chapter.

Installation instructions for the other software we need will be given throughout the book at the appropriate time. At the end of this chapter, you will find pointers on how to find additional information online if you get stuck or are uncertain about the best way to solve problems.

In this chapter, we will cover:

- Installing Python, SciPy, matplotlib, IPython, and NumPy on Windows, Linux, and Macintosh
- Writing a simple application using NumPy arrays
- Getting to know IPython
- Online resources and help

Software used in this book

The software used in this book is based on Python, so you are required to have Python installed. On some operating systems, Python is already installed. You, however, need to check whether the Python version is compatible with the software version you want to install. There are many implementations of Python, including commercial implementations and distributions. In this book, we will focus on the standard CPython implementation, which is guaranteed to be compatible with NumPy.

 You can download Python from `https://www.python.org/download/`. On this website, we can find installers for Windows and Mac OS X as well as source archives for Linux, Unix, and Mac OS X.

The software we will install in this chapter has binary installers for Windows, various Linux distributions, and Mac OS X. There are also source distributions if you prefer that. You need to have Python 2.4.x or above installed on your system. Python 2.7.x is currently the best Python version to have because most Scientific Python libraries support it. Python 2.7 will be supported and maintained until 2020. After that, we will have to switch to Python 3.

Installing software and setup

We will learn how to install and set up NumPy, SciPy, matplotlib, and IPython on Windows, Linux and Mac OS X. Let's look at the process in detail.

On Windows

Installing on Windows is, fortunately, a straightforward task that we will cover in detail. You only need to download an installer and a wizard will guide you through the installation steps. We will give you steps to install NumPy here. The steps to install the other libraries are similar. The actions we will take are as follows:

1. Download installers for Windows from the SourceForge website (refer to the following table). The latest release versions may change, so just choose the one that fits your setup best.

Library	URL	Latest version
NumPy	`http://sourceforge.net/projects/numpy/files/`	1.8.1
SciPy	`http://sourceforge.net/projects/scipy/files/`	0.14.0
matplotlib	`http://sourceforge.net/projects/matplotlib/files/`	1.3.1
IPython	`http://archive.ipython.org/release/`	2.0.0

2. Choose the appropriate version. In this example, we chose
    `numpy-1.8.1-win32-superpack-python2.7.exe`.

3. Open the EXE installer by double-clicking on it.

4. Now, we can see a description of NumPy and its features. Click on the
    Next button.

    If you have Python installed, it should automatically be detected. If it is
    not detected, maybe your path settings are wrong.

 At the end of this chapter, resources are listed just in case you have
problems installing NumPy.

5. Click on the **Next** button if Python is found; otherwise, click on the **Cancel**
    button and install Python (NumPy cannot be installed without Python).
    Click on the **Next** button. This is the point of no return. Well, kind of, but
    it is best to make sure that you are installing to the proper directory, and
    so on and so forth. Now the real installation starts. This may take a while.

 The situation around installers is rapidly evolving. Other alternatives
exist in various stages of maturity (see `http://www.scipy.org/`
`install.html`). It might be necessary to put the `msvcp71.dll` file
in your `system32` directory located at `C:\Windows\`. You can get
it from `http://www.dll-files.com/dllindex/dll-files.`
`shtml?msvcp71`.

On Linux

Installing the recommended software on Linux depends on the distribution you have. We will discuss how you would install NumPy from the command line; you could probably use graphical installers depending on your distribution (distro). The commands to install matplotlib, SciPy, and IPython are the same; only the package names are different. Installing matplotlib, SciPy, and IPython is recommended but optional.

Most Linux distributions have NumPy packages. We will go through the necessary commands for some of the popular Linux distributions as follows:

- Run the following instructions from the command line to install NumPy on Red Hat:

  ```
  $ yum install python-numpy
  ```

- To install NumPy on Mandriva, run the following command-line instruction:

  ```
  $ urpmi python-numpy
  ```

- To install NumPy on Gentoo, run the following command-line instruction:

  ```
  $ sudo emerge numpy
  ```

- To install NumPy on Debian or Ubuntu, we need to type the following:

  ```
  $ sudo apt-get install python-numpy
  ```

The following table gives an overview of the Linux distributions and corresponding package names for NumPy, SciPy, matplotlib, and IPython:

Linux distribution	NumPy	SciPy	matplotlib	IPython
Arch Linux	python-numpy	python-scipy	python-matplotlib	Ipython
Debian	python-numpy	python-scipy	python-matplotlib	Ipython
Fedora	numpy	python-scipy	python-matplotlib	Ipython
Gentoo	dev-python/numpy	scipy	matplotlib	ipython
openSUSE	python-numpy, python-numpy-devel	python-scipy	python-matplotlib	ipython
Slackware	numpy	scipy	matplotlib	ipython

On Mac OS X

You can install NumPy, matplotlib, and SciPy on Mac OS X with a graphical installer or from the command line with a port manager, such as MacPorts or Fink, depending on your preference. The prerequisite is to install XCode, as it is not part of OS X releases. We will install NumPy with a GUI installer using the following steps:

1. We can get a NumPy installer from the SourceForge website at `http://sourceforge.net/projects/numpy/files/`. Similar files exist for matplotlib and SciPy.

2. Just change `numpy` in the previous URL to `scipy` or `matplotlib` to get installers of the respective libraries. IPython didn't have a GUI installer at the time of writing this.

3. Download the appropriate DMG file; usually the latest one is the best.

    Another alternative is SciPy Superpack (`https://github.com/fonnesbeck/ScipySuperpack`).

Whichever option you choose, it is important to make sure that updates that impact the system Python library don't negatively influence already-installed software by not building against the Python library provided by Apple. Install NumPy, matplotlib, and SciPy using the following steps:

1. Open the DMG file (in this example, `numpy-1.8.1-py2.7-python.org-macosx10.6.dmg`).

2. Double-click on the icon of the opened box — the one with a subscript that ends with `.mpkg`. We will be presented with the welcome screen of the installer.

3. Click on the **Continue** button to go to the **Read Me** screen, where we will be presented with a short description of NumPy.

4. Click on the **Continue** button to go to the **License** screen.

5. Read the license, click on the **Continue** button, and then click on the **Accept** button when prompted to accept the license. Continue through the screens that follow from there, and click on the **Finish** button at the end.

Alternatively, we can install the libraries through the MacPorts route, with Fink or Homebrew. The following installation commands install all these packages. We only need NumPy for all the tutorials in this book, so please omit the packages you are not interested in.

- To install with MacPorts, type in the following command:

  ```
  $ sudo port install py-numpy py-scipy py-matplotlib py-ipython
  ```

- Fink also has packages for NumPy, such as `scipy-core-py24`, `scipy-core-py25`, and `scipy-core-py26`. The SciPy packages are `scipy-py24`, `scipy-py25`, and `scipy-py26`. We can install NumPy and other recommended packages that we will be using in this book for Python 2.6 with the following command:

  ```
  $ fink install scipy-core-py26 scipy-py26 matplotlib-py26
  ```

Building NumPy, SciPy, matplotlib, and IPython from source

As a last resort or if we want to have the latest code, we can build from source. In practice, it shouldn't be that hard, although depending on your operating system, you might run into problems. As operating systems and related software are rapidly evolving, in such cases, the best you can do is search online or ask for help. In this chapter, we give pointers on good places to look for help.

The source code can be retrieved with `git` or as an archive from GitHub. The steps to install NumPy from source are straightforward and given here. We can retrieve the source code for NumPy with `git` as follows:

```
$ git clone git://github.com/numpy/numpy.git numpy
```

 There are similar commands for SciPy, matplotlib, and IPython (refer to the table that follows after this piece of information). The IPython source code can be downloaded from https://github.com/ipython/ipython/releases as a source archive or ZIP file. You can then unpack it with your favorite tool or with the following command:

```
$ tar -xzf ipython.tar.gz
```

Please refer to the following table for the `git` commands and source archive/zip links:

Library	Git command	Tarball/zip URL
NumPy	`git clone git://github.com/` `numpy/numpy.git numpy`	`https://github.com/numpy/` `numpy/releases`
SciPy	`git clone http://github.com/` `scipy/scipy.git scipy`	`https://github.com/scipy/` `scipy/releases`

matplotlib	`git clone git://github.com/`
	`matplotlib/matplotlib.git`
		`https://github.com/`
		`matplotlib/matplotlib/`
		`releases`

IPython	`git clone --recursive`
	`https://github.com/ipython/`
	`ipython.git`
		`https://github.com/ipython/`
		`ipython/releases`

Install on `/usr/local` with the following command from the source code directory:

```
$ python setup.py build
$ sudo python setup.py install --prefix=/usr/local
```

To build, we need a C compiler such as GCC and the Python header files in the `python-dev` or `python-devel` package.

Installing with setuptools

If you have `setuptools` or `pip`, you can install NumPy, SciPy, matplotlib, and IPython with the following commands. For each library, we give two commands, one for `setuptools` and one for `pip`. You only need to choose one command per pair:

```
$ easy_install numpy
$ pip install numpy

$ easy_install scipy
$ pip install scipy

$ easy_install matplotlib
$ pip install matplotlib

$ easy_install ipython
$ pip install ipython
```

It may be necessary to prepend `sudo` to these commands if your current user doesn't have sufficient rights on your system.

NumPy arrays

After going through the installation of NumPy, it's time to have a look at NumPy arrays. NumPy arrays are more efficient than Python lists when it comes to numerical operations. NumPy arrays are, in fact, specialized objects with extensive optimizations. NumPy code requires less explicit loops than equivalent Python code. This is based on vectorization.

If we go back to highschool mathematics, then we should remember the concepts of scalars and vectors. The number 2, for instance, is a scalar. When we add 2 to 2, we are performing scalar addition. We can form a vector out of a group of scalars. In Python programming terms, we will then have a one-dimensional array. This concept can, of course, be extended to higher dimensions. Performing an operation on two arrays, such as addition, can be reduced to a group of scalar operations. In straight Python, we will do that with loops going through each element in the first array and adding it to the corresponding element in the second array. However, this is more verbose than the way it is done in mathematics. In mathematics, we treat the addition of two vectors as a single operation. That's the way NumPy arrays do it too, and there are certain optimizations using low-level C routines, which make these basic operations more efficient. We will cover NumPy arrays in more detail in the following chapter, *Chapter 2, NumPy Arrays*.

A simple application

Imagine that we want to add two vectors called a and b. The word *vector* is used here in the mathematical sense, which means a one-dimensional array. We will learn in *Chapter 3, Statistics and Linear Algebra*, about specialized NumPy arrays that represent matrices. The vector a holds the squares of integers 0 to n; for instance, if n is equal to 3, a contains 0, 1, or 4. The vector b holds the cubes of integers 0 to n, so if n is equal to 3, then the vector b is equal to 0, 1, or 8. How would you do that using plain Python? After we come up with a solution, we will compare it with the NumPy equivalent.

The following function solves the vector addition problem using pure Python without NumPy:

```
def pythonsum(n):
    a = range(n)
    b = range(n)
    c = []

    for i in range(len(a)):
        a[i] = i ** 2
        b[i] = i ** 3
```

```
        c.append(a[i] + b[i])

    return c
```

The following is a function that solves the vector addition problem with NumPy:

```
def numpysum(n):
    a = numpy.arange(n) ** 2
    b = numpy.arange(n) ** 3
    c = a + b
    return c
```

Notice that `numpysum()` does not need a `for` loop. Also, we used the `arange()` function from NumPy, which creates a NumPy array for us with integers from 0 to *n*. The `arange()` function was imported; that is why it is prefixed with `numpy`.

Now comes the fun part. Remember that it was mentioned in the *Preface* that NumPy is faster when it comes to array operations. How much faster is Numpy, though? The following program will show us by measuring the elapsed time in microseconds for the `numpysum()` and `pythonsum()` functions. It also prints the last two elements of the vector sum. Let's check that we get the same answers using Python and NumPy:

```
#!/usr/bin/env/python

import sys
from datetime import datetime
import numpy as np

"""
    This program demonstrates vector addition the Python way.
    Run from the command line as follows

      python vectorsum.py n

    where n is an integer that specifies the size of the vectors.

    The first vector to be added contains the squares of 0 up to n.
    The second vector contains the cubes of 0 up to n.
    The program prints the last 2 elements of the sum and the elapsed
    time.
"""

def numpysum(n):
    a = np.arange(n) ** 2
```

```
        b = np.arange(n) ** 3
        c = a + b

        return c

    def pythonsum(n):
        a = range(n)
        b = range(n)
        c = []

        for i in range(len(a)):
            a[i] = i ** 2
            b[i] = i ** 3
            c.append(a[i] + b[i])

        return c

    size = int(sys.argv[1])

    start = datetime.now()
    c = pythonsum(size)
    delta = datetime.now() - start
    print "The last 2 elements of the sum", c[-2:]
    print "PythonSum elapsed time in microseconds", delta.microseconds

    start = datetime.now()
    c = numpysum(size)
    delta = datetime.now() - start
    print "The last 2 elements of the sum", c[-2:]
    print "NumPySum elapsed time in microseconds", delta.microseconds
```

The output of the program for 1000, 2000, and 3000 vector elements is as follows:

```
$ python vectorsum.py 1000
The last 2 elements of the sum [995007996, 998001000]
PythonSum elapsed time in microseconds 707
The last 2 elements of the sum [995007996 998001000]
NumPySum elapsed time in microseconds 171


$ python vectorsum.py 2000
The last 2 elements of the sum [7980015996, 7992002000]
```

```
PythonSum elapsed time in microseconds 1420

The last 2 elements of the sum [7980015996 7992002000]

NumPySum elapsed time in microseconds 168


$ python vectorsum.py 4000

The last 2 elements of the sum [63920031996, 63968004000]

PythonSum elapsed time in microseconds 2829

The last 2 elements of the sum [63920031996 63968004000]

NumPySum elapsed time in microseconds 274
```

Clearly, NumPy is much faster than the equivalent normal Python code. One thing is certain; we get the same results whether we are using NumPy or not. However, the result that is printed differs in representation. Notice that the result from the numpysum() function does not have any commas. How come? Obviously, we are not dealing with a Python list but with a NumPy array. We will learn more about NumPy arrays in the next chapter, *Chapter 2, NumPy Arrays*.

Using IPython as a shell

Scientists, data analysts, and engineers are used to experimenting. IPython was created by scientists with experimentation in mind. The interactive environment that IPython provides is viewed by many as a direct answer to MATLAB, Mathematica, and Maple.

The following is a list of features of the IPython shell:

- Tab completion, which helps you find a command
- History mechanism
- Inline editing
- Ability to call external Python scripts with %run
- Access to system commands
- The pylab switch
- Access to the Python debugger and profiler

The following list describes how to use the IPython shell:

- **The pylab switch**: The pylab switch automatically imports all the Scipy, NumPy, and matplotlib packages. Without this switch, we would have to import these packages ourselves.

All we need to do is enter the following instruction on the command line:

```
$ ipython -pylab
Type "copyright", "credits" or "license" for more information.


IPython 2.0.0-dev -- An enhanced Interactive Python.
?           -> Introduction and overview of IPython's features.
%quickref -> Quick reference.
help       -> Python's own help system.
object?    -> Details about 'object', use 'object??' for extra
details.


Welcome to pylab, a matplotlib-based Python environment
[backend: MacOSX].
For more information, type 'help(pylab)'.


In [1]: quit()
```

 The quit () function or *Ctrl* + *D* quits the IPython shell.

- **Saving a session**: We might want to be able to go back to our experiments. In IPython, it is easy to save a session for later use, with the following command:

```
In [1]: %logstart
Activating auto-logging. Current session state plus future
input saved.
Filename      : ipython_log.py
Mode          : rotate
Output logging : False
Raw input log  : False
Timestamping  : False
State         : active
```

Logging can be switched off as follows:

```
In [9]: %logoff
Switching logging OFF
```

- **Executing system shell command**: Execute a system shell command in the default IPython profile by prefixing the command with the ! symbol. For instance, the following input will get the current date:

```
In [1]: !date
```

In fact, any line prefixed with ! is sent to the system shell. Also, we can store the command output as shown here:

```
In [2]: thedate = !date
In [3]: thedate
```

- **Displaying history**: We can show the history of commands with the %hist command, for example:

```
In [1]: a = 2 + 2

In [2]: a
Out[2]: 4

In [3]: %hist
a = 2 + 2

a

%hist
```

This is a common feature in **Command Line Interface (CLI)** environments. We can also search through the history with the -g switch as follows:

```
In [5]: %hist -g a = 2
   1: a = 2 + 2
```

Downloading the example code

You can download the example code files for all the Packt books you have purchased from your account at http://www.packtpub.com. If you purchased this book elsewhere, you can visit http://www.packtpub.com/support and register to have the files e-mailed directly to you.

We saw a number of so-called magic functions in action. These functions start with the % character. If the magic function is used on a line by itself, the % prefix is optional.

Reading manual pages

When we are in IPython's pylab mode (`$ ipython -pylab`), we can open manual pages for NumPy functions with the `help` command. It is not necessary to know the name of a function. We can type a few characters and then let tab completion do its work. Let's, for instance, browse the available information for the `arange()` function.

We can browse the available information in either of the following two ways:

- **Calling the help function**: Call the `help` command. Type in a few characters of the function and press the *Tab* key.

```
In [1]: help ar
arange        arcsin        arctan2       argmin        around        array_equal   array_split
arccos        arcsinh       arctanh       argsort       array         array_equiv   array_str
arccosh       arctan        argmax        argwhere      array2string  array_repr    arrow
```

- **Querying with a question mark**: Another option is to append a question mark to the function name. You will then, of course, need to know the function name, but you don't have to type `help`, for example:

  In [3]: arange?

  Tab completion is dependent on `readline`, so you need to make sure that it is installed. It can be installed with `setuptools` with one of the following commands:

  $ easy_install readline

  $ pip install readline

  The question mark gives you information from docstrings.

IPython notebooks

If you have browsed the Internet looking for information on Python, it is very likely that you have seen IPython notebooks. These are web pages with text, charts, and Python code in a special format. Have a look at these notebook collections at the following links:

- `https://github.com/ipython/ipython/wiki/A-gallery-of-interesting-IPython-Notebooks`
- `http://nbviewer.ipython.org/github/ipython/ipython/tree/2.x/examples/`

Often, the notebooks are used as an educational tool or to demonstrate Python software. We can import or export notebooks either from plain Python code or using the special notebook format. The notebooks can be run locally, or we can make them available online by running a dedicated notebook server. Certain cloud computing solutions, such as Wakari and PiCloud, allow you to run notebooks in the Cloud. Cloud computing is one of the topics of *Chapter 11, Environments Outside the Python Ecosystem and Cloud Computing*.

Where to find help and references

The main documentation website for NumPy and SciPy is at `http://docs.scipy.org/doc/`. Through this web page, we can browse the NumPy reference guide at `http://docs.scipy.org/doc/numpy/reference/` and the user guide as well as several tutorials.

The popular Stack Overflow software development forum has hundreds of questions tagged `numpy`. To view them, go to `http://stackoverflow.com/questions/tagged/numpy`.

This might be stating the obvious, but `numpy` can also be substituted with `scipy`, `ipython`, or almost anything of interest. If you are really stuck with a problem or you want to be kept informed of NumPy development, you can subscribe to the NumPy discussion mailing list. The e-mail address is `numpy-discussion@scipy.org`. The number of e-mails per day is not too high, and there is almost no spam to speak of. Most importantly, developers actively involved with NumPy also answer questions asked on the discussion group. The complete list can be found at `http://www.scipy.org/Mailing_Lists`.

For IRC users, there is an IRC channel on `irc://irc.freenode.net`. The channel is called `#scipy`, but you can also ask NumPy questions since SciPy users also have knowledge of NumPy, as SciPy is based on NumPy. There are at least 50 members on the SciPy channel at all times.

Summary

In this chapter, we installed NumPy, SciPy, matplotlib, and IPython that we will be using in tutorials. We got a vector addition program working and convinced ourselves that NumPy offers superior performance. In addition, we explored the available documentation and online resources.

In the next chapter, *Chapter 2, NumPy Arrays*, we will take a look under the hood of NumPy and explore some fundamental concepts including arrays and data types.

2
NumPy Arrays

After installing NumPy and other key Python-programming libraries and getting some code to work, it's time to pass over NumPy arrays. This chapter acquaints you with the fundamentals of NumPy and arrays. At the end of this chapter, you will have a basic understanding of NumPy arrays and their related functions.

The topics we will address in this chapter are as follows:

- Data types
- Array types
- Type conversions
- Creating arrays
- Indexing
- Fancy indexing
- Slicing
- Manipulating shapes

The NumPy array object

NumPy has a multidimensional array object called `ndarray`. It consists of two parts, which are as follows:

- The actual data
- Some metadata describing the data

The bulk of array procedures leaves the raw information unaffected; the sole facet that varies is the metadata.

We have already discovered in the preceding chapter how to produce an array by applying the `arange()` function. Actually, we made a one-dimensional array that held a set of numbers. The `ndarray` can have more than a single dimension.

The advantages of NumPy arrays

The NumPy array is, in general, homogeneous (there is a particular record array type that is heterogeneous) — the items in the array have to be of the same type. The advantage is that if we know that the items in an array are of the same type, it is easy to ascertain the storage size needed for the array. NumPy arrays can execute vectorized operations, processing a complete array, in contrast to Python lists, where you usually have to loop through the list and execute the operation on each element. Also, NumPy utilizes an optimized C API to make them particularly quick.

NumPy arrays are indexed just like in Python, commencing from 0. Data types are represented by special objects. These objects will be discussed comprehensively further in this chapter.

We will make an array with the `arange()` subroutine again (examine `arrayattributes.py` from this book's code). In this chapter, you will see snippets from IPython sessions where NumPy is already imported. Here's how to get the data type of an array:

```
In: a = arange(5)
In: a.dtype
Out: dtype('int64')
```

The data type of the array a is `int64` (at least on my computer), but you may get `int32` as the output if you are using 32-bit Python. In both the cases, we are dealing with integers (64 bit or 32 bit). Besides the data type of an array, it is crucial to know its shape. The example in *Chapter 1, Getting Started with Python Libraries*, demonstrated how to create a vector (actually, a one-dimensional NumPy array). A vector is commonly used in mathematics but most of the time we need higher-dimensional objects. Let's find out the shape of the vector we produced a few minutes ago:

```
In: a
Out: array([0, 1, 2, 3, 4])
In: a.shape
Out: (5,)
```

As you can see, the vector has five components with values ranging from 0 to 4. The `shape` property of the array is a tuple; in this instance, a tuple of 1 element, which holds the length in each dimension.

Creating a multidimensional array

Now that we know how to create a vector, we are set to create a multidimensional NumPy array. After we produce the matrix, we will again need to show its shape (check `arrayattributes.py` from this book's code bundle), as demonstrated in the following code snippets:

1. Create a multidimensional array as follows:

```
In: m = array([arange(2), arange(2)])
In: m
Out:
array([[0, 1],
       [0, 1]])
```

2. Show the array shape as follows:

```
In: m.shape
Out: (2, 2)
```

We made a 2 x 2 array with the `arange()` subroutine. The `array()` function creates an array from an object that you pass to it. The object has to be an array, for example, a Python list. In the previous example, we passed a list of arrays. The object is the only required parameter of the `array()` function. NumPy functions tend to have a heap of optional arguments with predefined default options.

Selecting NumPy array elements

From time to time, we will wish to select a specific constituent of an array. We will take a look at how to do this, but to kick off, let's make a 2 x 2 matrix again (see the `elementselection.py` file in this book's code bundle):

```
In: a = array([[1,2],[3,4]])
In: a
Out:
array([[1, 2],
       [3, 4]])
```

The matrix was made this time by giving the `array()` function a list of lists. We will now choose each item of the matrix one at a time, as shown in the following code snippet. Recall that the index numbers begin from `0`:

```
In: a[0,0]
Out: 1
```

```
In: a[0,1]
Out: 2
In: a[1,0]
Out: 3
In: a[1,1]
Out: 4
```

As you can see, choosing elements of an array is fairly simple. For the array a, we just employ the notation a[m,n], where m and n are the indices of the item in the array. Have a look at the following figure for your reference:

NumPy numerical types

Python has an integer type, a float type, and complex type; nonetheless, this is not sufficient for scientific calculations. In practice, we still demand more data types with varying precisions and, consequently, different storage sizes of the type. For this reason, NumPy has many more data types. The bulk of the NumPy mathematical types ends with a number. This number designates the count of bits related to the type. The following table (adapted from the NumPy user guide) presents an overview of NumPy numerical types:

Type	Description
bool	Boolean (True or False) stored as a bit
inti	Platform integer (normally either int32 or int64)
int8	Byte (-128 to 127)
int16	Integer (-32768 to 32767)
int32	Integer (-2 ** 31 to 2 ** 31 -1)
int64	Integer (-2 ** 63 to 2 ** 63 -1)
uint8	Unsigned integer (0 to 255)
uint16	Unsigned integer (0 to 65535)
uint32	Unsigned integer (0 to 2 ** 32 - 1)
uint64	Unsigned integer (0 to 2 ** 64 - 1)
float16	Half precision float: sign bit, 5 bits exponent, and 10 bits mantissa
float32	Single precision float: sign bit, 8 bits exponent, and 23 bits mantissa

Type	Description
`float64` or `float`	Double precision float: sign bit, 11 bits exponent, and 52 bits mantissa
`complex64`	Complex number, represented by two 32-bit floats (real and imaginary components)
`complex128` or `complex`	Complex number, represented by two 64-bit floats (real and imaginary components)

For each data type, there exists a matching conversion function (look at the `numericaltypes.py` script of this book's code bundle):

```
In: float64(42)
Out: 42.0
In: int8(42.0)
Out: 42
In: bool(42)
Out: True
In: bool(0)
Out: False
In: bool(42.0)
Out: True
In: float(True)
Out: 1.0
In: float(False)
Out: 0.0
```

Many functions have a data type argument, which is frequently optional:

```
In: arange(7, dtype=uint16)
Out: array([0, 1, 2, 3, 4, 5, 6], dtype=uint16)
```

It is important to be aware that you are not allowed to change a complex number into an integer. Attempting to do that sparks off a `TypeError`:

```
In: float(42.0 + 1.j)
Traceback (most recent call last):
  File "numericaltypes.py", line 45, in <module>
    print float(42.0 + 1.j)
TypeError: can't convert complex to float
```

The same goes for conversion of a complex number into a floating-point number. By the way, the j component is the imaginary coefficient of a complex number. Even so, you can convert a floating-point number to a complex number, for example, `complex(1.0)`. The real and imaginary pieces of a complex number can be pulled out with the `real()` and `imag()` functions, respectively.

Data type objects

Data type objects are instances of the numpy.dtype class. Once again, arrays have a data type. To be exact, each element in a NumPy array has the same data type. The data type object can tell you the size of the data in bytes. The size in bytes is given by the itemsize property of the dtype class (refer to dtypeattributes.py):

```
In: a.dtype.itemsize
Out: 8
```

Character codes

Character codes are included for backward compatibility with **Numeric**. Numeric is the predecessor of NumPy. Its use is not recommended, but the code is supplied here because it pops up in various locations. You should use the dtype object instead. The following table lists several different data types and character codes related to them:

Type	Character code
integer	i
Unsigned integer	u
Single precision float	f
Double precision float	d
bool	b
complex	D
string	S
unicode	U
Void	V

Take a look at the following code to produce an array of single precision floats (refer to charcodes.py in this book's code bundle):

```
In: arange(7, dtype='f')
Out: array([ 0.,   1.,   2.,   3.,   4.,   5.,   6.], dtype=float32)
```

Likewise, this creates an array of complex numbers:

```
In: arange(7, dtype='D')
Out: array([ 0.+0.j,   1.+0.j,   2.+0.j,   3.+0.j,   4.+0.j,   5.+0.j,
6.+0.j])
```

The dtype constructors

We have a variety of means to create data types. Take the case of floating-point data (have a look at `dtypeconstructors.py` in this book's code bundle):

- We can use the general Python float, as shown in the following lines of code:
  ```
  In: dtype(float)
  Out: dtype('float64')
  ```

- We can specify a single precision float with a character code:
  ```
  In: dtype('f')
  Out: dtype('float32')
  ```

- We can use a double precision float with a character code:
  ```
  In: dtype('d')
  Out: dtype('float64')
  ```

- We can pass the `dtype` constructor a two-character code. The first character stands for the type; the second character is a number specifying the number of bytes in the type (the numbers 2, 4, and 8 correspond to floats of 16, 32, and 64 bits, respectively):
  ```
  In: dtype('f8')
  Out: dtype('float64')
  ```

A (truncated) list of all the full data type codes can be found by applying `sctypeDict.keys()`:

```
In: sctypeDict.keys()
Out: [0, …
 'i2',
 'int0']
```

The dtype attributes

The `dtype` class has a number of useful properties. For instance, we can get information about the character code of a data type through the properties of `dtype` (refer to `dtypeattributes2.py` in this book's code bundle):

```
In: t = dtype('Float64')
In: t.char
Out: 'd'
```

The type attribute corresponds to the type of object of the array elements:

```
In: t.type
Out: <type 'numpy.float64'>
```

The str attribute of dtype gives a string representation of a data type. It begins with a character representing endianness, if appropriate, then a character code, succeeded by a number corresponding to the number of bytes that each array item needs. Endianness, here, entails the way bytes are ordered inside a 32- or 64-bit word. In the big-endian order, the most significant byte is stored first, indicated by >. In the little-endian order, the least significant byte is stored first, indicated by <, as exemplified in the following lines of code:

```
In: t.str
Out: '<f8'
```

One-dimensional slicing and indexing

Slicing of one-dimensional NumPy arrays works just like the slicing of standard Python lists. Let's define an array containing the numbers 0, 1, 2, and so on up to and including 8. We can select a part of the array from indexes 3 to 7, which extracts the elements of the arrays 3 through 6 (have a look at slicing1d.py in this book's code bundle):

```
In: a = arange(9)
In: a[3:7]
Out: array([3, 4, 5, 6])
```

We can choose elements from indexes the 0 to 7 with an increment of 2:

```
In: a[:7:2]
Out: array([0, 2, 4, 6])
```

Just as in Python, we can use negative indices and reverse the array:

```
In: a[::-1]
Out: array([8, 7, 6, 5, 4, 3, 2, 1, 0])
```

Manipulating array shapes

We have already learned about the reshape() function. Another repeating chore is the flattening of arrays. Flattening in this setting entails transforming a multidimensional array into a one-dimensional array. The code for this example is in the shapemanipulation.py file in this book's code bundle.

```
import numpy as np

# Demonstrates multi dimensional arrays slicing.
#
# Run from the commandline with
```

```
#
#  python shapemanipulation.py
print "In: b = arange(24).reshape(2,3,4)"
b = np.arange(24).reshape(2,3,4)

print "In: b"
print b
#Out:
#array([[[ 0,  1,  2,  3],
#        [ 4,  5,  6,  7],
#        [ 8,  9, 10, 11]],
#
#        [[12, 13, 14, 15],
#        [16, 17, 18, 19],
#        [20, 21, 22, 23]]])

print "In: b.ravel()"
print b.ravel()
#Out:
#array([ 0,  1,  2,  3,  4,  5,  6,  7,  8,  9, 10, 11, 12, 13,
14, 15, 16,
#       17, 18, 19, 20, 21, 22, 23])

print "In: b.flatten()"
print b.flatten()
#Out:
#array([ 0,  1,  2,  3,  4,  5,  6,  7,  8,  9, 10, 11, 12, 13,
14, 15, 16,
#       17, 18, 19, 20, 21, 22, 23])

print "In: b.shape = (6,4)"
b.shape = (6,4)

print "In: b"
print b
#Out:
#array([[ 0,  1,  2,  3],
#        [ 4,  5,  6,  7],
#        [ 8,  9, 10, 11],
#        [12, 13, 14, 15],
#        [16, 17, 18, 19],
#        [20, 21, 22, 23]])

print "In: b.transpose()"
```

```
print b.transpose()
#Out:
#array([[ 0,  4,  8, 12, 16, 20],
#       [ 1,  5,  9, 13, 17, 21],
#       [ 2,  6, 10, 14, 18, 22],
#       [ 3,  7, 11, 15, 19, 23]])


print "In: b.resize((2,12))"
b.resize((2,12))

print "In: b"
print b
#Out:
#array([[ 0,  1,  2,  3,  4,  5,  6,  7,  8,  9, 10, 11],
#       [12, 13, 14, 15, 16, 17, 18, 19, 20, 21, 22, 23]])
```

We can manipulate array shapes using the following functions:

- **Ravel**: We can accomplish this with the `ravel()` function as follows:

```
In: b
Out:
array([[[ 0,  1,  2,  3],
        [ 4,  5,  6,  7],
        [ 8,  9, 10, 11]],
       [[12, 13, 14, 15],
        [16, 17, 18, 19],
        [20, 21, 22, 23]]])
In: b.ravel()
Out:
array([ 0,  1,  2,  3,  4,  5,  6,  7,  8,  9, 10, 11, 12,
13, 14, 15, 16, 17, 18, 19, 20, 21, 22, 23])
```

- **Flatten**: The appropriately named function, `flatten()`, does the same as `ravel()`. However, `flatten()` always allocates new memory, whereas `ravel` might give back a view of the array. This means that we can directly manipulate the array as follows:

```
In: b.flatten()
Out:
array([ 0,  1,  2,  3,  4,  5,  6,  7,  8,  9, 10, 11, 12,
13, 14, 15, 16,
       17, 18, 19, 20, 21, 22, 23])
```

- **Setting the shape with a tuple**: Besides the `reshape()` function, we can also define the shape straightaway with a tuple, which is exhibited as follows:

```
In: b.shape = (6,4)
In: b
Out:
array([[ 0,  1,  2,  3],
       [ 4,  5,  6,  7],
       [ 8,  9, 10, 11],
       [12, 13, 14, 15],
       [16, 17, 18, 19],
       [20, 21, 22, 23]])
```

As you can understand, the preceding code alters the array immediately. Now, we have a 6 x 4 array.

- **Transpose**: In linear algebra, it is common to transpose matrices. Transposing is a way to transform data. For a two-dimensional table, transposing means that rows become columns and columns become rows. We can do this too by using the following code:

```
In: b.transpose()
Out:
array([[ 0,  4,  8, 12, 16, 20],
       [ 1,  5,  9, 13, 17, 21],
       [ 2,  6, 10, 14, 18, 22],
       [ 3,  7, 11, 15, 19, 23]])
```

- **Resize**: The `resize()` method works just like the `reshape()` method, but changes the array it works on:

```
In: b.resize((2,12))
In: b
Out:
array([[ 0,  1,  2,  3,  4,  5,  6,  7,  8,  9, 10, 11],
       [12, 13, 14, 15, 16, 17, 18, 19, 20, 21, 22, 23]])
```

Stacking arrays

Arrays can be stacked horizontally, depth wise, or vertically. We can use, for this goal, the `vstack()`, `dstack()`, `hstack()`, `column_stack()`, `row_stack()`, and `concatenate()` functions. To start with, let's set up some arrays (refer to `stacking.py` in this book's code bundle):

```
In: a = arange(9).reshape(3,3)
In: a
```

```
Out:
array([[0, 1, 2],
       [3, 4, 5],
       [6, 7, 8]])
In: b = 2 * a
In: b
Out:
array([[ 0,  2,  4],
       [ 6,  8, 10],
       [12, 14, 16]])
```

As mentioned previously, we can stack arrays using the following techniques:

- **Horizontal stacking**: Beginning with horizontal stacking, we will shape a tuple of ndarrays and hand it to the hstack() function to stack the arrays. This is shown as follows:

```
In: hstack((a, b))
Out:
array([[ 0,  1,  2,  0,  2,  4],
       [ 3,  4,  5,  6,  8, 10],
       [ 6,  7,  8, 12, 14, 16]])
```

We can attain the same thing with the concatenate() function, which is shown as follows:

```
In: concatenate((a, b), axis=1)
Out:
array([[ 0,  1,  2,  0,  2,  4],
       [ 3,  4,  5,  6,  8, 10],
       [ 6,  7,  8, 12, 14, 16]])
```

The following diagram depicts horizontal stacking:

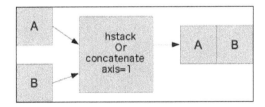

- **Vertical stacking**: With vertical stacking, a tuple is formed again. This time it is given to the vstack() function to stack the arrays. This can be seen as follows:

```
In: vstack((a, b))
Out:
```

```
array([[ 0,   1,   2],
       [ 3,   4,   5],
       [ 6,   7,   8],
       [ 0,   2,   4],
       [ 6,   8,  10],
       [12,  14,  16]])
```

The concatenate() function gives the same outcome with the axis
parameter fixed to 0. This is the default value for the axis parameter,
as portrayed in the following code:

```
In: concatenate((a, b), axis=0)
Out:
array([[ 0,   1,   2],
       [ 3,   4,   5],
       [ 6,   7,   8],
       [ 0,   2,   4],
       [ 6,   8,  10],
       [12,  14,  16]])
```

Refer to the following figure for vertical stacking:

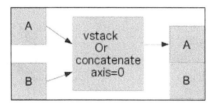

- **Depth stacking**: To boot, there is the depth-wise stacking employing
  dstack() and a tuple, of course. This entails stacking a list of arrays
  along the third axis (depth). For example, we could stack 2D arrays
  of image data on top of each other as follows:

```
In: dstack((a, b))
Out:
array([[[ 0,   0],
        [ 1,   2],
        [ 2,   4]],
       [[ 3,   6],
        [ 4,   8],
        [ 5,  10]],
       [[ 6,  12],
        [ 7,  14],
        [ 8,  16]]])
```

- **Column stacking**: The `column_stack()` function stacks 1D arrays column-wise. This is shown as follows:

```
In: oned = arange(2)
In: oned
Out: array([0, 1])
In: twice_oned = 2 * oned
In: twice_oned
Out: array([0, 2])
In: column_stack((oned, twice_oned))
Out:
array([[0, 0],
       [1, 2]])
```

2D arrays are stacked the way the `hstack()` function stacks them, as demonstrated in the following lines of code:

```
In: column_stack((a, b))
Out:
array([[ 0,  1,  2,  0,  2,  4],
       [ 3,  4,  5,  6,  8, 10],
       [ 6,  7,  8, 12, 14, 16]])
In: column_stack((a, b)) == hstack((a, b))
Out:
array([[ True,  True,  True,  True,  True,  True],
       [ True,  True,  True,  True,  True,  True],
       [ True,  True,  True,  True,  True,  True]],
dtype=bool)
```

Yes, you guessed it right! We compared two arrays with the `==` operator.

- **Row stacking**: NumPy, naturally, also has a function that does row-wise stacking. It is named `row_stack()` and for 1D arrays, it just stacks the arrays in rows into a 2D array:

```
In: row_stack((oned, twice_oned))
Out:
array([[0, 1],
       [0, 2]])
```

The `row_stack()` function results for 2D arrays are equal to the `vstack()` function results:

```
In: row_stack((a, b))
Out:
```

```
array([[ 0,   1,   2],
       [ 3,   4,   5],
       [ 6,   7,   8],
       [ 0,   2,   4],
       [ 6,   8,  10],
       [12,  14,  16]])
In: row_stack((a,b)) == vstack((a, b))
Out:
array([[ True,   True,   True],
       [ True,   True,   True],
       [ True,   True,   True],
       [ True,   True,   True],
       [ True,   True,   True],
       [ True,   True,   True]], dtype=bool)
```

Splitting NumPy arrays

Arrays can be split vertically, horizontally, or depth wise. The functions involved are hsplit(), vsplit(), dsplit(), and split(). We can split arrays either into arrays of the same shape or indicate the location after which the split should happen. Let's look at each of the functions in detail:

- **Horizontal splitting**: The following code splits a 3 x 3 array on its horizontal axis into three parts of the same size and shape (see splitting.py in this book's code bundle):

```
In: a
Out:
array([[0, 1, 2],
       [3, 4, 5],
       [6, 7, 8]])
In: hsplit(a, 3)
Out:
[array([[0],
        [3],
        [6]]),
 array([[1],
        [4],
        [7]]),
 array([[2],
        [5],
        [8]])]
```

Liken it with a call of the `split()` function, with an additional argument, `axis=1`:

```
In: split(a, 3, axis=1)
Out:
[array([[0],
        [3],
        [6]]),
 array([[1],
        [4],
        [7]]),
 array([[2],
        [5],
        [8]])]
```

- **Vertical splitting**: `vsplit()` splits along the vertical axis:

```
In: vsplit(a, 3)
Out: [array([[0, 1, 2]]), array([[3, 4, 5]]), array([[6, 7,
8]])]
```

The `split()` function, with `axis=0`, also splits along the vertical axis:

```
In: split(a, 3, axis=0)
Out: [array([[0, 1, 2]]), array([[3, 4, 5]]), array([[6, 7,
8]])]
```

- **Depth-wise splitting**: The `dsplit()` function, unsurprisingly, splits depth-wise. We will require an array of rank 3 to begin with:

```
In: c = arange(27).reshape(3, 3, 3)
In: c
Out:
array([[[ 0,  1,  2],
        [ 3,  4,  5],
        [ 6,  7,  8]],
       [[ 9, 10, 11],
        [12, 13, 14],
        [15, 16, 17]],
       [[18, 19, 20],
        [21, 22, 23],
        [24, 25, 26]]])
In: dsplit(c, 3)
Out:
[array([[[ 0],
```

```
             [ 3],
             [ 6]]],
            [[ 9],
             [12],
             [15]],
            [[18],
             [21],
             [24]]]),
     array([[[ 1],
             [ 4],
             [ 7]],
            [[10],
             [13],
             [16]],
            [[19],
             [22],
             [25]]]),
     array([[[ 2],
             [ 5],
             [ 8]],
            [[11],
             [14],
             [17]],
            [[20],
             [23],
             [26]]])]
```

NumPy array attributes

Let's learn more about the NumPy array attributes with the help of an example.
For this example, see `arrayattributes2.py` provided in the book's code bundle:

```
import numpy as np

# Demonstrates ndarray attributes.
#
# Run from the commandline with
#
#   python arrayattributes2.py
b = np.arange(24).reshape(2, 12)
print "In: b"
print b
```

```
#Out:
#array([[ 0,  1,  2,  3,  4,  5,  6,  7,  8,  9, 10, 11],
#       [12, 13, 14, 15, 16, 17, 18, 19, 20, 21, 22, 23]])

print "In: b.ndim"
print b.ndim
#Out: 2

print "In: b.size"
print b.size
#Out: 24

print "In: b.itemsize"
print b.itemsize
#Out: 8

print "In: b.nbytes"
print b.nbytes
#Out: 192

print "In: b.size * b.itemsize"
print b.size * b.itemsize
#Out: 192

print "In: b.resize(6,4)"
print b.resize(6,4)

print "In: b"
print b
#Out:
#array([[ 0,  1,  2,  3],
#       [ 4,  5,  6,  7],
#       [ 8,  9, 10, 11],
#       [12, 13, 14, 15],
#       [16, 17, 18, 19],
#       [20, 21, 22, 23]])

print "In: b.T"
print b.T
#Out:
#array([[ 0,  4,  8, 12, 16, 20],
#       [ 1,  5,  9, 13, 17, 21],
```

```
#         [ 2,   6, 10, 14, 18, 22],
#         [ 3,   7, 11, 15, 19, 23]])

print "In: b.ndim"
print b.ndim
#Out: 1

print "In: b.T"
print b.T
#Out: array([0, 1, 2, 3, 4])


print "In: b = array([1.j + 1, 2.j + 3])"
b = np.array([1.j + 1, 2.j + 3])

print "In: b"
print b
#Out: array([ 1.+1.j,   3.+2.j])

print "In: b.real"
print b.real
#Out: array([ 1.,   3.])

print "In: b.imag"
print b.imag
#Out: array([ 1.,   2.])

print "In: b.dtype"
print b.dtype
#Out: dtype('complex128')

print "In: b.dtype.str"
print b.dtype.str
#Out: '<c16'


print "In: b = arange(4).reshape(2,2)"
b = np.arange(4).reshape(2,2)

print "In: b"
print b
#Out:
```

```
#array([[0, 1],
#        [2, 3]])

print "In: f = b.flat"
f = b.flat

print "In: f"
print f
#Out: <numpy.flatiter object at 0x103013e00>

print "In: for it in f: print it"
for it in f:
    print it
#0
#1
#2
#3

print "In: b.flat[2]"
print b.flat[2]
#Out: 2


print "In: b.flat[[1,3]]"
print b.flat[[1,3]]
#Out: array([1, 3])


print "In: b"
print b
#Out:
#array([[7, 7],
#        [7, 7]])

print "In: b.flat[[1,3]] = 1"
b.flat[[1,3]] = 1

print "In: b"
print b
#Out:
#array([[7, 1],
#        [7, 1]])
```

Besides the shape and dtype attributes, ndarray has a number of other properties, as shown in the following list:

- ndim gives the number of dimensions, as shown in the following code snippet:

```
In: b
Out:
array([[ 0,  1,  2,  3,  4,  5,  6,  7,  8,  9, 10, 11],
       [12, 13, 14, 15, 16, 17, 18, 19, 20, 21, 22, 23]])
In: b.ndim
Out: 2
```

- size holds the count of elements. This is shown as follows:

```
In: b.size
Out: 24
```

- itemsize returns the count of bytes for each element in the array, as shown in the following code snippet:

```
In: b.itemsize
Out: 8
```

- If you require the full count of bytes the array needs, you can have a look at nbytes. This is just a product of the itemsize and size properties:

```
In: b.nbytes
Out: 192
In: b.size * b.itemsize
Out: 192
```

- The T property has the same result as the transpose() function, which is shown as follows:

```
In: b.resize(6,4)
In: b
Out:
array([[ 0,  1,  2,  3],
       [ 4,  5,  6,  7],
       [ 8,  9, 10, 11],
       [12, 13, 14, 15],
       [16, 17, 18, 19],
       [20, 21, 22, 23]])
In: b.T
Out:
array([[ 0,  4,  8, 12, 16, 20],
       [ 1,  5,  9, 13, 17, 21],
       [ 2,  6, 10, 14, 18, 22],
       [ 3,  7, 11, 15, 19, 23]])
```

- If the array has a rank of less than 2, we will just get a view of the array:

```
In: b.ndim
Out: 1
In: b.T
Out: array([0, 1, 2, 3, 4])
```

- Complex numbers in NumPy are represented by j. For instance, we can produce an array with complex numbers as follows:

```
In: b = array([1.j + 1, 2.j + 3])
In: b
Out: array([ 1.+1.j,  3.+2.j])
```

- The real property returns to us the real part of the array, or the array itself if it only holds real numbers:

```
In: b.real
Out: array([ 1.,  3.])
```

- The imag property holds the imaginary part of the array:

```
In: b.imag
Out: array([ 1.,  2.])
```

- If the array holds complex numbers, then the data type will automatically be complex as well:

```
In: b.dtype
Out: dtype('complex128')
In: b.dtype.str
Out: '<c16'
```

- The flat property gives back a numpy.flatiter object. This is the only means to get a flatiter object; we do not have access to a flatiter constructor. The flat iterator enables us to loop through an array as if it were a flat array, as shown in the following code snippet:

```
In: b = arange(4).reshape(2,2)
In: b
Out:
array([[0, 1],
       [2, 3]])
In: f = b.flat
In: f
Out: <numpy.flatiter object at 0x103013e00>
```

```
In: for item in f: print item
    .....:
0
1
2
3
```

It is possible to straightaway obtain an element with the `flatiter` object:

```
In: b.flat[2]
Out: 2
```

Also, you can obtain multiple elements as follows:

```
In: b.flat[[1,3]]
Out: array([1, 3])
```

The `flat` property can be set. Setting the value of the `flat` property leads to overwriting the values of the entire array:

```
In: b.flat = 7
In: b
Out:
array([[7, 7],
       [7, 7]])
```

We can also obtain selected elements as follows:

```
In: b.flat[[1,3]] = 1
In: b
Out:
array([[7, 1],
       [7, 1]])
```

The next diagram illustrates various properties of `ndarray`:

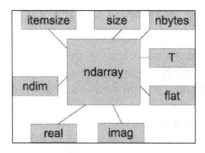

Converting arrays

We can convert a NumPy array to a Python list with the `tolist()` function (refer to `arrayconversion.py` in this book's code bundle). The following is a brief explanation:

- Convert to a list:

```
In: b
Out: array([ 1.+1.j,  3.+2.j])
In: b.tolist()
Out: [(1+1j), (3+2j)]
```

- The `astype()` function transforms the array to an array of the specified data type:

```
In: b
Out: array([ 1.+1.j,  3.+2.j])
In: b.astype(int)
/usr/local/bin/ipython:1: ComplexWarning: Casting complex
values to real discards the imaginary part
  #!/usr/bin/python
Out: array([1, 3])
In: b.astype('complex')
Out: array([ 1.+1.j,  3.+2.j])
```

> We are dropping off the imaginary part when casting from the `complex` type to `int`. The `astype()` function takes the name of a data type as a string too.

The preceding code won't display a warning this time because we used the right data type.

Creating array views and copies

In the example about `ravel()`, views were brought up. Views should not be confused with the construct of database views. Views in the NumPy universe are not read only and you don't have the possibility to protect the underlying information. It is crucial to know when we are handling a shared array view and when we have a replica of the array data. A slice of an array, for example, will produce a view. This entails that if you assign the slice to a variable and then alter the underlying array, the value of this variable will change. We will create an array from the famed *Lena picture*, and then create a view and alter it at the final stage. The Lena image array comes from a SciPy function.

1. Create a copy of the Lena array:

    ```
    acopy = lena.copy()
    ```

2. Create a view of the array:

    ```
    aview = lena.view()
    ```

3. Set all the values in the view to 0 with a `flat` iterator:

    ```
    aview.flat = 0
    ```

The final outcome is that only one of the pictures depicts the model. The other ones are censored altogether, as shown in the following screenshot:

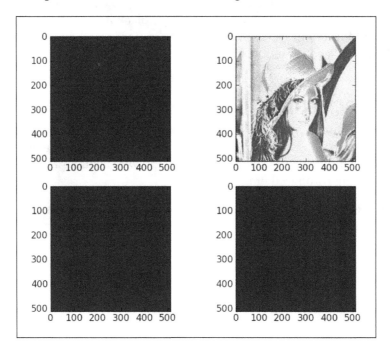

Refer to the following code of this tutorial (it is without comments to save space; for the full code, have a look at `copy_view.py`), which shows the behavior of array views and copies:

```
import scipy.misc
import matplotlib.pyplot as plt

lena = scipy.misc.lena()
acopy = lena.copy()
aview = lena.view()
```

```
plt.subplot(221)
plt.imshow(lena)
plt.subplot(222)
plt.imshow(acopy)
plt.subplot(223)
plt.imshow(aview)
aview.flat = 0
plt.subplot(224)
plt.imshow(aview)
plt.show()
```

As you can see, by altering the view at the end of the program, we modified the original Lena array. This resulted in three blue (or black if you are reading the print version of this book) pictures. The copied array was unchanged. It is crucial to remember that views are not read only.

Fancy indexing

Fancy indexing is indexing that does not involve integers or slices, which is *conventional* indexing. In this tutorial, we will practice fancy indexing to set the diagonal values of the Lena photo to 0. This will draw black lines along the diagonals, crossing through them.

The following is the code for this tutorial with comments taken away. The full code is in `fancy.py` of this book's code bundle:

```
import scipy.misc
import matplotlib.pyplot as plt

lena = scipy.misc.lena()
xmax = lena.shape[0]
ymax = lena.shape[1]
lena[range(xmax), range(ymax)] = 0
lena[range(xmax-1,-1,-1), range(ymax)] = 0
plt.imshow(lena)
plt.show()
```

The following is a brief explanation of the preceding code:

1. Set the values of the first diagonal to 0.

   To set the diagonal values to 0, we need to specify two different ranges for the x and y values (coordinates in a Cartesian coordinate system):

   ```
   lena[range(xmax), range(ymax)] = 0
   ```

2. Set the values of the other diagonal to `0`.

   To set the values of the other diagonal, we need a different set of ranges, but the rules remain the same:

   ```
   lena[range(xmax-1,-1,-1), range(ymax)] = 0
   ```

   At the final stage, we produce the following picture with the diagonals crossed out:

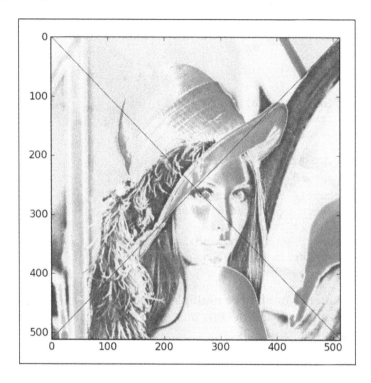

We specified different ranges for the x values and y values. These ranges were used to index the Lena array. Fancy indexing is done based on an internal NumPy iterator object. The following three steps are performed:

1. The iterator object is created.
2. The iterator object gets bound to the array.
3. Array elements are accessed via the iterator.

Indexing with a list of locations

Let's apply the `ix_()` function to shuffle the Lena photo. The following is the code for this example without comments. The finished code for the recipe can be found in `ix.py` in this book's code bundle:

```
import scipy.misc
import matplotlib.pyplot as plt
import numpy as np

lena = scipy.misc.lena()
xmax = lena.shape[0]
ymax = lena.shape[1]

def shuffle_indices(size):
    arr = np.arange(size)
    np.random.shuffle(arr)

    return arr

xindices = shuffle_indices(xmax)
np.testing.assert_equal(len(xindices), xmax)
yindices = shuffle_indices(ymax)
np.testing.assert_equal(len(yindices), ymax)
plt.imshow(lena[np.ix_(xindices, yindices)])
plt.show()
```

This function produces a mesh from multiple sequences. We hand in parameters as one-dimensional sequences and the function gives back a tuple of NumPy arrays, for instance, as follows:

```
In : ix_([0,1], [2,3])
Out:
(array([[0],[1]]), array([[2, 3]]))
```

To index the NumPy array with a list of locations, execute the following steps:

1. Shuffle array indices.

   Make an array with random index numbers with the `shuffle()` function of the `numpy.random` subpackage. The function modifies the array in place.

   ```
   def shuffle_indices(size):
       arr = np.arange(size)
       np.random.shuffle(arr)

       return arr
   ```

2. Plot the shuffled indices, as shown in the following code:

```
plt.imshow(lena[np.ix_(xindices, yindices)])
```

3. What we obtain is a totally scrambled Lena:

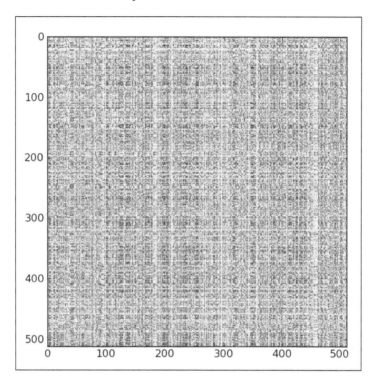

Indexing NumPy arrays with Booleans

Boolean indexing is indexing based on a Boolean array and falls in the family of fancy indexing. Since Boolean indexing is a kind of fancy indexing, the way it works is essentially the same.

The following is the code for this segment (refer to `boolean_indexing.py` in this book's code bundle):

```
import scipy.misc
import matplotlib.pyplot as plt
import numpy as np

lena = scipy.misc.lena()

def get_indices(size):
```

```
    arr = np.arange(size)
    return arr % 4 == 0

lena1 = lena.copy()
xindices = get_indices(lena.shape[0])
yindices = get_indices(lena.shape[1])
lena1[xindices, yindices] = 0
plt.subplot(211)
plt.imshow(lena1)
lena2 = lena.copy()
lena2[(lena > lena.max()/4) & (lena < 3 * lena.max()/4)] = 0
plt.subplot(212)
plt.imshow(lena2)
plt.show()
```

The preceding code implies that indexing occurs with the aid of a special iterator object. The following steps will give you a brief explanation of the preceding code:

1. Image with dots on the diagonal.

   This is in some manner similar to the *Fancy indexing* section. This time we choose modulo 4 points on the diagonal of the picture:

   ```
   def get_indices(size):
       arr = np.arange(size)
       return arr % 4 == 0
   ```

   Then, we just use this selection and plot the points:

   ```
   lena1 = lena.copy()
   xindices = get_indices(lena.shape[0])
   yindices = get_indices(lena.shape[1])
   lena1[xindices, yindices] = 0
   plt.subplot(211)
   plt.imshow(lena1)
   ```

2. Set to 0 based on value.

   Select array values between one quarter and three quarters of the maximum value and set them to 0:

   ```
   lena2[(lena > lena.max()/4) & (lena < 3 * lena.max()/4)] =
   0
   ```

3. The diagram with the two new pictures is presented as follows:

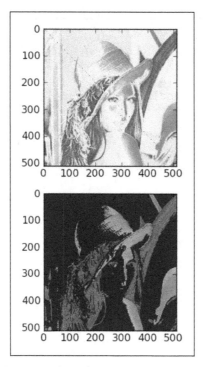

Broadcasting NumPy arrays

NumPy attempts to execute a procedure even though the operands do not have the same shape.

In this recipe, we will multiply an array and a scalar. The scalar is *broadened* to the shape of the array operand and then the multiplication is executed. The process described here is called **broadcasting**. The following is the entire code for this recipe (refer to `broadcasting.py` in this book's code bundle):

```
import scipy.io.wavfile
import matplotlib.pyplot as plt
import urllib2
import numpy as np
```

```
response =
urllib2.urlopen('http://www.thesoundarchive.com/austinpowers/smash
ingbaby.wav')
print response.info()
WAV_FILE = 'smashingbaby.wav'
filehandle = open(WAV_FILE, 'w')
filehandle.write(response.read())
filehandle.close()
sample_rate, data = scipy.io.wavfile.read(WAV_FILE)
print "Data type", data.dtype, "Shape", data.shape
plt.subplot(2, 1, 1)
plt.title("Original")
plt.plot(data)
newdata = data * 0.2
newdata = newdata.astype(np.uint8)
print "Data type", newdata.dtype, "Shape", newdata.shape
scipy.io.wavfile.write("quiet.wav",
    sample_rate, newdata)
plt.subplot(2, 1, 2)
plt.title("Quiet")
plt.plot(newdata)
plt.show()
```

We will download a sound file and create a new version that is quieter:

1. Reading a WAV file.

   We will use standard Python code to download a sound file of Austin Powers exclaiming *Smashing, baby*. SciPy has a `wavfile` subpackage, which lets you load audio data or generate WAV files. If SciPy is installed, then we should already have this subpackage. The `read()` function delivers a data array and sample rate. In this exercise, we are only concerned about the data.

   ```
   sample_rate, data = scipy.io.wavfile.read(WAV_FILE)
   ```

2. Plot the original WAV data.

   Plot the original WAV data with matplotlib and give the subplot the title `Original`:

   ```
   plt.subplot(2, 1, 1)
   plt.title("Original")
   plt.plot(data)
   ```

3. Create a new array.

   Now, we will use NumPy to produce a hushed sound sample. It is just a matter of making a new array with smaller values by multiplying it with a constant. This is where the trick of broadcasting happens. At the end, we want to be certain that we have the same data type as in the original array because of the WAV format.

   ```
   newdata = data * 0.2
   newdata = newdata.astype(np.uint8)
   ```

4. Write to a WAV file.

   This new array can be saved in a new WAV file as follows:

   ```
   scipy.io.wavfile.write("quiet.wav",
       sample_rate, newdata)
   ```

5. Plot the new WAV data.

   Plot the new data array with matplotlib as follows:

   ```
   plt.subplot(2, 1, 2)
   plt.title("Quiet")
   plt.plot(newdata)
   plt.show()
   ```

6. The result is a diagram of the original WAV file data and a new array with smaller values, as depicted in the following figure:

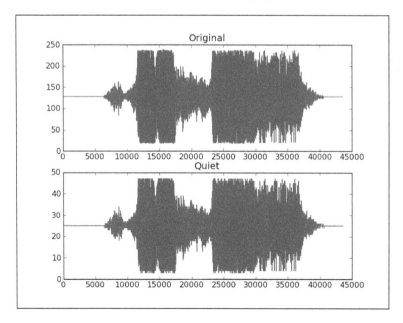

Summary

In this chapter, we found out a heap about the NumPy basics: data types and arrays. Arrays have various properties that describe them. You learned that one of these properties is the data type, which, in NumPy, is represented by a full-fledged object.

NumPy arrays can be sliced and indexed in an effective way, compared to standard Python lists. NumPy arrays have the extra ability to work with multiple dimensions.

The shape of an array can be modified in multiple ways, such as stacking, resizing, reshaping, and splitting. A large number of convenience functions for shape manipulation were presented in this chapter.

Having picked up the fundamentals, it's time to proceed to data analysis with the commonly used functions in *Chapter 3, Statistics and Linear Algebra*. This includes the usage of staple statistical and numerical functions.

3

Statistics and Linear Algebra

Statistics and linear algebra are branches of mathematics that are especially useful for data analysis. That's why we will focus on them in this chapter. Statistics is needed to make inferences from raw data. For instance, we can compute that the data for a variable has a certain arithmetic mean and standard deviation. From these numbers, we can then infer a range and the expected value for this variable. Then, we can run statistical tests to check how likely it is that we made the right conclusion.

Linear algebra concerns itself with systems of linear equations. These are easy to solve with NumPy and SciPy using the `linalg` package. Linear algebra is useful, for instance, to fit data to a model. We shall introduce other NumPy and SciPy packages in this chapter for random number generation and masked arrays.

In this chapter, we will cover the following topics:

- Descriptive statistics
- The `linalg` package
- Polynomials
- Matrices as specialized `ndarray` subclasses
- Random numbers
- Continuous and discrete distributions
- Masked arrays

NumPy and SciPy modules

First, let's take a look at the NumPy and SciPy module documentation. What will be described here is not a topic specific to data analysis, but more of a general Python item.

The following code prints the descriptions of subpackages for NumPy and SciPy:

```
import pkgutil as pu
import numpy as np
import matplotlib as mpl
import scipy as sp
import pydoc


print "NumPy version", np.__version__
print "SciPy version", sp.__version__
print "Matplotlib version", mpl.__version__

def clean(astr):
    s = astr
    # remove multiple spaces
    s = ' '.join(s.split())
    s = s.replace('=','')

    return s

def print_desc(prefix, pkg_path):
    for pkg in pu.iter_modules(path=pkg_path):
        name = prefix + "." + pkg[1]

        if pkg[2] == True:
            try:
                docstr = pydoc.plain(pydoc.render_doc(name))
                docstr = clean(docstr)
                start = docstr.find("DESCRIPTION")
                docstr = docstr[start: start + 140]
                print name, docstr
            except:
                continue

print_desc("numpy", np.__path__)
print
print
print
print_desc("scipy", sp.__path__)
```

Using the standard Python modules pkgutil and pydoc, we can iterate through subpackages in NumPy and SciPy and extract short descriptions of these subpackages. We will also print the SciPy, matplotlib, and NumPy versions.

The versions for the various software used in this chapter can be obtained from the `__version__` attribute of the corresponding module as follows:

```
print "NumPy version", np.__version__
print "SciPy version", sp.__version__
print "Matplotlib version", mpl.__version__
```

I have tested the code with the following versions (of course, you don't need to have the exact same versions):

- NumPy Version 1.9.0.dev-e886943
- SciPy Version 0.13.2
- matplotlib Version 1.4.x

We can iterate through subpackages given a path with the `iter_modules()` function of `pkgutil`. The result of the function call is a list of tuples containing three elements each. For us, only the second and third elements are interesting right now. The second element contains the name of the subpackage and the third element is a Boolean indicating a subpackage.

```
for pkg in pu.iter_modules(path=pkg_path):
```

The `pydoc.render_doc()` function returns the documentation string for a given subpackage or function. It returns a string that can contains non-printable characters, so we use the `pydoc.plain()` function to get rid of them. From this string, we will extract a part of the text, following the DESCRIPTION heading (not the whole text to save space).

```
docstr = pydoc.plain(pydoc.render_doc(name))
```

The preceding code should make it easy to find information for locally installed Python modules. For NumPy, we get the following subpackage descriptions:

```
numpy.compat DESCRIPTION This module contains duplicated code from
Python itself or 3rd party extensions, which may be included for the
following reasons
numpy.core DESCRIPTION Functions - array - NumPy Array construction -
zeros - Return an array of all zeros - empty - Return an unitialized
array - shap
numpy.distutils
numpy.doc DESCRIPTION Topical documentation  The following topics are
available: - basics - broadcasting - byteswapping - constants - creation
- gloss
numpy.f2py
numpy.fft DESCRIPTION Discrete Fourier Transform (:mod:`numpy.fft`)
.. currentmodule:: numpy.fft Standard FFTs ------------- ..
autosummary:: :toctre
```

numpy.lib DESCRIPTION Basic functions used by several sub-packages and useful to have in the main name-space. Type Handling ------------ - iscomplexo

numpy.linalg DESCRIPTION Core Linear Algebra Tools ------------------ ------- Linear algebra basics: - norm Vector or matrix norm - inv Inverse of a squar

numpy.ma DESCRIPTION Masked Arrays Arrays sometimes contain invalid or missing data. When doing operations on such arrays, we wish to suppress inva

numpy.matrixlib

numpy.polynomial DESCRIPTION Within the documentation for this sub-package, a "finite power series," i.e., a polynomial (also referred to simply as a "series

numpy.random DESCRIPTION Random Number Generation Utility functions random_sample Uniformly distributed floats over ``[0, 1)``. random Alias for `ra

numpy.testing DESCRIPTION This single module should provide all the common functionality for numpy tests in a single location, so that test scripts can ju

For SciPy, we get the following subpackage descriptions:

scipy._build_utils

scipy.cluster DESCRIPTION Clustering package (:mod:`scipy.cluster`) .. currentmodule:: scipy.cluster :mod:`scipy.cluster.vq` Clustering algorithms are u

scipy.constants DESCRIPTION Constants (:mod:`scipy.constants`) .. currentmodule:: scipy.constants Physical and mathematical constants and units. Mathemati

scipy.fftpack DESCRIPTION Discrete Fourier transforms (:mod:`scipy.fftpack`) Fast Fourier Transforms (FFTs) .. autosummary:: :toctree: generated/ fft -

scipy.integrate DESCRIPTION Integration and ODEs (:mod:`scipy.integrate`) .. currentmodule:: scipy.integrate Integrating functions, given function object

scipy.interpolate DESCRIPTION Interpolation (:mod:`scipy.interpolate`) .. currentmodule:: scipy.interpolate Sub-package for objects used in interpolation. A

scipy.io DESCRIPTION Input and output (:mod:`scipy.io`) .. currentmodule:: scipy.io SciPy has many modules, classes, and functions available to rea

scipy.lib DESCRIPTION Python wrappers to external libraries - lapack -- wrappers for `LAPACK/ATLAS <http://netlib.org/lapack/>`_ libraries - blas --

```
scipy.linalg DESCRIPTION  Linear algebra (:mod:`scipy.linalg`) ..
currentmodule:: scipy.linalg Linear algebra functions. .. seealso::
`numpy.linalg` for

scipy.misc DESCRIPTION  Miscellaneous routines (:mod:`scipy.misc`)
.. currentmodule:: scipy.misc Various utilities that don't have
another home. Note

scipy.ndimage DESCRIPTION  Multi-dimensional image processing
(:mod:`scipy.ndimage`) .. currentmodule:: scipy.ndimage This package
contains various funct

scipy.odr DESCRIPTION  Orthogonal distance regression
(:mod:`scipy.odr`) .. currentmodule:: scipy.odr Package Content ..
autosummary:: :toctree: gen

scipy.optimize DESCRIPTION  Optimization and root finding
(:mod:`scipy.optimize`) .. currentmodule:: scipy.optimize
Optimization  General-purpose --------

scipy.signal DESCRIPTION  Signal processing (:mod:`scipy.signal`) ..
module:: scipy.signal Convolution  .. autosummary:: :toctree:
generated/ convolve -

scipy.sparse DESCRIPTION  Sparse matrices (:mod:`scipy.sparse`) ..
currentmodule:: scipy.sparse SciPy 2-D sparse matrix package for
numeric data. Conten

scipy.spatial DESCRIPTION  Spatial algorithms and data structures
(:mod:`scipy.spatial`) .. currentmodule:: scipy.spatial Nearest-
neighbor Queries  .. au

scipy.special DESCRIPTION  Special functions (:mod:`scipy.special`)
.. module:: scipy.special Nearly all of the functions below are
universal functions a

scipy.stats DESCRIPTION  Statistical functions (:mod:`scipy.stats`)
.. module:: scipy.stats This module contains a large number of
probability distribu

scipy.weave DESCRIPTION C/C++ integration  inline -- a function for
including C/C++ code within Python blitz -- a function for compiling
Numeric express
```

Basic descriptive statistics with NumPy

In this book, we will try to use as many varied datasets as possible. This depends on the availability of the data. Unfortunately, this means that the subject of the data might not exactly match your interests. Every dataset has its own quirks, but the general skills you acquire in this book should transfer to your own field. In this chapter, we will load a number of **Comma-separated Value (CSV)** files into NumPy arrays in order to analyze the data.

To load the data, we will use the NumPy `loadtxt()` function as follows:

 The code for this example can be found in `basic_stats.py` in the code bundle.

```
import numpy as np
from scipy.stats import scoreatpercentile

data = np.loadtxt("mdrtb_2012.csv", delimiter=',', usecols=(1,),
skiprows=1, unpack=True)

print "Max method", data.max()
print "Max function", np.max(data)

print "Min method", data.min()
print "Min function", np.min(data)

print "Mean method", data.mean()
print "Mean function", np.mean(data)

print "Std method", data.std()
print "Std function", np.std(data)

print "Median", np.median(data)
print "Score at percentile 50", scoreatpercentile(data, 50)
```

Next, we will compute the mean, median, maximum, minimum, and standard deviations of a NumPy array.

 If these terms sound unfamiliar to you, please take some time to learn about them from Wikipedia or any other source. As mentioned in the *Preface*, we will assume familiarity with basic mathematical and statistical concepts.

The data comes from the `mdrtb_2012.csv` file, which can be found in the code bundle. This is an edited version of the CSV file, which can be downloaded from the WHO website at `https://extranet.who.int/tme/generateCSV.asp?ds=mdr_estimates`. It contains data about a type of tuberculosis. The file we are going to use is a reduced version of the original file containing only two columns: the country and percentage of new cases. Here are the first two lines of the file:

```
country,e_new_mdr_pcnt
Afghanistan,3.5
```

Now, let's compute the mean, median, maximum, minimum, and standard deviations of a NumPy array:

1. First, we will load the data with the following function call:

    ```
    data = np.loadtxt("mdrtb_2012.csv", delimiter=',',
    usecols=(1,), skiprows=1, unpack=True)
    ```

    In the preceding call, we specify a comma as a delimiter, the second column to load data from, and that we want to skip the header. We also specify the name of the file and assume that the file is in the current directory; otherwise, we will have to specify the correct path.

2. The maximum of an array can be obtained via a method of the `ndarray` and NumPy functions. The same goes for the minimum, mean, and standard deviations. The following code snippet prints the various statistics:

    ```
    print "Max method", data.max()
    print "Max function", np.max(data)

    print "Min method", data.min()
    print "Min function", np.min(data)

    print "Mean method", data.mean()
    print "Mean function", np.mean(data)

    print "Std method", data.std()
    print "Std function", np.std(data)
    ```

    The output is as follows:

    ```
    Max method 50.0
    Max function 50.0
    Min method 0.0
    Min function 0.0
    Mean method 3.2787037037
    Mean function 3.2787037037
    Std method 5.76332073654
    Std function 5.76332073654
    ```

3. The median can be retrieved with a NumPy or SciPy function, which can estimate the 50th percentile of the data with the following lines:

    ```
    print "Median", np.median(data)
    print "Score at percentile 50", scoreatpercentile(data, 50)
    ```

    The following is printed:

    ```
    Median 1.8
    Score at percentile 50 1.8
    ```

Linear algebra with NumPy

Linear algebra is an important subdivision of mathematics. We can use linear algebra, for instance, to perform linear regression. The `numpy.linalg` subpackage holds linear algebra routines. With this subpackage, you can invert matrices, compute eigenvalues, solve linear equations, and find determinants among other matters. Matrices in NumPy are represented by a subclass of `ndarray`.

Inverting matrices with NumPy

The inverse of a square and invertible matrix `A` in linear algebra is the matrix `A-1`, which when multiplied with the original matrix is equal to the identity matrix `I`. This can be written down as the following mathematical equation:

```
A A-1 = I
```

The `inv()` function in the `numpy.linalg` subpackage can do this for us. Let's invert an example matrix. To invert matrices, follow the ensuing steps:

1. Create the example matrix.

    We will create the demonstration matrix with the `mat()` function:

    ```
    A = np.mat("2 4 6;4 2 6;10 -4 18")
    print "A\n", A
    ```

    The `A` matrix is printed as follows:

    ```
    A
    [[ 2  4  6]
     [ 4  2  6]
     [10 -4 18]]]
    ```

2. Invert the matrix.

    Now, we can view the `inv()` subroutine in action:

    ```
    inverse = np.linalg.inv(A)
    print "inverse of A\n", inverse
    ```

    The inverse matrix is displayed as follows:

    ```
    inverse of A
    [[-0.41666667  0.66666667 -0.08333333]
     [ 0.08333333  0.16666667 -0.08333333]
     [ 0.25       -0.33333333  0.08333333]]
    ```

If the matrix is singular, or not square, a `LinAlgError` is raised. If you wish, you can check the solution manually. This is left as a drill for you. The `pinv()` NumPy function performs a pseudo inversion, which can be applied to any matrix, including matrices that are not square.

3. Check by multiplication.

    Let's check what we get when we multiply the original matrix with the result of the `inv()` function:

    ```
    print "Check\n", A * inverse
    ```

    The result is the identity matrix, as expected (ignoring small differences):

    ```
    Check
    [[  1.00000000e+00   0.00000000e+00  -5.55111512e-17]
     [ -2.22044605e-16   1.00000000e+00  -5.55111512e-17]
     [ -8.88178420e-16   8.88178420e-16   1.00000000e+00]]
    ```

By subtracting the 3 x 3 identity matrix from the previous result, we get the errors of the inversion process:

```
print "Error\n", A * inverse - np.eye(3)
```

The errors should be negligible in general, but in some cases small errors could be propagated with undesirable side effects:

```
[[ -1.11022302e-16   0.00000000e+00  -5.55111512e-17]
 [ -2.22044605e-16   4.44089210e-16  -5.55111512e-17]
 [ -8.88178420e-16   8.88178420e-16  -1.11022302e-16]]
```

In such cases, higher precision data types might help or switch to a superior algorithm. We computed the inverse of a matrix with the `inv()` routine of the `numpy.linalg` subpackage. We made certain, with matrix multiplication, whether this is indeed the inverse matrix (see `inversion.py` in this book's code bundle):

```
import numpy as np

A = np.mat("2 4 6;4 2 6;10 -4 18")
print "A\n", A

inverse = np.linalg.inv(A)
print "inverse of A\n", inverse

print "Check\n", A * inverse
print "Error\n", A * inverse - np.eye(3)
```

Solving linear systems with NumPy

A matrix transforms a vector into another vector in a linear fashion. This operation numerically corresponds to a system of linear equations. The `solve()` subroutine of `numpy.linalg` solves systems of linear equations of the form `Ax = b`; here, A is a matrix, b can be a one-dimensional or two-dimensional array, and x is an unknown quantity. We will witness the `dot()` subroutine in action. This function computes the dot product of two floating-point numbers' arrays.

Let's solve an instance of a linear system. To solve a linear system, follow the ensuing steps:

1. Create the matrix A and array b.

    The following code will create A and b:

    ```
    A = np.mat("1 -2 1;0 2 -8;-4 5 9")
    print "A\n", A
    b = np.array([0, 8, -9])
    print "b\n", b
    ```

    The matrix A and array (vector) b are defined as follows:

    ```
    A
    [[ 1 -2  1]
     [ 0  2 -8]
     [-4  5  9]]
    b
    [ 0  8 -9]
    ```

2. Call the `solve()` function.

    Solve this linear system with the `solve()` function:

    ```
    x = np.linalg.solve(A, b)
    print "Solution", x
    ```

    The solution of the linear system is as follows:

    ```
    Solution [ 29.  16.   3.]
    ```

3. Check with the `dot()` function.

    Check whether the solution is correct with the `dot()` function:

    ```
    print "Check\n", np.dot(A , x)
    ```

The result is as expected:

```
Check
[[ 0.   8.  -9.]]
```

We solved a linear system by applying the `solve()` function from the `linalg` subpackage of NumPy and checking the result with the `dot()` function (please refer to `solution.py` in this book's code bundle):

```
import numpy as np

A = np.mat("1 -2 1;0 2 -8;-4 5 9")
print "A\n", A

b = np.array([0, 8, -9])
print "b\n", b

x = np.linalg.solve(A, b)
print "Solution", x

print "Check\n", np.dot(A , x)
```

Finding eigenvalues and eigenvectors with NumPy

Eigenvalues are scalar solutions to the equation Ax = ax, where A is a two-dimensional matrix and x is a one-dimensional vector. **Eigenvectors** are vectors corresponding to eigenvalues.

 Eigenvalues and eigenvectors are fundamental in mathematics and are used in many important algorithms, such as **Principal Component Analysis** (**PCA**). PCA can be used to simplify the analysis of large datasets.

The `eigvals()` subroutine in the `numpy.linalg` package computes eigenvalues. The `eig()` function gives back a tuple holding eigenvalues and eigenvectors.

We will obtain the eigenvalues and eigenvectors of a matrix with the `eigvals()` and `eig()` functions of the `numpy.linalg` subpackage. We will check the outcome by applying the `dot()` function (see `eigenvalues.py` in this book's code):

```
import numpy as np

A = np.mat("3 -2;1 0")
```

```
print "A\n", A

print "Eigenvalues", np.linalg.eigvals(A)

eigenvalues, eigenvectors = np.linalg.eig(A)
print "First tuple of eig", eigenvalues
print "Second tuple of eig\n", eigenvectors

for i in range(len(eigenvalues)):
    print "Left", np.dot(A, eigenvectors[:,i])
    print "Right", eigenvalues[i] * eigenvectors[:,i]
    print
```

Let's calculate the eigenvalues of a matrix:

1. Create the matrix.

    The following code will create a matrix:

    ```
    A = np.mat("3 -2;1 0")
    print "A\n", A
    ```

    The matrix we created looks like this:

    ```
    A
    [[ 3 -2]
     [ 1  0]]
    ```

2. Calculate eigenvalues with the `eig()` function.

    Apply the `eig()` subroutine:

    ```
    print "Eigenvalues", np.linalg.eigvals(A)
    ```

    The eigenvalues of the matrix are as follows:

    ```
    Eigenvalues [ 2.  1.]
    ```

3. Get eigenvalues and eigenvectors with `eig()`.

    Get the eigenvalues and eigenvectors with the `eig()` function. This routine returns a tuple, where the first element holds eigenvalues and the second element contains matching `eigenvectors`, set up column-wise:

    ```
    eigenvalues, eigenvectors = np.linalg.eig(A)
    print "First tuple of eig", eigenvalues
    print "Second tuple of eig\n", eigenvectors
    ```

    The `eigenvalues` and `eigenvectors` values will be:

    ```
    First tuple of eig [ 2.  1.]
    ```

```
Second tuple of eig
[[ 0.89442719  0.70710678]
 [ 0.4472136   0.70710678]]
```

4. Check the result.

Check the answer with the dot() function by computing both sides of the eigenvalues equation Ax = ax:

```
for i in range(len(eigenvalues)):
    print "Left", np.dot(A, eigenvectors[:,i])
    print "Right", eigenvalues[i] * eigenvectors[:,i]
    print
```

The output is as follows:

```
Left [[ 1.78885438]
 [ 0.89442719]]
Right [[ 1.78885438]
 [ 0.89442719]]
Left [[ 0.70710678]
 [ 0.70710678]]
Right [[ 0.70710678]
 [ 0.70710678]]
```

NumPy random numbers

Random numbers are used in Monte Carlo methods, stochastic calculus, and more. Real random numbers are difficult to produce, so in practice, we use pseudo-random numbers. Pseudo-random numbers are sufficiently random for most intents and purposes, except for some very exceptional instances, such as very accurate simulations. The random-numbers-associated routines can be located in the NumPy random subpackage.

> The core random-number generator is based on the Mersenne Twister algorithm (refer to https://en.wikipedia.org/wiki/Mersenne_twister).

Random numbers can be produced from discrete or continuous distributions. The distribution functions have an optional size argument, which informs NumPy how many numbers are to be created. You can specify either an integer or a tuple as the size. This will lead to an array of appropriate shapes filled with random numbers. Discrete distributions include the geometric, hypergeometric, and binomial distributions. Continuous distributions include the normal and lognormal distributions.

Gambling with the binomial distribution

The binomial distribution models the number of successes in an integer number of independent runs of an experiment, where the chance of success in each experiment is a set number.

Envisage a 17th-century gambling house where you can wager on tossing pieces of eight. Nine coins are flipped in a popular game. If less than five coins are heads, then you lose one piece of eight; otherwise, you earn one. Let's simulate this, commencing with one thousand coins in our possession. We will use the `binomial()` function from the `random` module for this purpose:

 If you want to follow the code, have a look at `headortail.py` in this book's code bundle.

```
import numpy as np
from matplotlib.pyplot import plot, show

cash = np.zeros(10000)
cash[0] = 1000
outcome = np.random.binomial(9, 0.5, size=len(cash))

for i in range(1, len(cash)):

    if outcome[i] < 5:
        cash[i] = cash[i - 1] - 1
    elif outcome[i] < 10:
        cash[i] = cash[i - 1] + 1
    else:
        raise AssertionError("Unexpected outcome " + outcome)

print outcome.min(), outcome.max()

plot(np.arange(len(cash)), cash)
show()
```

In order to understand the `binomial()` function, take a look at the following steps:

1. Calling the binomial() function.

   Initialize an array, which acts as the cash balance, to zero. Call the `binomial()` function with a size of `10000`. This represents 10,000 coin flips in our casino:

   ```
   cash = np.zeros(10000)
   cash[0] = 1000
   outcome = np.random.binomial(9, 0.5, size=len(cash))
   ```

2. Updating the cash balance.

   Go through the results of the coin tosses and update the `cash` array. Display the highest and lowest value of the `outcome` array, just to make certain we don't have any unusual outliers:

```
for i in range(1, len(cash)):
    if outcome[i] < 5:
        cash[i] = cash[i - 1] - 1
    elif outcome[i] < 10:
        cash[i] = cash[i - 1] + 1
    else:
        raise AssertionError("Unexpected outcome " + outcome)
print outcome.min(), outcome.max()
```

   As expected, the values are between 0 and 9:

```
0 9
```

3. Plotting the cash array with matplotlib:

```
plot(np.arange(len(cash)), cash)
show()
```

You can determine in the following plot that our cash balance executes a random walk (random movement not following a pattern):

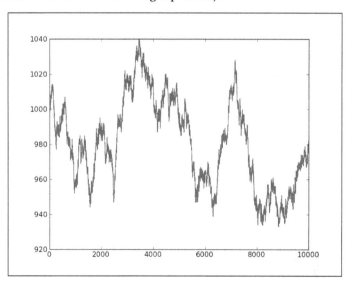

Of course, each time we execute the code, we will have a different random walk. If you want to always receive the same results, you will want to hand a seed value to the `binomial()` function from the NumPy random subpackage.

Sampling the normal distribution

Continuous distributions are modeled by the **probability density functions (pdf)**. The chance for a specified interval is found by integration of the probability density function. The NumPy `random` module has a number of functions that represent continuous distributions, such as `beta`, `chisquare`, `exponential`, `f`, `gamma`, `gumbel`, `laplace`, `lognormal`, `logistic`, `multivariate_normal`, `noncentral_chisquare`, `noncentral_f`, `normal`, and others.

We will visualize the normal distribution by applying the `normal()` function from the `random` NumPy subpackage. We will do this by drawing a bell curve and histogram of randomly generated values (refer to `normaldist.py` in this book's code bundle):

```
import numpy as np
import matplotlib.pyplot as plt


N=10000

normal_values = np.random.normal(size=N)
dummy, bins, dummy = plt.hist(normal_values, np.sqrt(N), normed=True,
lw=1)
sigma = 1
mu = 0
plt.plot(bins, 1/(sigma * np.sqrt(2 * np.pi)) * np.exp( - (bins -
mu)**2 / (2 * sigma**2) ),lw=2)
plt.show()
```

Random numbers can be produced from a normal distribution and their distribution might be displayed with a histogram. To plot a normal distribution, follow the ensuing steps:

1. Generate values.

   Create random numbers for a certain sample size with the aid of the `normal()` function from the `random` NumPy subpackage:

   ```
   N=100.00
   normal_values = np.random.normal(size=N)
   ```

2. Draw the histogram and theoretical pdf.

   Plot the histogram and theoretical pdf with a central value of 0 and a standard deviation of 1. We will use matplotlib for this goal:

   ```
   dummy, bins, dummy = plt.hist(normal_values,
     np.sqrt(N), normed=True, lw=1)
   sigma = 1
   ```

```
mu = 0
plt.plot(bins, 1/(sigma * np.sqrt(2 * np.pi))
   * np.exp( - (bins - mu)**2 / (2 * sigma**2) ),lw=2)
plt.show()
```

In the following plot, we see the famed bell curve:

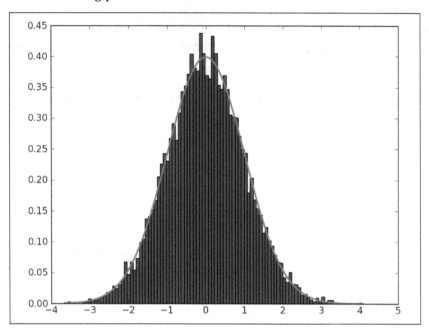

Performing a normality test with SciPy

The normal distribution is widely used in science and statistics. According to the central limit theorem, a large, random sample with independent observations will converge towards the normal distribution. The properties of the normal distribution are well known and it is considered convenient to use. However, there are a number of requirements that need to be met such as a sufficiently large number of data points, and these data points must be independent. It is a good practice to check whether data conforms to the normal distribution or not. A great number of normality tests exist, some of which have been implemented in the scipy.stats package. We will apply these tests in this section. As sample data, we will use flu trends data from https://www.google.org/flutrends/data.txt. The original file has been reduced to include only two columns: a date and values for Argentina. A few lines are given as follows:

```
Date,Argentina
29/12/02,
05/01/03,
```

```
12/01/03,
19/01/03,
26/01/03,
02/02/03,136
```

The data can be found in the `goog_flutrends.csv` file of the code bundle. We will also sample data from the normal distribution as we did in the previous tutorial. The resulting array will have the same size as the flu trends array and will serve as the golden standard, which should pass the normality test with flying colors.

 Refer to `normality_test.py` in the code bundle for the code.

```
import numpy as np
from scipy.stats import shapiro
from scipy.stats import anderson
from scipy.stats import normaltest



flutrends = np.loadtxt("goog_flutrends.csv", delimiter=',',
usecols=(1,), skiprows=1, converters = {1: lambda s: float(s or 0)},
unpack=True)
N = len(flutrends)
normal_values = np.random.normal(size=N)
zero_values = np.zeros(N)

print "Normal Values Shapiro", shapiro(normal_values)
print "Zeroes Shapiro", shapiro(zero_values)
print "Flu Shapiro", shapiro(flutrends)
print

print "Normal Values Anderson", anderson(normal_values)
print "Zeroes Anderson", anderson(zero_values)
print "Flu Anderson", anderson(flutrends)
print

print "Normal Values normaltest", normaltest(normal_values)
print "Zeroes normaltest", normaltest(zero_values)
print "Flu normaltest", normaltest(flutrends)
```

As a negative example, we will use an array of the same size as the two previously mentioned arrays filled with zeros. In real life, we could get this kind of values if we were dealing with a rare event (for instance, a pandemic outbreak).

In the data file, some cells are empty. Of course, these types of issues occur frequently, so we have to get used to cleaning our data. We are going to assume that the correct value should be 0. A converter can fill in those 0 values for us as follows:

```
flutrends = np.loadtxt("goog_flutrends.csv", delimiter=',',
usecols=(1,), skiprows=1, converters = {1: lambda s:
float(s or 0)}, unpack=True)
```

The Shapiro-Wilk test can check for normality. The corresponding SciPy function returns a tuple of which the first number is a test statistic and the second number is a p-value. It should be noted that the zeros-filled array caused a warning. In fact, all the three functions used in this example had trouble with this array and gave warnings. We get the following result:

```
Normal Values Shapiro (0.9967482686042786,
0.2774980068206787)
Zeroes Shapiro (1.0, 1.0)
Flu Shapiro (0.9351990818977356, 2.2945883254311397e-15)
```

The result for the zeros-filled array is a bit strange. Since we get a warning, it might be advisable to even ignore it altogether. The p-values we get are similar to the results of the third test later in this example. The analysis is basically the same.

The Anderson-Darling test can check for normality and also for other distributions such as Exponential, Logistic, and Gumbel. The related SciPy function related a test statistic and an array containing critical values for the 15, 10, 5, 2.5, and 1 percentage significance levels. If the statistic is larger than the critical value at a significance level, we can reject normality. We get the following values:

```
Normal Values Anderson (0.31201465602225653, array([ 0.572,
0.652,  0.782,  0.912,  1.085]), array([ 15. ,  10. ,   5.
,   2.5,   1. ]))

Zeroes Anderson (nan, array([ 0.572,  0.652,  0.782,
0.912,  1.085]), array([ 15. ,  10. ,   5. ,   2.5,   1.
]))

Flu Anderson (8.258614154768793, array([ 0.572,  0.652,
0.782,  0.912,  1.085]), array([ 15. ,  10. ,   5. ,   2.5,
1. ]))
```

For the zeros-filled array, we cannot say anything sensible because the statistic returned is not a number. We are not allowed to reject normality for our golden standard array, as we would have expected. However, the statistic returned for the flu trends data is larger than all the corresponding critical values. We can, therefore, confidently reject normality. Out of the three test functions, this one seems to be the easiest to use.

The D'Agostino and Pearson's test is also implemented in SciPy as the `normaltest()` function. This function returns a tuple with a statistic and p-value just like the `shapiro()` function. The p-value is a two-sided Chi-squared probability. Chi-squared is another well-known distribution. The test itself is based on z-scores of the skewness and kurtosis tests. Skewness measures how symmetric a distribution is. The normal distribution is symmetric and has zero skewness. Kurtosis tells us something about the shape of the distribution (high peak, fat tail). The normal distribution has a kurtosis of three (the excess kurtosis is zero). The following values are obtained by the test:

```
Normal Values normaltest (3.102791866779639, 0.21195189649335339)
Zeroes normaltest (1.0095473240349975, 0.60364218712103535)
Flu normaltest (99.643733363569538, 2.3048264115368721e-22)
```

Since we are dealing with a probability for the p-value, we want this probability to be as high as possible and close to one. For the zeros-filled array, this has strange consequences, but since we got warnings, the result for that particular array is not reliable. Further, we can accept normality if the p-value is at least 0.5. For the golden standard array, we get a lower value, which means that we probably need to have more observations. It is left as an exercise for you to confirm this.

Creating a NumPy-masked array

Data is often messy and contains gaps or characters that we do not deal with often. Masked arrays can be utilized to disregard absent or invalid data points. A masked array from the `numpy.ma` subpackage is a subclass of `ndarray` with a mask. In this section, we will use the Lena Soderberg photo as the data source and act as if some of this data is corrupt. The following is the full code for the masked-array example from the `masked.py` file in this book's code bundle:

```
import numpy
import scipy
```

```
import matplotlib.pyplot as plt

lena = scipy.misc.lena()
random_mask = numpy.random.randint(0, 2, size=lena.shape)

plt.subplot(221)
plt.title("Original")
plt.imshow(lena)
plt.axis('off')

masked_array = numpy.ma.array(lena, mask=random_mask)
print masked_array

plt.subplot(222)
plt.title("Masked")
plt.imshow(masked_array)
plt.axis('off')

plt.subplot(223)
plt.title("Log")
plt.imshow(numpy.log(lena))
plt.axis('off')

plt.subplot(224)
plt.title("Log Masked")
plt.imshow(numpy.log(masked_array))
plt.axis('off')

plt.show()
```

Finally, we will display the original picture, logarithm values of the original image, the masked array, and logarithm values thereof:

1. Create a mask.

   To produce a masked array, we have to stipulate a mask. Let's create a random mask. This mask will have values that are either 0 or 1:

   ```
   random_mask = numpy.random.randint(0, 2, size=lena.shape)
   ```

2. Create a masked array.

   By applying the mask in the former step, create a masked array:

   ```
   masked_array = numpy.ma.array(lena, mask=random_mask)
   ```

The resulting pictures are exhibited as follows:

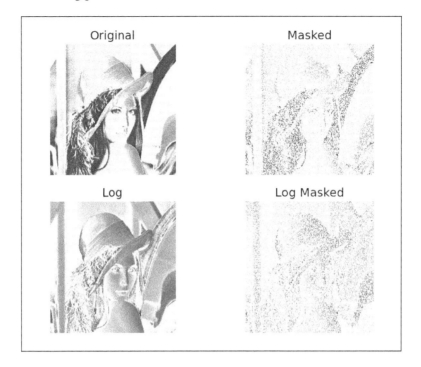

We applied a random mask to NumPy arrays. This resulted in disregarding the data matching the mask. There is an entire range of masked-array procedures to be discovered in the numpy.ma subpackage. In this tutorial, we only presented how to produce a masked array.

Disregarding negative and extreme values

Masked arrays are useful when we desire to ignore negative values, for example, when taking the logarithm of array values. A second use case for masked arrays is rejecting outliers. This works based on a higher and lower limit for extreme values. In this tutorial, we will apply these techniques to the salary data of players in the MLB. The data comes originally from http://www.exploredata.net/Downloads/ Baseball-Data-Set. The data was edited to contain two columns: the player name and salary. This resulted in MLB2008.csv, which can be found in the code bundle. The full script for this tutorial is in the masked_funcs.py file in this book's code bundle:

```
import numpy as np
from matplotlib.finance import quotes_historical_yahoo
from datetime import date
```

```
import sys
import matplotlib.pyplot as plt

salary = np.loadtxt("MLB2008.csv", delimiter=',', usecols=(1,),
skiprows=1, unpack=True)
triples = np.arange(0, len(salary), 3)
print "Triples", triples[:10], "..."

signs = np.ones(len(salary))
print "Signs", signs[:10], "..."

signs[triples] = -1
print "Signs", signs[:10], "..."

ma_log = np.ma.log(salary * signs)
print "Masked logs", ma_log[:10], "..."

dev = salary.std()
avg = salary.mean()
inside = np.ma.masked_outside(salary, avg - dev, avg + dev)
print "Inside", inside[:10], "..."

plt.subplot(311)
plt.title("Original")
plt.plot(salary)

plt.subplot(312)
plt.title("Log Masked")
plt.plot(np.exp(ma_log))

plt.subplot(313)
plt.title("Not Extreme")
plt.plot(inside)

plt.show()
```

The following are the steps that will help you execute the aforementioned commands:

1. Taking the logarithm of negative numbers.

   We will take the logarithm of an array that holds negative numbers. Firstly, let's create an array holding numbers divisible by three:

   ```
   triples = numpy.arange(0, len(salary), 3)
   print "Triples", triples[:10], "..."
   ```

Next, we will produce an array with ones that have the same size as the salary data array:

```
signs = numpy.ones(len(salary))
print "Signs", signs[:10], "..."
```

We will set up each third array element to be negative with the aid of indexing tricks we acquired in *Chapter 2, NumPy Arrays*:

```
signs[triples] = -1
print "Signs", signs[:10], "..."
```

In conclusion, we will take the logarithm of this array:

```
ma_log = numpy.ma.log(salary * signs)
print "Masked logs", ma_log[:10], "..."
```

This ought to print the following for the salary data:

```
Triples [ 0  3  6  9 12 15 18 21 24 27] ...
Signs [ 1.  1.  1.  1.  1.  1.  1.  1.  1.  1.] ...
Signs [-1.  1.  1. -1.  1.  1. -1.  1.  1. -1.] ...
Masked logs [-- 14.970818190308929 15.830413578506539 --
13.458835614025542
 15.319587954740548 -- 15.648092021712584
13.864300722133706 --] ...
```

2. Ignoring extreme values.

   Let's specify outliers as being one standard deviation below the mean or one standard deviation above the mean (this is not necessarily a correct definition that is given here because it is easy to compute). This definition directs us to compose the following code, which will mask extreme points:

   ```
   dev = salary.std()
   avg = salary.mean()
   inside = numpy.ma.masked_outside(salary, avg - dev, avg +
   dev)
   print "Inside", inside[:10], "..."
   ```

   The following code displays the output for the initial 10 elements:

   ```
   Inside [3750000.0 3175000.0 7500000.0 3000000.0 700000.0
   4500000.0 3000000.0
    6250000.0 1050000.0 4600000.0] ...
   ```

   Let's plot the original salary data, the data after taking the logarithm and the exponent back again, and finally the data after applying the standard deviation-based mask.

It will look something like this:

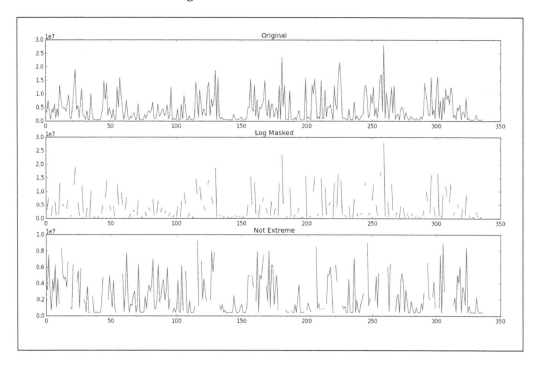

Functions in the `numpy.ma` subpackage mask array elements, which we view as invalid. For example, negative values are not allowed for the `log()` and `sqrt()` functions. A masked value is like a `NULL` value in relational databases and programming. All operations with a masked value deliver a masked value.

Summary

In this chapter, you learned a lot about NumPy and SciPy subpackages. We went over linear algebra, statistics, continuous and discrete distributions, masked arrays, and random numbers.

In the next chapter, *Chapter 4, pandas Primer*, we will discover pandas, which is a Python data analysis and manipulation library.

4
pandas Primer

pandas is named after **panel data** (an econometric term) and Python data analysis, and is a popular open source Python project. This chapter is a tutorial on basic pandas functionalities, where we will learn about pandas data structures and operations.

 The official pandas documentation insists on naming the project *pandas* in all lowercase letters. The other convention they insist on is this import statement: `import pandas as pd`. We will try to follow these conventions as much as possible.

In this chapter, we will install and explore pandas. Then, we will acquaint ourselves with the two central pandas data structures: `DataFrame` and `Series`. After this, you will learn how to perform SQL-like operations on the data contained in these data structures. pandas has statistical utilities including time-series routines, some of which will be demonstrated. The topics we will pursue are as follows:

- Installing and exploring pandas
- `DataFrame` and `Series` data structures
- Querying data in pandas
- Statistics with pandas DataFrames
- Data aggregation with pandas DataFrames
- Concatenating, joining, and appending DataFrames
- Handling missing values
- Dealing with dates
- Pivot tables
- Remote data access

Installing and exploring pandas

The minimal dependency set requirements for pandas is given as follows:

- **NumPy**: This is the fundamental numerical array package that we installed and covered extensively in the preceding chapters

- **python-dateutil**: This is a date-handling library

- **pytz**: This handles time zone definitions

This list is the bare minimum; a longer list of optional dependencies can be located at `http://pandas.pydata.org/pandas-docs/stable/install.html`. We can install pandas via PyPI with `pip` or `easy_install`, using a binary installer, with the aid of our operating system package manager, or from the source by checking out the code. The binary installers can be downloaded from `http://pandas.pydata.org/getpandas.html`.

The command to install pandas with `pip` is as follows:

```
$ pip install pandas
```

You may have to prepend the preceding command with `sudo` if your user account doesn't have sufficient rights. For most, if not all, Linux distributions, the pandas package name is `python-pandas`. Please refer to the manual pages of your package manager for the correct command to install. These commands should be the same as the ones summarized in *Chapter 1, Getting Started with Python Libraries*. To install from the source, we need to execute the following commands from the command line:

```
$ git clone git://github.com/pydata/pandas.git
$ cd pandas
$ python setup.py install
```

This procedure requires the correct setup of the compiler and other dependencies; therefore, it is recommended only if you really need the most up-to-date version of pandas. Once we have installed pandas, we can explore it further by adding pandas-related lines to our documentation-scanning script `pkg_check.py` of the previous chapter. The program prints the following output:

```
pandas version 0.13.1

pandas.compat DESCRIPTION compat  Cross-compatible functions for Python 2
and 3. Key items to import for 2/3 compatible code: * iterators: range(),
map(),

pandas.computation

pandas.core
```

```
pandas.io
pandas.rpy
pandas.sandbox
pandas.sparse
pandas.stats
pandas.tests
pandas.tools
pandas.tseries
pandas.util
```

Unfortunately, the documentation of the pandas subpackages lacks informative descriptions; however, the subpackage names are descriptive enough to get an idea of what they are about.

pandas DataFrames

A pandas `DataFrame` is a data structure, which is a labeled two-dimensional object and is similar in spirit to an Excel worksheet or a relational database table. A similar concept, by the way, was invented originally in the R programming language. (For more information, refer to `http://www.r-tutor.com/r-introduction/data-frame`.) A `DataFrame` can be created in the following ways:

- From another `DataFrame`.
- From a NumPy array or a composite of arrays that has a two-dimensional shape.
- Likewise, we can create a `DataFrame` out of another pandas data structure called `Series`. We will learn about `Series` in the following section.
- A `DataFrame` can also be produced from a file, such as a CSV file.

As an example, we will use data that can be retrieved from `http://www.exploredata.net/Downloads/WHO-Data-Set`. The original datafile is quite big and has many columns, so we will use an edited file instead, which only contains the first nine columns and is called `WHO_first9cols.csv`; the file is in the code bundle of this book. These are the first two lines including the header:

```
Country,CountryID,Continent,Adolescent fertility rate (%),Adult
literacy rate (%),Gross national income per capita (PPP
international $),Net primary school enrolment ratio female (%),Net
primary school enrolment ratio male (%),Population (in thousands)
total

Afghanistan,1,1,151,28,,,,26088
```

In the next steps, we will take a look at pandas DataFrames and its attributes:

1. To kick off, load the datafile into a `DataFrame` and print it on the screen:

```
from pandas.io.parsers import import read_csv

df = read_csv("WHO_first9cols.csv")
print "Dataframe", df
```

The printout is a summary of the `DataFrame`. It is too long to be displayed entirely, so we will just grab the last few lines:

```
57                         1340
58                        81021
59                          833

                          . . .


[202 rows x 9 columns]
```

2. The `DataFrame` has an attribute that holds its shape as a tuple, similar to `ndarray`. Query the number of rows of a `DataFrame` as follows:

```
print "Shape", df.shape
print "Length", len(df)
```

The values we obtain comply with the printout of the preceding step:

```
Shape (202, 9)
Length 202
```

3. Check the column's header and data types with the other attributes:

```
print "Column Headers", df.columns
print "Data types", df.dtypes
```

We receive the column headers in a special data structure:

```
Column Headers Index([u'Country', u'CountryID',
u'Continent', u'Adolescent fertility rate (%)', u'Adult
literacy rate (%)', u'Gross national income per capita (PPP
international $)', u'Net primary school enrolment ratio
female (%)', u'Net primary school enrolment ratio male
(%)', u'Population (in thousands) total'], dtype='object')
```

The data types are printed as follows:

```
Data types Country                                              object
CountryID                                                        int64
Continent                                                        int64
Adolescent fertility rate (%)                                  float64
Adult literacy rate (%)                                        float64
Gross national income per capita (PPP international $)         float64
Net primary school enrolment ratio female (%)                  float64
Net primary school enrolment ratio male (%)                    float64
Population (in thousands) total                                float64
```

4. The pandas `DataFrame` has an index, which is like the primary key of
    relational database tables. We can either specify the index or have pandas
    create it automatically. The index can be accessed with a corresponding
    property as follows:

    ```
    print "Index", df.index
    ```

    An index helps us search for items quickly, just like the index in this book.
    The index in this case is a wrapper around an array starting at 0, with an
    increment of one for each row:

    ```
    Index Int64Index([0, 1, 2, 3, 4, 5, 6, 7, 8, 9, 10, 11, 12,
    13, 14, 15, 16, 17, 18, 19, 20, 21, 22, 23, 24, 25, 26, 27,
    28, 29, 30, 31, 32, 33, 34, 35, 36, 37, 38, 39, 40, 41, 42,
    43, 44, 45, 46, 47, 48, 49, 50, 51, 52, 53, 54, 55, 56, 57,
    58, 59, 60, 61, 62, 63, 64, 65, 66, 67, 68, 69, 70, 71, 72,
    73, 74, 75, 76, 77, 78, 79, 80, 81, 82, 83, 84, 85, 86, 87,
    88, 89, 90, 91, 92, 93, 94, 95, 96, 97, 98, 99, ...],
    dtype='int64')
    ```

5. Sometimes, we wish to iterate over the underlying data of a `DataFrame`.
    Iterating over column values can be inefficient if we utilize the pandas
    iterators. It's much better to extract the underlying NumPy arrays and
    work with those. The pandas `DataFrame` has an attribute that can aid
    with this as well:

    ```
    print "Values", df.values
    ```

Please note that some values are designated nan in the output, for not a number. These values come from empty fields in the input datafile:

```
Values [['Afghanistan' 1 1 ..., nan nan 26088.0]
  ['Albania' 2 2 ..., 93.0 94.0 3172.0]
  ['Algeria' 3 3 ..., 94.0 96.0 33351.0]
  ...,
  ['Yemen' 200 1 ..., 65.0 85.0 21732.0]
  ['Zambia' 201 3 ..., 94.0 90.0 11696.0]
  ['Zimbabwe' 202 3 ..., 88.0 87.0 13228.0]]
```

The code for the following example can be located in the df_demo.py file of this book's code bundle:

```
from pandas.io.parsers import import read_csv

df = read_csv("WHO_first9cols.csv")
print "Dataframe", df
print "Shape", df.shape
print "Length", len(df)
print "Column Headers", df.columns
print "Data types", df.dtypes
print "Index", df.index
print "Values", df.values
```

pandas Series

The pandas Series data structure is a one-dimensional heterogeneous array with labels. We can create a pandas Series data structure as follows:

- From a Python dict
- From a NumPy array
- From a single scalar value

When creating a Series, we can hand the constructor a list of axis labels, which is commonly referred to as the index. The index is an optional parameter. By default, if we use a NumPy array as the input data, pandas will index values by autoincrementing the index commencing from 0. If the data handed to the constructor is a Python dict, the sorted dict keys will become the index. In the case of a scalar value as the input data, we are required to supply the index. For each new value in the index, the scalar input value will be reiterated. The pandas Series and DataFrame interfaces have features and behaviors borrowed from NumPy arrays and Python dictionaries, such as slicing, lookup using a key, and vectorized operations. Performing a lookup on a DataFrame column returns a Series. We will demonstrate this and other features of Series by going back to the previous section and loading the CSV file again.

1. We will start by selecting the `Country` column, which happens to be the first column in the datafile. Then, show the type of the object currently in the local scope:

```
country_col = df["Country"]
print "Type df", type(df)
print "Type country col", type(country_col)
```

We can now confirm that we get a Series when we select a column of a data frame:

```
Type df <class 'pandas.core.frame.DataFrame'>
Type country col <class 'pandas.core.series.Series'>
```

 If you want, you can open a Python or IPython shell, import pandas, and view with the `dir()` function, a list of functions and attributes for the classes of the previous printout. However, be aware that you will get a long list of functions in both cases.

2. The pandas `Series` data structure shares some of the attributes of `DataFrame` and also has a name attribute. Explore these properties as follows:

```
print "Series shape", country_col.shape
print "Series index", country_col.index
print "Series values", country_col.values
print "Series name", country_col.name
```

The output (truncated to save space) is given as follows:

```
Series shape (202,)
Series index Int64Index([0, 1, 2, 3, 4, 5, 6, 7, 8, 9, 10,
11, 12, ...], dtype='int64')

Series values ['Afghanistan' … 'Vietnam' 'West Bank and
Gaza' 'Yemen' 'Zambia' 'Zimbabwe']
Series name Country
```

3. To demonstrate the slicing of a Series, select the last two countries of the `Country` Series and print the type:

```
print "Last 2 countries", country_col[-2:]
print "Last 2 countries type", type(country_col[-2:])
```

Slicing yields another Series as demonstrated:

```
Last 2 countries 200      Zambia
201     Zimbabwe
Name: Country, dtype: object
Last 2 countries type <class 'pandas.core.series.Series'>
```

4. NumPy functions can operate on pandas `DataFrame` and `Series`. We can, for instance, apply the NumPy `sign()` function, which yields the sign of a number. `1` is returned for positive numbers, `-1` for negative numbers, and `0` for zeros. Apply the function to the `DataFrame` and last column, which happens to be the population for each country in the dataset:

```
print "df signs", np.sign(df)
last_col = df.columns[-1]
print "Last df column signs", last_col,
np.sign(df[last_col])
```

The output is truncated here to save space and is as follows:

```
df signs    Country CountryID Continent Adolescent
fertility rate (%)  \
0          1         1          1
1
[TRUNCATED]
59                                              1
1
                                            ...

...


[202 rows x 9 columns]
Last df column signs Population (in thousands) total 0
1
1     1
[TRUNCATED]
198    NaN
199     1
200     1
201     1
Name: Population (in thousands) total, Length: 202, dtype:
float64
```

Please note that the population value at index 198 is NaN. The matching record is given as follows:

```
West Bank and Gaza,199,1,,,,,,
```

We can perform all sorts of numerical operations between DataFrames, Series, and NumPy arrays. If we get the underlying NumPy array of a pandas Series and subtract this array from the Series, we can reasonably expect the following two outcomes:

- An array filled with zeros and at least one NaN (we saw one NaN in the previous step)
- We can also expect to get only zeros

The rule for NumPy functions is to produce NaNs for most operations involving NaNs, as illustrated by the following IPython session:

```
In: np.sum([0, np.nan])
Out: nan
```

Write the following code to perform the subtraction:

```
print np.sum(df[last_col] - df[last_col].values)
```

The snippet yields the result predicted by the second option:

```
0.0
```

Please refer to the `series_demo.py` file in the book's code bundle:

```python
from pandas.io.parsers import import read_csv
import numpy as np

df = read_csv("WHO_first9cols.csv")
country_col = df["Country"]
print "Type df", type(df)
print "Type country col", type(country_col)

print "Series shape", country_col.shape
print "Series index", country_col.index
print "Series values", country_col.values
print "Series name", country_col.name

print "Last 2 countries", country_col[-2:]
print "Last 2 countries type", type(country_col[-2:])

print "df signs", np.sign(df)
last_col = df.columns[-1]
print "Last df column signs", last_col, np.sign(df[last_col])

print np.sum(df[last_col] - df[last_col].values)
```

Querying data in pandas

Since a pandas DataFrame is structured similarly to a relational database, we can view operations that read data from a DataFrame as a query. In this example, we will retrieve the annual sunspot data from Quandl. We can either use the Quandl API or download the data manually as a CSV file from `http://www.quandl.com/SIDC/SUNSPOTS_A-Sunspot-Numbers-Annual`. If you want to install the API, you can do so by downloading installers from `https://pypi.python.org/pypi/Quandl` or running the following command:

```
$ pip install Quandl
```

 Using the API is free, but is limited to 50 API calls per day. If you require more API calls, you will have to request an authentication key. The code in this tutorial is not using a key. It should be simple to change the code to either use a key or read a downloaded CSV file. If you have difficulties, refer to the *Where to find help and references* section in *Chapter 1, Getting Started with Python Libraries*, or search through the Python docs at `https://docs.python.org/2/`.

Without further preamble, let's take a look at how to query data in a pandas DataFrame:

1. As a first step, we obviously have to download the data. After importing the Quandl API, get the data as follows:

   ```
   import Quandl

   # Data from http://www.quandl.com/SIDC/SUNSPOTS_A-Sunspot-
   Numbers-Annual
   # PyPi url https://pypi.python.org/pypi/Quandl
   sunspots = Quandl.get("SIDC/SUNSPOTS_A")
   ```

2. The `head()` and `tail()` methods have a purpose similar to that of the Unix commands with the same name. Select the first n and last n records of a DataFrame, where n is an integer parameter:

   ```
   print "Head 2", sunspots.head(2)
   print "Tail 2", sunspots.tail(2)
   ```

   This gives us the first two and last two rows of the sunspot data:

   ```
   Head 2          Number
   Year
   1700-12-31        5
   1701-12-31       11

   [2 rows x 1 columns]
   ```

```
Tail 2                  Number
Year
2012-12-31    57.7
2013-12-31    64.9
```

```
[2 rows x 1 columns]
```

Please note that we only have one column holding the number of sunspots per year. The dates are a part of the DataFrame index.

3. The following is the query for the last value using the last date:

```
last_date = sunspots.index[-1]
print "Last value", sunspots.loc[last_date]
```

You can check the following output with the result from the previous step:

```
Last value Number    64.9
Name: 2013-12-31 00:00:00, dtype: float64
```

4. Query the date with date strings in the YYYYMMDD format as follows:

```
print "Values slice by date", sunspots["20020101":
"20131231"]
```

This gives the records from 2002 through 2013:

```
Values slice by date            Number
Year
2002-12-31    104.0
[TRUNCATED]
2013-12-31     64.9
```

```
[12 rows x 1 columns]
```

5. A list of indices can be used to query as well:

```
print "Slice from a list of indices", sunspots.iloc[[2, 4,
-4, -2]]
```

The preceding code selects the following rows:

```
Slice from a list of indices            Number
Year
1702-12-31    16.0
1704-12-31    36.0
2010-12-31    16.0
2012-12-31    57.7
```

```
[4 rows x 1 columns]
```

6. To select scalar values, we have two options. The second option given here should be faster. Two integers are required, the first for the row and the second for the column:

```
print "Scalar with Iloc", sunspots.iloc[0, 0]
print "Scalar with iat", sunspots.iat[1, 0]
```

This gives us the first and second values of the dataset as scalars:

```
Scalar with Iloc 5.0
Scalar with iat 11.0
```

7. Querying with Booleans works much like the `Where` clause of SQL. The following code queries for values larger than the arithmetic mean. Notice that there is a difference when we perform the query on the whole DataFrame and when we perform it on a single column:

```
print "Boolean selection", sunspots[sunspots >
sunspots.mean()]
print "Boolean selection with column label",
sunspots[sunspots. Number > sunspots.Number.mean()]
```

The notable difference is that the first query yields all the rows, with rows not conforming to the condition that has a value of `NaN`. The second query returns only the rows where the value is larger than the mean:

```
Boolean selection                       Number
Year
1700-12-31      NaN
[TRUNCATED]
1759-12-31      54.0

                      ...

[314 rows x 1 columns]
Boolean selection with column label              Number
Year
1705-12-31      58.0
[TRUNCATED]
1870-12-31      139.1

                      ...

[127 rows x 1 columns]
```

The example code is in the `query_demo.py` file of this book's code bundle:

```
import Quandl

# Data from http://www.quandl.com/SIDC/SUNSPOTS_A-Sunspot-Numbers-
Annual
```

```
# PyPi url https://pypi.python.org/pypi/Quandl
sunspots = Quandl.get("SIDC/SUNSPOTS_A")
print "Head 2", sunspots.head(2)
print "Tail 2", sunspots.tail(2)

last_date = sunspots.index[-1]
print "Last value", sunspots.loc[last_date]

print "Values slice by date", sunspots["20020101": "20131231"]

print "Slice from a list of indices", sunspots.iloc[[2, 4, -4, -2]]

print "Scalar with Iloc", sunspots.iloc[0, 0]
print "Scalar with iat", sunspots.iat[1, 0]

print "Boolean selection", sunspots[sunspots > sunspots.mean()]
print "Boolean selection with column label",
sunspots[sunspots.Number > sunspots.Number.mean()]
```

Statistics with pandas DataFrames

The pandas `DataFrame` has a dozen statistical methods. The following table lists these methods along with a short description:

Method	Description
describe	This method returns a small table with descriptive statistics.
count	This method returns the number of non-NaN items.
mad	This method calculates the mean absolute deviation, which is a robust measure similar to the standard deviation.
median	This method returns the median. This is equivalent to the value at the 50th percentile.
min	This method returns the lowest value.
max	This method returns the highest value.
mode	This method returns the mode, which is the most frequently occurring value.
std	This method returns the standard deviation, which measures dispersion. It is the square root of the variance.
var	This method returns the variance.
skew	This method returns skewness. Skewness is indicative of the distribution symmetry.
kurt	This method returns kurtosis. Kurtosis is indicative of the distribution shape.

Using the same data as in the previous example, we will demonstrate these statistical methods. The full script is in the `stats_demo.py` of this book's code bundle:

```
import Quandl

# Data from http://www.quandl.com/SIDC/SUNSPOTS_A-Sunspot-Numbers-
Annual
# PyPi url https://pypi.python.org/pypi/Quandl
sunspots = Quandl.get("SIDC/SUNSPOTS_A")
print "Describe", sunspots.describe()
print "Non NaN observations", sunspots.count()
print "MAD", sunspots.mad()
print "Median", sunspots.median()
print "Min", sunspots.min()
print "Max", sunspots.max()
print "Mode", sunspots.mode()
print "Standard Deviation", sunspots.std()
print "Variance", sunspots.var()
print "Skewness", sunspots.skew()
print "Kurtosis", sunspots.kurt()
```

The following is the output of the script:

```
Describe               Number
count  314.000000
mean    49.528662
std     40.277766
min      0.000000
25%     16.000000
50%     40.000000
75%     69.275000
max    190.200000

[8 rows x 1 columns]
Non NaN observations Number      314
dtype: int64
MAD Number     32.483184
dtype: float64
Median Number     40
```

```
dtype: float64
Min Number    0
dtype: float64
Max Number    190.2
dtype: float64
Mode    Number
0       47

[1 rows x 1 columns]
Standard Deviation Number    40.277766
dtype: float64
Variance Number    1622.298473
dtype: float64
Skewness Number    0.994262
dtype: float64
Kurtosis Number    0.469034
dtype: float64
```

Data aggregation with pandas DataFrames

Data aggregation is a term known from relational databases. In a database query, we can group data by the value in a column or columns. We can then perform various operations on each of these groups. The pandas DataFrame has similar capabilities. We will generate data held in a Python dict and then use this data to create a pandas DataFrame. We will then practice the pandas aggregation features:

1. Seed the NumPy random generator to make sure that the generated data will not differ between repeated program runs. The data will have four columns:

   ° Weather (a string)

   ° Food (also a string)

   ° Price (a random float)

   ° Number (a random integer between one and nine)

The use case is that we have the results for some sort of a consumer-purchase research, combined with weather and market pricing, where we calculate the average of prices and keep a track of the sample size and parameters:

```
import pandas as pd
from numpy.random import seed
from numpy.random import rand
from numpy.random import random_integers
import numpy as np

seed(42)

df = pd.DataFrame({'Weather' : ['cold', 'hot', 'cold', 'hot',
    'cold', 'hot', 'cold'],
    'Food' : ['soup', 'soup', 'icecream', 'chocolate',
    'icecream', 'icecream', 'soup'],
    'Price' : 10 * rand(7), 'Number' : random_integers(1, 9,
size=(7,))})

print df
```

You should get an output similar to the following:

```
        Food   Number      Price Weather
0       soup        8   3.745401    cold
1       soup        5   9.507143     hot
2   icecream        4   7.319939    cold
3  chocolate        8   5.986585     hot
4   icecream        8   1.560186    cold
5   icecream        3   1.559945     hot
6       soup        6   0.580836    cold

[7 rows x 4 columns]
```

Please note that the column labels come from the lexically ordered keys of the Python dict.

 Lexical or lexicographical order is based on the alphabetic order of characters in a string.

2. Group the data by the `Weather` column and then iterate through the groups as follows:

```
weather_group = df.groupby('Weather')

i = 0

for name, group in weather_group:
```

```
i = i + 1
print "Group", i, name
print group
```

We have two types of weather, hot and cold, so we get two groups:

```
Group 1 cold
        Food  Number      Price Weather
0        soup       8  3.745401    cold
2    icecream       4  7.319939    cold
4    icecream       8  1.560186    cold
6        soup       6  0.580836    cold

[4 rows x 4 columns]
Group 2 hot
        Food  Number      Price Weather
1        soup       5  9.507143     hot
3   chocolate       8  5.986585     hot
5    icecream       3  1.559945     hot

[3 rows x 4 columns]
```

3. The `weather_group` variable is a special pandas object that we get as a result of the `groupby()` method. This object has aggregation methods, which are demonstrated as follows:

```
print "Weather group first\n", weather_group.first()
print "Weather group last\n", weather_group.last()
print "Weather group mean\n", weather_group.mean()
```

The preceding code snippet prints the first row, last row, and mean of each group:

```
Weather group first
          Food  Number      Price
Weather
cold      soup       8  3.745401
hot       soup       5  9.507143

[2 rows x 3 columns]
Weather group last
           Food  Number      Price
Weather
cold       soup       6  0.580836
hot    icecream       3  1.559945

[2 rows x 3 columns]
Weather group mean
```

```
          Number     Price
Weather
cold     6.500000  3.301591
hot      5.333333  5.684558


[2 rows x 2 columns]
```

4. Just as in a database query, we are allowed to group on multiple columns. The groups attribute will then tell us the groups that are formed and the rows in each group:

```
wf_group = df.groupby(['Weather', 'Food'])
print "WF Groups", wf_group.groups
```

For each possible combination of weather and food values, a new group is created. The membership of each row is indicated by their index values as follows:

```
WF Groups {('hot', 'chocolate'): [3], ('cold', 'icecream'):
[2, 4], ('hot', 'icecream'): [5], ('hot', 'soup'): [1],
('cold', 'soup'): [0, 6]}
```

5. Apply a list of NumPy functions on groups with the agg() method:

```
print "WF Aggregated\n", wf_group.agg([np.mean, np.median])
```

Obviously, we could apply even more functions, but it would look messier than the following output:

```
WF Aggregated
                     Number            Price
                  mean  median      mean    median
Weather Food
cold    icecream     6       6   4.440063  4.440063
        soup         7       7   2.163119  2.163119
hot     chocolate    8       8   5.986585  5.986585
        icecream     3       3   1.559945  1.559945
        soup         5       5   9.507143  9.507143


[5 rows x 4 columns]
```

The full data aggregation example code is in the data_aggregation.py file, which can be found in this book's code bundle:

```
import pandas as pd
from numpy.random import seed
```

```
from numpy.random import rand
from numpy.random import random_integers
import numpy as np

seed(42)

df = pd.DataFrame({'Weather' : ['cold', 'hot', 'cold', 'hot',
   'cold', 'hot', 'cold'],
   'Food' : ['soup', 'soup', 'icecream', 'chocolate',
   'icecream', 'icecream', 'soup'],
   'Price' : 10 * rand(7), 'Number' : random_integers(1, 9,
size=(7,))})

print df
weather_group = df.groupby('Weather')

i = 0

for name, group in weather_group:
   i = i + 1
   print "Group", i, name
   print group

print "Weather group first\n", weather_group.first()
print "Weather group last\n", weather_group.last()
print "Weather group mean\n", weather_group.mean()

wf_group = df.groupby(['Weather', 'Food'])
print "WF Groups", wf_group.groups

print "WF Aggregated\n", wf_group.agg([np.mean, np.median])
```

Concatenating and appending DataFrames

The pandas DataFrame allows operations that are similar to the inner and outer joins of database tables. We can append and concatenate rows as well. To practice appending and concatenating of rows, we will reuse the DataFrame from the previous section. Let's select the first three rows:

```
print "df :3\n", df[:3]
```

Check that these are indeed the first three rows:

```
df :3
        Food  Number      Price Weather
0        soup      8   3.745401    cold
1        soup      5   9.507143     hot
2    icecream      4   7.319939    cold
```

The `concat()` function concatenates DataFrames. For example, we can concatenate a DataFrame that consists of three rows to the rest of the rows, in order to recreate the original DataFrame:

```
print "Concat Back together\n", pd.concat([df[:3], df[3:]])
```

The concatenation output appears as follows:

```
Concat Back together
        Food  Number      Price Weather
0        soup      8   3.745401    cold
1        soup      5   9.507143     hot
2    icecream      4   7.319939    cold
3   chocolate      8   5.986585     hot
4    icecream      8   1.560186    cold
5    icecream      3   1.559945     hot
6        soup      6   0.580836    cold

[7 rows x 4 columns]
```

To append rows, use the `append()` function:

```
print "Appending rows\n", df[:3].append(df[5:])
```

The result is a `DataFrame` with the first three rows of the original `DataFrame` and the last two rows appended to it:

```
Appending rows
        Food  Number      Price Weather
0        soup      8   3.745401    cold
1        soup      5   9.507143     hot
2    icecream      4   7.319939    cold
5    icecream      3   1.559945     hot
6        soup      6   0.580836    cold

[5 rows x 4 columns]
```

Joining DataFrames

To demonstrate joining, we will use two CSV files: `dest.csv` and `tips.csv`. The use case behind it is that we are running a taxi company. Every time a passenger is dropped off at his or her destination, we add a row to the `dest.csv` file with the employee number of the driver and the destination:

```
EmpNr,Dest
5,The Hague
3,Amsterdam
9,Rotterdam
```

Sometimes drivers get a tip, so we want that registered in the `tips.csv` file (if this doesn't seem realistic, please feel free to come up with your own story):

```
EmpNr,Amount
5,10
9,5
7,2.5
```

Database-like joins in pandas can be done with either the `merge()` function or the `join()` DataFrame method. The `join()` method joins on indices by default, which might not be what you want. In SQL—a relational database query language—we have the inner join, left outer join, right outer join, and full outer join.

> An inner join selects rows from two tables, if and only if values match, for columns specified in the join condition. Outer joins do not require a match and can potentially return more rows. Please refer to the following Wikipedia page on joins: http://en.wikipedia.org/wiki/Join_%28SQL%29.

All these join types are supported by pandas, but we will only take a look at inner joins and full outer joins.

- A join on the employee number with the `merge()` function is performed as follows:

  ```
  print "Merge() on key\n", pd.merge(dests, tips, on='EmpNr')
  ```

  This gives an inner join as the outcome:

  ```
  Merge() on key
      EmpNr         Dest  Amount
  0       5    The Hague      10
  1       9    Rotterdam       5

  [2 rows x 3 columns]
  ```

- Joining with the `join()` method requires providing suffixes for the left and right operands:

```
print "Dests join() tips\n", dests.join(tips,
lsuffix='Dest', rsuffix='Tips')
```

This method call joins index values so that the result is different from a SQL inner join:

```
Dests join() tips
    EmpNrDest        Dest  EmpNrTips  Amount
0           5   The Hague          5    10.0
1           3   Amsterdam          9     5.0
2           9   Rotterdam          7     2.5

[3 rows x 4 columns]
```

- An even more explicit way to execute an inner join with `merge()` is as follows:

```
print "Inner join with merge()\n", pd.merge(dests, tips,
how='inner')
```

The output is as follows:

```
Inner join with merge()
   EmpNr        Dest  Amount
0      5   The Hague      10
1      9   Rotterdam       5

[2 rows x 3 columns]
```

To make this a full outer join requires only a small change:

```
print "Outer join\n", pd.merge(dests, tips, how='outer')
```

The outer join adds rows with NaN values:

```
Outer join
   EmpNr        Dest  Amount
0      5   The Hague    10.0
1      3   Amsterdam     NaN
2      9   Rotterdam     5.0
3      7         NaN     2.5

[4 rows x 3 columns]
```

In a relational database query, these values would have been set to NULL. The demo code is in the `join_demo.py` file of this book's code bundle:

```python
import pandas as pd
from numpy.random import seed
from numpy.random import rand
from numpy.random import random_integers
import numpy as np

seed(42)

df = pd.DataFrame({'Weather' : ['cold', 'hot', 'cold', 'hot',
    'cold', 'hot', 'cold'],
    'Food' : ['soup', 'soup', 'icecream', 'chocolate',
    'icecream', 'icecream', 'soup'],
    'Price' : 10 * rand(7), 'Number' : random_integers(1, 9,
size=(7,))})

print "df :3\n", df[:3]
print "Concat Back together\n", pd.concat([df[:3], df[3:]])

print "Appending rows\n", df[:3].append(df[5:])

dests = pd.read_csv('dest.csv')
print "Dests\n", dests

tips = pd.read_csv('tips.csv')
print "Tips\n", tips

print "Merge() on key\n", pd.merge(dests, tips, on='EmpNr')
print "Dests join() tips\n", dests.join(tips, lsuffix='Dest',
rsuffix='Tips')

print "Inner join with merge()\n", pd.merge(dests, tips,
how='inner')
print "Outer join\n", pd.merge(dests, tips, how='outer')
```

Handling missing values

We regularly encounter empty fields in data records. It's best that we accept this and learn how to handle this kind of issue in a robust manner. Real data can not only have gaps, it can also have wrong values because of faulty measuring equipment, for example. In pandas, missing numerical values will be designated as NaN, objects as None, and the datetime64 objects as NaT. The outcome of arithmetic operations with NaN values is NaN as well. Descriptive statistics methods, such as summation and average, behave differently. As we observed in an earlier example, in such a case, NaN values are treated as zero values. However, if all the values are NaN during summation, for example, the sum returned is still NaN. In aggregation operations, NaN values in the column that we group are ignored. We will again load the WHO_first9cols.csv file into a DataFrame. Recall that this file contains empty fields. Let's only select the first three rows, including the headers of the Country and Net primary school enrolment ratio male (%) columns as follows:

```
df = df[['Country', df.columns[-2]]][:2]
print "New df\n", df
```

We get a DataFrame with two NaN values:

```
New df
        Country  Net primary school enrolment ratio male (%)
0   Afghanistan                                          NaN
1       Albania                                           94

[2 rows x 2 columns]
```

The pandas isnull() function checks for missing values as follows:

```
print "Null Values\n", pd.isnull(df)
```

The output for our DataFrame is as follows:

```
Null Values
  Country Net primary school enrolment ratio male (%)
0   False                                        True
1   False                                       False
```

To count the number of NaN values for each column, we can sum the Boolean values returned by isnull(). This works because during summation, True values are considered as ones and False values are treated as zeros:

```
Total Null Values
Country                                        0
Net primary school enrolment ratio male (%)    1
dtype: int64
```

Likewise, we can check with the DataFrame `notnull()` method for any non-missing values that are present:

```
print "Not Null Values\n", df.notnull()
```

The result of the `notnull()` method is the opposite of the `isnull()` function:

```
Not Null Values
    Country Net primary school enrolment ratio male (%)
0    True                                          False
1    True                                           True
```

When we double values in a DataFrame that has NaN values, the product will still contain NaN values, since doubling is an arithmetic operation:

```
print "Last Column Doubled\n", 2 * df[df.columns[-1]]
```

We double the last column, which contains numerical values (doubling string values repeats the string):

```
Last Column Doubled
0       NaN
1       188
Name: Net primary school enrolment ratio male (%), dtype: float64
```

If we add a NaN value, however, the NaN value wins:

```
print "Last Column plus NaN\n", df[df.columns[-1]] + np.nan
```

As you can see, the NaN values declared total victory:

```
Last Column plus NaN
0      NaN
1      NaN
Name: Net primary school enrolment ratio male (%), dtype: float64
```

Replace the missing values by a scalar value, for example, 0 (we can't always replace missing values with zeros, but sometimes this is good enough) with the `fillna()` method:

```
print "Zero filled\n", df.fillna(0)
```

The effect of the preceding line is to replace the NaN value with 0:

```
Zero filled
          Country    Net primary school enrolment ratio male (%)
0    Afghanistan                                              0
1        Albania                                             94
```

The code for this section is in the `missing_values.py` file of this book's code bundle:

```
import pandas as pd
import numpy as np

df = pd.read_csv('WHO_first9cols.csv')
# Select first 3 rows of country and Net primary school enrolment
ratio male (%)
df = df[['Country', df.columns[-2]]][:2]
print "New df\n", df
print "Null Values\n", pd.isnull(df)
print "Total Null Values\n", pd.isnull(df).sum()
print "Not Null Values\n", df.notnull()
print "Last Column Doubled\n", 2 * df[df.columns[-1]]
print "Last Column plus NaN\n", df[df.columns[-1]] + np.nan
print "Zero filled\n", df.fillna(0)
```

Dealing with dates

Dates are complicated. Just think of the Y2K bug, the pending Year 2038 problem, and time zones. It's a mess. We encounter dates naturally when dealing with the time-series data. pandas can create date ranges, resample time-series data, and perform date arithmetic operations.

Create a range of dates starting from January 1, 1900 with 42 days as follows:

```
print "Date range", pd.date_range('1/1/1900', periods=42,
freq='D')
```

January has less than 42 days, so the end date falls in February as you can check for yourself:

```
Date range <class 'pandas.tseries.index.DatetimeIndex'>
[1900-01-01, ..., 1900-02-11]
Length: 42, Freq: D, Timezone: None
```

The following table from the pandas official documentation (refer to `http://pandas.pydata.org/pandas-docs/stable/timeseries.html#offset-aliases`) describes frequencies used in pandas:

Short code	Description
B	Business day frequency
C	Custom business day frequency (experimental)
D	Calendar day frequency

Short code	Description
W	Weekly frequency
M	Month end frequency
BM	Business month end frequency
MS	Month start frequency
BMS	Business month start frequency
Q	Quarter end frequency
BQ	Business quarter end frequency
QS	Quarter start frequency
BQS	Business quarter start frequency
A	Year end frequency
BA	Business year end frequency
AS	Year start frequency
BAS	Business year start frequency
H	Hourly frequency
T	Minutely frequency
S	Secondly frequency
L	Milliseconds
U	Microseconds

Date ranges have their limits in pandas. Timestamps in pandas (based on the NumPy `datetime64` data type) are represented by a 64-bit integer with nanosecond resolution (a billionth of a second). This limits legal timestamps to dates in the range approximately between the year 1677 and 2262 (not all dates in these years are valid). The exact midpoint of this range is at January 1, 1970. For example, January 1, 1677 cannot be defined with a pandas timestamp, while September 30, 1677 can, as demonstrated in the following code snippet:

```
try:
    print "Date range", pd.date_range('1/1/1677', periods=4,
freq='D')
except:
    etype, value, _ = sys.exc_info()
    print "Error encountered", etype, value
```

The code snippet prints the following error message:

```
Date range Error encountered <class
'pandas.tslib.OutOfBoundsDatetime'> Out of bounds nanosecond
timestamp: 1677-01-01 00:00:00
```

Given all the previous information, calculate the allowed date range with pandas `DateOffset` as follows:

```
offset = DateOffset(seconds=2 ** 63/10 ** 9)
mid = pd.to_datetime('1/1/1970')
print "Start valid range", mid - offset
print "End valid range", mid + offset'
```

We get the following range values:

Start valid range 1677-09-21 00:12:44

End valid range 2262-04-11 23:47:16

We can convert a list of strings to dates with pandas. Of course, not all strings can be converted. If pandas is unable to convert a string, an error is often reported. Sometimes, ambiguities can arise due to differences in the way dates are defined in different locales. Use a format string in this case, as follows:

```
print "With format", pd.to_datetime(['19021112', '19031230'],
format='%Y%m%d')
```

The strings should be converted without an error occurring:

With format [datetime.datetime(1902, 11, 12, 0, 0)
 datetime.datetime(1903, 12, 30, 0, 0)]

If we try to convert a string, which is clearly not a date, by default the string is not converted:

```
print "Illegal date", pd.to_datetime(['1902-11-12', 'not a date'])
```

The second string in the list should not be converted:

Illegal date ['1902-11-12' 'not a date']

To force conversion, set the `coerce` parameter to `True`:

```
print "Illegal date coerced", pd.to_datetime(['1902-11-12', 'not a
date'], coerce=True)
```

Obviously, the second string still cannot be converted to a date, so the only valid value we can give it is `NaT` (not a time):

Illegal date coerced <class 'pandas.tseries.index.DatetimeIndex'>
[1902-11-12, NaT]
Length: 2, Freq: None, Timezone: None

The code for this example is in `date_handling.py` of this book's code bundle:

```
import pandas as pd
import sys

print "Date range", pd.date_range('1/1/1900', periods=42,
freq='D')

try:
    print "Date range", pd.date_range('1/1/1677', periods=4,
freq='D')
except:
    etype, value, _ = sys.exc_info()
    print "Error encountered", etype, value

print pd.to_datetime(['1900/1/1', '1901.12.11'])

print "With format", pd.to_datetime(['19021112', '19031230'],
format='%Y%m%d')

print "Illegal date", pd.to_datetime(['1902-11-12', 'not a date'])
print "Illegal date coerced", pd.to_datetime(['1902-11-12', 'not a
date'], coerce=True)
```

Pivot tables

A **pivot** table, as known from Excel, summarizes data. The data in CSV files that we have seen in this chapter so far has been in flat files. The pivot table aggregates data from a flat file for certain columns and rows. The aggregating operation can be sum, mean, standard deviations, and so on. We will reuse the data generating code from `data_aggregation.py`. The pandas API has a top-level `pivot_table()` function and corresponding DataFrame method. With the `aggfunc` parameter, we can specify the aggregation function to use the NumPy `sum()` function, for instance. The `cols` parameter tells pandas the column to be aggregated. Create a pivot table on the Food column as follows:

```
print pd.pivot_table(df, cols=['Food'], aggfunc=np.sum)
```

The pivot table we get contains totals for each food item:

```
Food      chocolate   icecream      soup
Number    8.000000    15.000000   19.00000
Price     5.986585    10.440071   13.83338

[2 rows x 3 columns]
```

The following code can be found in `pivot_demo.py` in this book's code bundle:

```
import pandas as pd
from numpy.random import seed
from numpy.random import rand
from numpy.random import random_integers
import numpy as np

seed(42)
N = 7
df = pd.DataFrame({
    'Weather' : ['cold', 'hot', 'cold', 'hot',
    'cold', 'hot', 'cold'],
    'Food' : ['soup', 'soup', 'icecream', 'chocolate',
    'icecream', 'icecream', 'soup'],
    'Price' : 10 * rand(N), 'Number' : random_integers(1, 9,
size=(N,))})

print "DataFrame\n", df
print pd.pivot_table(df, cols=['Food'], aggfunc=np.sum)
```

Remote data access

The pandas module can retrieve econometric data from various websites on the Internet. The types of data that can be downloaded varies from stock prices and option prices to macroeconomic data. The websites in question are listed as follows:

- Yahoo! Finance at `http://finance.yahoo.com/`

- Google Finance at `https://www.google.com/finance`

- Federal Reserve Economic Data at `http://research.stlouisfed.org/fred2/`

- Kenneth R. French - Data Library at `http://mba.tuck.dartmouth.edu/pages/faculty/ken.french/data_library.html`

- World Bank Group at `http://www.worldbank.org/`

It's quite possible that you are not interested in all of this econometric data; therefore, in this section, we will only download option data from Yahoo! Finance with the purpose of calculating the price of a straddle.

Options are financial contracts that derive their price from other financial instruments, for instance, stocks. The two fundamental types of options are calls and puts. Calls give you the right to buy the underlying instrument, for example, shares in IBM at a predetermined price called the strike price. Puts give you the opposite right to sell at a given strike price.

Option contracts are also tied to an expiration date, after which the contract is no longer valid. The rules related to expiration are too complicated to explain fully here. For all the finance details, have a look at *Python for Finance, Yuxing Yan, Packt Publishing*, which is listed in the *Preface*. A straddle is an option combination consisting of a put and a call option with the same expiration date. For a straddle, these options are typically chosen to be at-the-money, meaning that the strike price is close to the current stock price. This option strategy is market neutral; it doesn't matter whether the stock price goes up or down. However, to make profit, the stock price has to move within the expiration period; more than the price of the call and put options combined. In other words, the stock price has to move more than the price of the straddle. The price of a straddle is, therefore, equal to the price change the market currently expects to occur.

In the following example, we will ignore holidays. You can check manually for holidays falling on a Friday using the tips from `https://stackoverflow.com/questions/9187215/datetime-python-next-business-day`. The market is closed on a couple of Fridays each year, such as Good Friday. To calculate the price of the AAPL straddle, expiring next Friday, follow these steps:

1. Import the pandas `Options` class:

    ```
    from pandas.io.data import Options
    ```

2. Define the following function to determine the next Friday starting from today with the standard Python code:

    ```
    def next_friday():
        today = datetime.date.today()
        return today + datetime.timedelta( (4-today.weekday()) % 7 )
    ```

3. For a straddle, we need to get the call and put options, which are closest to the current stock price. The AAPL option contracts are a bit problematic. For reasons that are too technical to explain here, it might not be possible to determine unique option contracts with the strike price closest to the current stock price. To be on the safer side, we will select the most popular options. By definition, these are the options with the highest *open interest*. Define the following function that retrieves the price of an at-the-money put or call as follows:

```
def get_price(options, is_call, is_put):
    fri = next_friday()
    option_list = options.get_near_stock_price(above_below=1,
call=is_call, put=is_put, expiry=fri)[0]
    option =  option_list[option_list["Open Int"] == option_
list["Open Int"].max()]

    return option["Last"].values[0]
```

Recall that an option can be either a put or call contract. Therefore, is_put and is_call are Boolean variables. We use the pandas get_near_stock_price() method of the Options class to get the options closest to the current stock price. In the pandas DataFrame that we obtain, there is a column named Open Int, which is indicative of how popular a given option contract is. We select the most popular contract with the max() method. The Last column in the DataFrame gives the last traded price. This is the price that we are interested in and, therefore, return.

4. Create an Options object for AAPL that gets data from Yahoo! Finance:

```
options = Options('AAPL', "yahoo")
```

The rest of the code is simple and self-explanatory. You can find the code in the price_straddle.py file in this book's code bundle:

```
from pandas.io.data import Options
import datetime


def next_friday():
    today = datetime.date.today()
```

```
        return today + datetime.timedelta( (4-today.weekday()) % 7 )

def get_price(options, is_call, is_put):
    fri = next_friday()
    option_list = options.get_near_stock_price(above_below=1, call=is_
call, put=is_put, expiry=fri)[0]
    option =  option_list[option_list["Open Int"] == option_list["Open
Int"].max()]

    return option["Last"].values[0]

def get_straddle():
    options = Options('AAPL', "yahoo")
    call =  get_price(options, True, False)
    put = get_price(options, False, True)

    return call + put

if __name__ == "__main__":
    print get_straddle()
```

Summary

In this chapter, we focused on pandas—a Python data analysis library. This was an introductory tutorial about the basic pandas features and data structures. We realized that a lot of the pandas functionality mimics relational database tables, allowing us to query, aggregate, and manipulate data efficiently. NumPy and pandas work well together and make it possible to perform basic statistical analysis. At this point, you might be tempted to think that pandas is all we need for data analysis. However, there is more to data analysis than meets the eye.

The next chapter, *Chapter 5, Retrieving, Processing, and Storing Data*, will teach us skills that are essential, though they may not be considered data analysis by some people. We will go with a broader definition that considers anything conceivably related to data analysis. Usually, when we analyze data, we don't have a whole team of assistants to help us with retrieving and storing data. However, since these tasks are important for a smooth data analysis flow, we will describe these activities in detail.

5
Retrieving, Processing, and Storing Data

Data can be found everywhere in all shapes and forms. We can get it from the Web, by e-mail and FTP, or create it ourselves in a lab experiment or marketing poll. An exhaustive overview of how to acquire data in various formats will require many more pages than what we have available. Sometimes, we need to store data before we can analyze it or after we are done with our analysis. We will also discuss storing data in this chapter. *Chapter 8, Working with Databases*, gives information about various databases (relational and NoSQL) and related APIs. The following is a list of the topics that we are going to cover in this chapter:

- Writing CSV files with NumPy and pandas
- The binary `.npy` and pickle formats
- Reading and writing to Excel with pandas
- JSON
- REST web services
- Parsing RSS feeds
- Scraping the Web
- Parsing HTML
- Storing data with PyTables
- HDF5 pandas I/O

Writing CSV files with NumPy and pandas

In the previous chapters, we learned about reading CSV files. Writing CSV files is just as straightforward, but uses different functions and methods. Let's first generate some data to be stored in the CSV format. Generate a 3 x 4 NumPy array after seeding the random generator in the following code snippet.

Set one of the array values to NaN:

```
np.random.seed(42)

a = np.random.randn(3, 4)
a[2][2] = np.nan
print a
```

This code will print the array as follows:

```
[[ 0.49671415 -0.1382643   0.64768854  1.52302986]
 [-0.23415337 -0.23413696  1.57921282  0.76743473]
 [-0.46947439  0.54256004         nan -0.46572975]]
```

The NumPy `savetxt()` function is the counterpart of the NumPy `loadtxt()` function and can save arrays in delimited file formats such as CSV. Save the array we created with the following function call:

```
np.savetxt('np.csv', a, fmt='%.2f', delimiter=',', header="
#1,  #2,  #3,  #4")
```

In the preceding function call, we specified the name of the file to be saved, the array, an optional format, a delimiter (the default is space), and an optional header.

 The format parameter is documented at http://docs.python.org/2/ library/string.html#format-specification-mini-language.

View the np.csv file we created with the `cat` command (cat np.csv) or an editor, such as Notepad on Windows. The contents of the file should be displayed as follows:

```
# #1,  #2,  #3,  #4
0.50,-0.14,0.65,1.52
-0.23,-0.23,1.58,0.77
-0.47,0.54,nan,-0.47
```

Create a pandas DataFrame from the random values array:

```
df = pd.DataFrame(a)
print df
```

As you can observe, pandas automatically comes up with column names for our data:

```
          0          1          2          3
0  0.496714  -0.138264   0.647689   1.523030
1 -0.234153  -0.234137   1.579213   0.767435
2 -0.469474   0.542560NaN -0.465730
```

Write a DataFrame to a CSV file with the pandas `to_csv()` method as follows:

```
df.to_csv('pd.csv', float_format='%.2f', na_rep="NAN!")
```

We gave this method the name of the file, an optional format string analogous to the format parameter of the NumPy `savetxt()` function, and an optional string that represents NaN. View the `pd.csv` file to see the following:

```
,0,1,2,3
0,0.50,-0.14,0.65,1.52
1,-0.23,-0.23,1.58,0.77
2,-0.47,0.54,NAN!,-0.47
```

Take a look at the code in the `writing_csv.py` file in this book's code bundle:

```
import numpy as np
import pandas as pd

np.random.seed(42)

a = np.random.randn(3, 4)
a[2][2] = np.nan
print a
np.savetxt('np.csv', a, fmt='%.2f', delimiter=',', header=" #1,
#2,  #3,  #4")
df = pd.DataFrame(a)
print df
df.to_csv('pd.csv', float_format='%.2f', na_rep="NAN!")
```

Comparing the NumPy .npy binary format and pickling pandas DataFrames

Saving data in the CSV format is fine most of the time. It is easy to exchange CSV files, since most programming languages and applications can handle this format. However, it is not very efficient; CSV and other plaintext formats take up a lot of space. Numerous file formats have been invented, which offer a high level of compression such as zip, bzip, and gzip.

The following is the complete code for this storage comparison exercise, which can also be found in the `binary_formats.py` file of this book's code bundle:

```
import numpy as np
import pandas as pd
from tempfile import NamedTemporaryFile
from os.path import getsize

np.random.seed(42)
a = np.random.randn(365, 4)

tmpf = NamedTemporaryFile()
np.savetxt(tmpf, a, delimiter=',')
print "Size CSV file", getsize(tmpf.name)

tmpf = NamedTemporaryFile()
np.save(tmpf, a)
tmpf.seek(0)
loaded = np.load(tmpf)
print "Shape", loaded.shape
print "Size .npy file", getsize(tmpf.name)

df = pd.DataFrame(a)
df.to_pickle(tmpf.name)
print "Size pickled dataframe", getsize(tmpf.name)
print "DF from pickle\n", pd.read_pickle(tmpf.name)
```

NumPy offers a NumPy-specific format called .npy, which can be used to store NumPy arrays. Before demonstrating this format, we will generate a 365 x 4 NumPy array filled with random values. This array simulates daily measurements for four variables for a year (for instance, a weather data station with sensors measuring temperature, humidity, precipitation, and atmospheric pressure). We will use a standard Python `NamedTemporaryFile` to store the data. The temporary file should be automatically deleted.

Store the array in a CSV file and check its size as follows:

```
tmpf = NamedTemporaryFile()
np.savetxt(tmpf, a, delimiter=',')
print "Size CSV file", getsize(tmpf.name)
```

The CSV file size is printed as follows:

Size CSV file 36864

Save the array in the NumPy .npy format, load the array, check its shape, and the size of the .npy file:

```
tmpf = NamedTemporaryFile()
np.save(tmpf, a)
tmpf.seek(0)
loaded = np.load(tmpf)
print "Shape", loaded.shape
print "Size .npy file", getsize(tmpf.name)
```

The call to the seek() method was needed to simulate closing and reopening the temporary file. The shape should be printed with the file size:

Shape (365, 4)
Size .npy file 11760

The .npy file is roughly three times smaller than the CSV file, as expected. Python lets us store data structures of practically arbitrary complexity. We can store a pandas DataFrame or Series as a pickle as well.

 The Python pickle is a format to store Python objects to disk or other medium. This is called **pickling**. We can recreate the Python objects from storage. This reverse process is called **unpickling** (refer to http://docs.python.org/2/library/pickle.html). Pickling has evolved over the years, so as a result, various pickle protocols exist. Not all Python objects can be pickled; however, alternative implementations such as **dill** exist, which allow more types of Python objects to be pickled. If possible, use cPickle (included in the standard Python distribution) because it is implemented in C and is, therefore, faster.

Create a DataFrame from the generated NumPy array, write it to a pickle with the to_pickle() method, and retrieve it from the pickle with the read_pickle() function:

```
df = pd.DataFrame(a)
df.to_pickle(tmpf.name)
print "Size pickled dataframe", getsize(tmpf.name)
print "DF from pickle\n", pd.read_pickle(tmpf.name)
```

The pickle of the `DataFrame` is slightly larger than the `.npy` file, as you can confirm in the following printout:

```
Size pickled dataframe 14991
DF from pickle
            0          1          2          3
0    0.496714  -0.138264   0.647689   1.523030
[TRUNCATED]
59  -2.025143   0.186454  -0.661786   0.852433
        ...        ...        ...        ...

[365 rows x 4 columns]
```

Storing data with PyTables

Hierarchical Data Format (**HDF**) is a specification and technology for the storage of big numerical data. HDF was created in the supercomputing community and is now an open standard. The latest version of HDF is **HDF5** and is the one we will be using. HDF5 structures data in groups and datasets. Datasets are multidimensional homogeneous arrays. Groups can contain other groups or datasets. Groups are like directories in a hierarchical filesystem.

The two main HDF5 Python libraries are:

* h5y
* PyTables

In this example, we will be using PyTables. PyTables has a number of dependencies:

* NumPy: We installed NumPy in *Chapter 1, Getting Started with Python Libraries*
* numexpr: This package claims that it evaluates multiple-operator array expressions many times faster than NumPy can
* HDF5

The parallel version of HDF5 also requires MPI. HDF5 can be installed by obtaining a distribution from `http://www.hdfgroup.org/HDF5/release/obtain5.html` and running the following commands (which could take a few minutes):

```
$ gunzip < hdf5-X.Y.Z.tar.gz | tar xf -
$ cd hdf5-X.Y.Z
$ make
$ make install
```

In all likelihood, your favorite package manager has a distribution for HDF5. Please choose the latest stable version. At the time of writing this book, the most recent version was 1.8.12.

The second dependency, numexpr, claims to be able to perform certain operations faster than NumPy. It supports multithreading and has its own virtual machine implemented in C. Numexpr and PyTables are available on PyPi, so we can install these with `pip` as follows:

```
$ pip install numexpr
$ pip install tables
```

Check the installed versions with the following command:

```
$ pip freeze|grep tables
tables==3.1.1
$ pip freeze|grep numexpr
numexpr==2.4
```

Again, we will generate random values and fill a NumPy array with those random values. Create an HDF5 file and attach the NumPy array to the root node with the following code:

```
tmpf = NamedTemporaryFile()
h5file = tables.openFile(tmpf.name, mode='w', title="NumPy Array")
root = h5file.root
h5file.createArray(root, "array", a)
h5file.close()
```

Read the HDF5 file and print its file size:

```
h5file = tables.openFile(tmpf.name, "r")
print getsize(tmpf.name)
```

The value that we get for the file size is `13824`. Once we read an HDF5 file and obtain a handle for it, we would normally traverse it to find the data we need. Since we only have one dataset, traversing is pretty simple. Call the `iterNodes()` and `read()` methods to get the NumPy array back:

```
for node in h5file.iterNodes(h5file.root):
    b = node.read()
    print type(b), b.shape
```

The type and shape of the dataset corresponds to our expectations:

```
<type 'numpy.ndarray'> (365, 4)
```

The following code can be found in the `hf5storage.py` file in this book's code bundle:

```
import numpy as np
import tables
from tempfile import NamedTemporaryFile
from os.path import getsize

np.random.seed(42)
a = np.random.randn(365, 4)

tmpf = NamedTemporaryFile()
h5file = tables.openFile(tmpf.name, mode='w', title="NumPy Array")
root = h5file.root
h5file.createArray(root, "array", a)
h5file.close()

h5file = tables.openFile(tmpf.name, "r")
print getsize(tmpf.name)

for node in h5file.iterNodes(h5file.root):
    b = node.read()
    print type(b), b.shape

h5file.close()
```

Reading and writing pandas DataFrames to HDF5 stores

The `HDFStore` class is the pandas abstraction responsible for dealing with HDF5 data. Using random data and temporary files, we will demonstrate this functionality. These are the steps to do so:

Give the `HDFStore` constructor the path to a temporary file and create a store:

```
store = pd.io.pytables.HDFStore(tmpf.name)
print store
```

The preceding code snippet will print the file path to the store and its contents, which is empty at the moment:

```
<class 'pandas.io.pytables.HDFStore'>
File path:
/var/folders/k_/xx_xz6xj0hx627654s3vld440000gn/T/tmpfmwPPB
Empty
```

`HDFStore` has a dict-like interface, meaning that we can store values, for instance, a pandas `DataFrame` with a corresponding lookup key. Store a `DataFrame` containing random data in `HDFStore` as follows:

```
store['df'] = df
print store
```

Now the store contains data as illustrated in the following output:

```
<class 'pandas.io.pytables.HDFStore'>
File path:
/var/folders/k_/xx_xz6xj0hx627654s3vld440000gn/T/tmpfwyLIN
/df               frame        (shape->[365,4])
```

We can access the `DataFrame` in three ways: with the `get()` method, a dict-like lookup, or dotted access. So let's try this out:

```
print "Get", store.get('df').shape
print "Lookup", store['df'].shape
print "Dotted", store.df.shape
```

The shape of the `DataFrame` is the same for all three access methods:

```
Get (365, 4)
Lookup (365, 4)
Dotted (365, 4)
```

We can delete an item in the store by calling the `remove()` method or with the `del` operator. Obviously, we can remove an item only once. Delete the `DataFrame` from the store:

```
del store['df']
print "After del\n", store
```

The store is now empty again:

```
After del
<class 'pandas.io.pytables.HDFStore'>
File path:
/var/folders/k_/xx_xz6xj0hx627654s3vld440000gn/T/tmpR6j_K5
Empty
```

The `is_open` attribute indicates whether the store is open or not. The store can be closed with the `close()` method. Close the store and check that it is closed:

```
print "Before close", store.is_open
store.close()
print "After close", store.is_open
```

Once closed, the store is no longer open as confirmed by the following:

```
Before close True
After close False
```

pandas also provides a DataFrame `to_hdf()` method and a top-level `read_hdf()` function to read and write HDF data. Call the `to_hdf()` method and read the data:

```
df.to_hdf(tmpf.name, 'data', format='table')
print pd.read_hdf(tmpf.name, 'data', where=['index>363'])
```

The arguments of the reading and writing API are a file path, an identifier for the group in the store, and an optional format string. The format can either be fixed or table. The fixed format is faster, but you cannot append or search. The table format corresponds to a PyTables `Table` structure and allows searching and selection. We get the following values for the query on the `DataFrame`:

```
            0          1          2          3
364   0.753342   0.381158   1.289753   0.673181
```

```
[1 rows x 4 columns]
```

The `pd_hdf.py` file in this book's code bundle contains the following code:

```
import numpy as np
import pandas as pd
from tempfile import NamedTemporaryFile

np.random.seed(42)
a = np.random.randn(365, 4)

tmpf = NamedTemporaryFile()
store = pd.io.pytables.HDFStore(tmpf.name)
print store

df = pd.DataFrame(a)
store['df'] = df
print store

print "Get", store.get('df').shape
print "Lookup", store['df'].shape
print "Dotted", store.df.shape

del store['df']
```

```
print "After del\n", store

print "Before close", store.is_open
store.close()
print "After close", store.is_open

df.to_hdf(tmpf.name, 'data', format='table')
print pd.read_hdf(tmpf.name, 'data', where=['index>363'])
```

Reading and writing to Excel with pandas

Excel files contain a lot of important data. Of course, we can export that data in other more portable formats such as CSV. However, it is more convenient to read and write Excel files with Python. As is common in the Python world, there is more than one project with the goal of providing Excel I/O capabilities. The modules that we will need to install to get Excel I/O to work with pandas are somewhat obscurely documented. The reason is that the projects that pandas depends on are independent and rapidly developing. The pandas package is picky about the files it accepts as Excel files. These files must have the `.xls` or `.xlsx` suffix; otherwise, we get the following error:

ValueError: No engine for filetype: ''

This is easy to fix. For instance, if we create a temporary file, we just give it the proper suffix. If you don't install anything, you will get the following error message:

ImportError: No module named openpyxl.workbook

The following command gets rid of the error by installing openpyxl:

$ pip install openpyxl

Check the version with the following command:

$ pip freeze|grep openpyxl

openpyxl==2.0.3

The openpyxl module is a port of PHPExcel and supports the reading and writing of `.xlsx` files.

 If for some reason the `pip install` method didn't work for you, you can find alternative installation instructions at `http://pythonhosted.org/openpyxl/`.

Even after installing openpyxl, you might get the following error:

```
ImportError: No module named style
```

Fix this by installing xlsxwriter:

```
$ pip install xlsxwriter
```

Also, we can check the xlsxwriter version again. I have installed version 0.5.5. The xlsxwriter module is also needed to read the .xlsx files. At this point, you will most likely get the following error:

```
ImportError: No module named xlrd
```

This module can be installed with pip as well:

```
$ pip install xlrd
$ pip freeze|grep xlrd
xlrd==0.9.3
```

The xlrd module is able to extract data from the .xls and .xlsx files. Let's generate random values to populate a pandas DataFrame, create an Excel file from the DataFrame, recreate the DataFrame from the Excel file, and apply the mean() method to it. For the sheet of the Excel file, we can either specify a zero-based index or name.

Refer to the pd_xls.py file in the book's code bundle, which will contain the following code:

```python
import numpy as np
import pandas as pd
from tempfile import NamedTemporaryFile

np.random.seed(42)
a = np.random.randn(365, 4)

tmpf = NamedTemporaryFile(suffix='.xlsx')
df = pd.DataFrame(a)
print tmpf.name
df.to_excel(tmpf.name, sheet_name='Random Data')
print "Means\n", pd.read_excel(tmpf.name, 'Random Data').mean()
```

Create an Excel file with the to_excel() method:

```python
df.to_excel(tmpf.name, sheet_name='Random Data')
```

Recreate the `DataFrame` with the top-level `read_excel()` function:

```
print "Means\n", pd.read_excel(tmpf.name, 'Random Data').mean()
```

The means are printed as follows:

```
/var/folders/k_/xx_xz6xj0hx627654s3vld440000gn/T/tmpeBEfn0.xlsx
Means
0    0.037860
1    0.024483
2    0.059836
3    0.058417
dtype: float64
```

Using REST web services and JSON

Representational State Transfer (REST) web services use the REST-architectural style (for more information refer to http://en.wikipedia.org/wiki/Representational_state_transfer). In the usual context of the HTTP(S) protocol, we have the **GET, POST, PUT,** and **DELETE** methods. These methods can be aligned with common operations on the data to create, request, update, or delete data items.

In a RESTful API, data items are identified by URIs such as http://example.com/resources or http://example.com/resources/item42. REST is not an official standard but is so widespread that we need to know about it. Web services often use **JavaScript Object Notation (JSON)** (for more information refer to http://en.wikipedia.org/wiki/JSON) to exchange data. In this format, data is written using the JavaScript notation. The notation is similar to the syntax for Python lists and dicts. In JSON, we can define arbitrarily complex data consisting of a combination of lists and dicts. To illustrate this, we will use a very simple JSON string that corresponds to a dictionary, which gives geographical information for a particular IP address:

```
{"country":"Netherlands","dma_code":"0","timezone":"Europe\/Amsterdam
","area_code":"0","ip":"46.19.37.108","asn":"AS196752","continent_cod
e":"EU","isp":"Tilaa
V.O.F.","longitude":5.75,"latitude":52.5,"country_code":"NL","country
_code3":"NLD"}
```

You can get this data from
http://www.telize.com/geoip/46.19.37.108.

The following is the code for the `json_demo.py` file:

```
import json

json_str = '{"country":"Netherlands","dma_
code":"0","timezone":"Europe\/Amsterdam","area_code":"0","ip":"46.1
9.37.108","asn":"AS196752","continent_code":"EU","isp":"Tilaa V.O.
F.","longitude":5.75,"latitude":52.5,"country_code":"NL","country_
code3":"NLD"}'

data = json.loads(json_str)
print "Country", data["country"]
data["country"] = "Brazil"
print json.dumps(data)
```

Python has a standard JSON API that is really easy to use. Parse a JSON string with the `loads()` function:

```
data = json.loads(json_str)
```

Access the `country` value with the following code:

```
print "Country", data["country"]
```

The previous line should print the following:

Country Netherlands

Overwrite the `country` value and create a string from the new JSON data:

```
data["country"] = "Brazil"
printjson.dumps(data)
```

The result is JSON with a new `country` value. The order is not preserved as it usually happens for dicts:

**{"longitude": 5.75, "ip": "46.19.37.108", "isp": "Tilaa V.O.F.",
"area_code": "0", "dma_code": "0", "country_code3": "NLD",
"continent_code": "EU", "country_code": "NL", "country": "Brazil",
"latitude": 52.5, "timezone": "Europe/Amsterdam", "asn": "AS196752"}**

Reading and writing JSON with pandas

We can easily create a pandas `Series` from the JSON string in the previous example. The pandas `read_json()` function can create a pandas `Series` or pandas `DataFrame`.

The following example code can be found in `pd_json.py` of this book's code bundle:

```
import pandas as pd

json_str = '{"country":"Netherlands","dma_
code":"0","timezone":"Europe\/Amsterdam","area_code":"0","ip":"46.1
9.37.108","asn":"AS196752","continent_code":"EU","isp":"Tilaa V.O.
F.","longitude":5.75,"latitude":52.5,"country_code":"NL","country_
code3":"NLD"}'

data = pd.read_json(json_str, typ='series')
print "Series\n", data

data["country"] = "Brazil"
print "New Series\n", data.to_json()
```

We can either specify a JSON string or the path of a JSON file. Call the `read_json()` function to create a pandas `Series` from the JSON string in the previous example:

```
data = pd.read_json(json_str, typ='series')
print "Series\n", data
```

In the resulting `Series`, the keys are ordered in alphabetical order:

```
Series
area_code                        0
asn                       AS196752
continent_code                  EU
country                Netherlands
country_code                    NL
country_code3                  NLD
dma_code                         0
ip                    46.19.37.108
ispTilaa V.O.F.
latitude                      52.5
longitude                     5.75
timezone         Europe/Amsterdam
dtype: object
```

Change the `country` value again and convert the pandas `Series` to a JSON string with the `to_json()` method:

```
data["country"] = "Brazil"
print "New Series\n", data.to_json()
```

In the new JSON string, the key order is preserved, but we also have a different `country` value:

New Series

```
{"area_code":"0","asn":"AS196752","continent_code":"EU","country":"Br
azil","country_code":"NL","country_code3":"NLD","dma_code":"0","ip":"
46.19.37.108","isp":"Tilaa
V.O.F.","latitude":52.5,"longitude":5.75,"timezone":"Europe\/Amsterda
m"}
```

Parsing RSS and Atom feeds

Really Simple Syndication (**RSS**) and Atom feeds (refer to http://en.wikipedia.org/wiki/RSS) are often used for blogs and news. These type of feeds follow the publish/subscribe model. For instance, Packt Publishing has an RSS feed with article and book announcements. We can subscribe to the feed to get timely updates. The Python feedparser module allows us to parse RSS and Atom feeds easily without dealing with a lot of technical details. The feedparser module can be installed with `pip` as follows:

```
$ sudo pip install feedparser
$ pip freeze|grep feedparser
feedparser==5.1.3
```

After parsing an RSS file, we can access the underlying data using a *dotted* notation. Parse the Packt Publishing RSS feed and print the number of entries:

```
import feedparser as fp

rss = fp.parse("http://www.packtpub.com/rss.xml")

print "# Entries", len(rss.entries)
```

The number of entries is printed (the number may vary for each program run):

```
# Entries 50
```

Print entry titles and summaries if the entry contains the word `Python` with the following code:

```
for i, entry in enumerate(rss.entries):
    if "Python" in entry.summary:
        print i, entry.title
        print entry.summary
```

On this particular run, the following was printed (if you try it for yourself, you may get something else or nothing at all if the filter is too restrictive):

```
42 Create interactive plots with matplotlib using Pack&#039;t new
book and eBook
```

```
About the author: Alexandre Devert is a scientist. He is an
enthusiastic Python coder as well and never gets enough of it! He
used to teach data mining, software engineering, and research in
numerical optimization.
```

```
Matplotlib is part of the Scientific Python modules collection. It
provides a large library of customizable plots and a comprehensive
set of backends. It tries to make easy things easy and make hard
things possible. It can help users generate plots, add dimensions to
plots, and also make plots interactive with just a few lines of code.
Also, matplotlib integrates well with all common GUI modules.
```

The following code can be found in the `rss.py` file of this book's code bundle:

```python
import feedparser as fp

rss = fp.parse("http://www.packtpub.com/rss.xml")

print "# Entries", len(rss.entries)

for i, entry in enumerate(rss.entries):
    if "Python" in entry.summary:
        print i, entry.title
        print entry.summary
```

Parsing HTML with Beautiful Soup

Hypertext Markup Language (**HTML**) is the fundamental technology used to create web pages. HTML is composed of HTML elements that consist of so-called tags enveloped in slanted brackets (for example, `<html>`). Often, tags are paired with a starting and closing tag in a hierarchical tree-like structure. An HTML-related draft specification was first published by Berners-Lee in 1991. Initially, there were only 18 HTML elements. The formal HTML definition was published by the **Internet Engineering Task Force** (**IETF**) in 1993. The IETF completed the HTML 2.0 standard in 1995. Around 2013, the latest HTML version, HTML5, was specified. HTML is not a very strict standard if compared to XHTML and XML.

Modern browsers tolerate a lot of violations of the standard, making web pages a form of unstructured data. We can treat HTML as a big string and perform string operations on it with regular expressions, for example. This approach works only for simple projects.

I have worked on web scraping projects in a professional setting; so from personal experience, I can tell you that we need more sophisticated methods. In a real world scenario, it may be necessary to submit HTML forms programmatically, for instance, to log in, navigate through pages, and manage cookies robustly. The problem with scraping data from the Web is that if we don't have full control of the web pages that we are scraping, we may have to change our code quite often. Also, programmatic access may be actively blocked by the website owner, or may even be illegal. For these reasons, you should always try to use other alternatives first, such as a REST API.

In the event that you must retrieve the data by scraping, it is recommended to use the Python Beautiful Soup API. This API can extract data from both HTML and XML files. New projects should use Beautiful Soup 4, since Beautiful Soup 3 is no longer developed. We can install Beautiful Soup 4 with the following command (similar to `easy_install`):

```
$ pip install beautifulsoup4
$ pip freeze|grep beautifulsoup
beautifulsoup4==4.3.2
```

> On Debian and Ubuntu, the package name is `python-bs4`. We can also download the source from `http://www.crummy.com/software/BeautifulSoup/download/4.x/`. After unpacking the source, we can install Beautiful Soup from the source directory with the following command:
> ```
> $ python setup.py install
> ```

If this doesn't work, you are allowed to simply package Beautiful Soup along with your own code. To demonstrate parsing HTML, I have generated the `loremIpsum.html` file in this book's code bundle with the generator from `http://loripsum.net/`. Then, I edited the file a bit. The content of the file is a first century BC text in Latin by Cicero, which is a traditional way to create mock-ups of websites. Refer to the following screenshot for the top part of the web page:

Ne in odium veniam, si amicum destitero tueri.

Generated with the generator from loripsum.net

Versions

Development

0.10.1 - July 2014

Official Release

0.10.0 June 2014

Previous Release

0.09.1 June 2013

Lorem ipsum dolor sit amet, consectetur adipiscing elit. Duo Reges: constructio interrete. Neque solum ea communia, verum etiam paria esse dixerunt. *Qui convenit?* Fatebuntur Stoici haec omnia dicta esse praeclare, neque eam causam Zenoni desciscendi fuisse. Est enim tanti

```
<html><head>
<title>Generated Lorem Ipsum</title>
</head>
<body>
<h1>Ne in odium veniam, si amicum destitero tueri.</h1>
<p>Generated with the generator from <a href="http://loripsum.net
/">loripsum.net</a>
</p><h3>Versions</h3>
<div class="tile">
<h4>Development</h4>
0.10.1 - July 2014<br>
</div>
<div class="tile" id="official">
<h4>Official Release</h4>
0.10.0 June 2014<br>
</div>
<div class="notile">
<h4>Previous Release</h4>
0.09.1 June 2013<br>
</div>
```

In this example, we will be using Beautiful Soup 4 and the standard Python regular expression library:

Import these libraries with the following lines:

```
from bs4 import BeautifulSoup
import re
```

Open the HTML file and create a BeautifulSoup object with the following line:

```
soup = BeautifulSoup(open('loremIpsum.html'))
```

Using a dotted notation, we can access the first <div> element. The <div> HTML element is used to organize and style elements. Access the first div element as follows:

```
print "First div\n", soup.div
```

The resulting output is an HTML snippet with the first <div> tag and all the tags it contains:

```
First div
<div class="tile">
<h4>Development</h4>
    0.10.1 - July 2014<br/>
</div>
```

This particular div element has a class attribute with the value tile. The class attribute pertains to the CSS style that is to be applied to this div element. **Cascading Style Sheets (CSS)** is a language used to style elements of a web page. CSS is a widespread specification that handles the look and feel of web pages through CSS classes. CSS aids in separating content and presentation by defining colors, fonts, and the layout of elements. The separation leads to a simpler and cleaner design.

Attributes of a tag can be accessed in a dict-like fashion. Print the class attribute value of the <div> tag as follows:

```
print "First div class", soup.div['class']
First div class ['tile']
```

The dotted notation allows us to access elements at an arbitrary depth. For instance, print the text of the first <dfn> tag as follows:

```
print "First dfn text", soup.dl.dt.dfn.text
```

A line with Latin text is printed (Solisten, I pray):

First dfn text Quareattende, quaeso.

Sometimes, we are only interested in the hyperlinks of an HTML document. For instance, we may only want to know which document links to which other documents. In HTML, links are specified with the <a> tag. The href attribute of this tag holds the URL the link points to. The BeautifulSoup class has a handy find_all() method, which we will use a lot. Locate all the hyperlinks with the find_all() method:

```
for link in soup.find_all('a'):
        print "Link text", link.string, "URL", link.get('href')
```

There are three links in the document with the same URL, but with three different texts:

```
Link text loripsum.net URL http://loripsum.net/
Link text Potera tautem inpune; URL http://loripsum.net/
Link text Is es profecto tu. URL http://loripsum.net/
```

We can omit the find_all() method as a shortcut. Access the contents of all the <div> tags as follows:

```
for i, div in enumerate(soup('div')):
    print i, div.contents
```

The `contents` attribute holds a list with HTML elements:

```
0 [u'\n', <h4>Development</h4>, u'\n       0.10.1 - July
2014', <br/>, u'\n']
1 [u'\n', <h4>Official Release</h4>, u'\n       0.10.0 June
2014', <br/>, u'\n']
2 [u'\n', <h4>Previous Release</h4>, u'\n       0.09.1 June
2013', <br/>, u'\n']
```

A tag with a unique ID is easy to find. Select the <div> element with the `official` ID and print the third element:

```
official_div = soup.find_all("div", id="official")
print "Official Version",
official_div[0].contents[2].strip()
```

Many web pages are created on the fly based on visitor input or external data. This is how most content from online shopping websites is served. If we are dealing with a dynamic website, we have to remember that any tag attribute value can change in a moment's notice. Typically, in a large website, IDs are automatically generated resulting in long alphanumeric strings. It's best to not look for exact matches but use regular expressions instead. We will see an example of a match based on a pattern later. The previous code snippet prints a version number and month as you might find on a website for a software product:

```
Official Version 0.10.0 June 2014
```

As you know, `class` is a Python keyword. To query the class attribute in a tag, we match it with `class_`. Get the number of <div> tags with a defined class attribute:

```
print "# elements with class",
len(soup.find_all(class_=True))
```

We find three tags as expected:

```
# elements with class 3
```

Find the number of <div> tags with the class `"tile"`:

```
tile_class = soup.find_all("div", class_="tile")
print "# Tile classes", len(tile_class)
```

There are two <div> tags with class `tile` and one <div> tag with class `notile`:

```
# Tile classes 2
```

Define a regular expression that will match all the `<div>` tags:

```
print "# Divs with class containing tile",
len(soup.find_all("div", class_=re.compile("tile")))
```

Again, three occurrences are found:

 # Divs with class containing tile 3

In CSS, we can define patterns in order to match elements. These patterns are called **CSS selectors** and are documented at `http://www.w3.org/TR/selectors/`. We can select elements with the CSS selector from the `BeautifulSoup` class too. Use the `select()` method to match the `<div>` element with class `notile`:

```
print "Using CSS selector\n", soup.select('div.notile')
```

The following is printed on the screen:

```
Using CSS selector
[<div class="notile">
<h4>Previous Release</h4>
    0.09.1 June 2013<br/>
</div>]
```

An HTML-ordered list looks like a numbered list of bullets. The ordered list consists of an `<ol>` tag and several `<li>` tags for each list item. The result from the `select()` method can be sliced as any Python list. Refer to the following screenshot of the ordered list:

Select the first two list items in the ordered list:

```
print "Selecting ordered list list items\n",
soup.select("ol> li")[:2]
```

The following two list items are shown:

```
Selecting ordered list list items
[<li>Cur id non ita fit?</li>, <li>In qua
si nihil est praeter rationem, sit in una virtute finis
bonorum;</li>]
```

In the CSS selector mini language, we start counting from 1. Select the second list item as follows:

```
print "Second list item in ordered list",
soup.select("ol>li:nth-of-type(2)")
```

The second list item can be translated in English as *In which, if there is nothing contrary to reason, let him be the power of the end of the good things in one:*

```
Second list item in ordered list [<li>In qua
si nihil est praeter rationem, sit in una virtute finis
bonorum;</li>]
```

If we are looking at a web page in a browser, we may decide to retrieve the text nodes that match a certain regular expression. Find all the text nodes containing the string 2014 with the text attribute:

```
print "Searching for text string",
soup.find_all(text=re.compile("2014"))
```

This prints the following text nodes:

```
Searching for text string [u'\n      0.10.1 - July 2014',
u'\n      0.10.0 June 2014']
```

This was just a brief overview of what the BeautifulSoup class can do for us. Beautiful Soup can also be used to modify HTML or XML documents. It has utilities to troubleshoot, pretty print, and deal with different character sets. Please refer to soup_request.py for the code:

```
from bs4 import BeautifulSoup
import re

soup = BeautifulSoup(open('loremIpsum.html'))

print "First div\n", soup.div
print "First div class", soup.div['class']

print "First dfn text", soup.dl.dt.dfn.text

for link in soup.find_all('a'):
    print "Link text", link.string, "URL", link.get('href')

# Omitting find_all
for i, div in enumerate(soup('div')):
    print i, div.contents


#Div with id=official
official_div = soup.find_all("div", id="official")
```

```
print "Official Version", official_div[0].contents[2].strip()

print "# elements with class", len(soup.find_all(class_=True))

tile_class = soup.find_all("div", class_="tile")
print "# Tile classes", len(tile_class)

print "# Divs with class containing tile", len(soup.find_all("div",
class_=re.compile("tile")))

print "Using CSS selector\n", soup.select('div.notile')
print "Selecting ordered list list items\n", soup.select("ol>
li")[:2]
print "Second list item in ordered list", soup.select("ol>li:nth-
of-type(2)")

print "Searching for text string", soup.find_all(text=re.
compile("2014"))
```

Summary

In this chapter, we learned about retrieving, processing, and storing data in different formats. The formats include the CSV, NumPy .npy format, Python pickle, JSON, RSS, and HTML. We used the NumPy pandas, json, feedparser, and Beautiful Soup libraries.

The next chapter *Chapter 6, Data Visualization*, is about the important topic of visualizing data with Python. Visualization is something we often do when we start analyzing data. It helps to display relations between variables in the data. By visualizing the data, we can also get an idea about its statistical properties.

6
Data Visualization

One of the first steps in data analysis is visualization. Even when looking at a table of values, we can form a mental image of what the data might look like when graphed. Data visualization calls for the conception and analysis of the visual representation of information, signifying data that has been abstracted in some formal pattern, including properties or quantities for units of measurements of the data. Data visualization is tightly associated with scientific visualization and statistical graphics. The Python matplotlib (all lowercase) library is a well-known plotting library based on NumPy, which we will be using in this chapter. It has an object-oriented and a procedural MATLAB-like API, which can be used in parallel. A gallery with matplotlib examples can be found at `http://matplotlib.org/gallery.html`. The following is a list of topics that will be covered in this chapter:

- Basic matplotlib plots
- Logarithmic plots
- Scatter plots
- Legends and annotations
- Three-dimensional plots
- Plotting in pandas
- Lag plots
- Autocorrelation plots
- Plot.ly

matplotlib subpackages

If we pick up our `pkg_check.py` file provided in the code bundle and change the code to list the matplotlib subpackages, we get the following result:

```
matplotlib version 1.3.1
matplotlib.axes
matplotlib.backends
matplotlib.compat
matplotlib.delaunay DESCRIPTION :Author: Robert Kern
<robert.kern@gmail.com> :Copyright: Copyright 2005 Robert Kern.
:License: BSD-style license. See LICENSE.tx
matplotlib.projections
matplotlib.sphinxext
matplotlib.style
matplotlib.testing
matplotlib.tests
matplotlib.tri
```

The subpackage names are pretty self-explanatory. Backends refers to the way the end result is output. This can be one of several file formats or on the screen in a graphical user interface. For completeness, refer to the following snippet with the changed lines in `pkg_check.py`:

```
import matplotlib as mpl

print "matplotlib version", mpl.__version__

print_desc("matplotlib", mpl.__path__)
```

Basic matplotlib plots

We installed matplotlib and IPython in *Chapter 1, Getting Started with Python Libraries*. Please go back to that chapter if you need to. The procedural MATLAB-like matplotlib API is considered by many as simpler to use than the object-oriented API, so we will demonstrate this procedural API first. To create a very basic plot in matplotlib, we need to invoke the `plot()` function in the `matplotlib.pyplot` subpackage. This function produces a two-dimensional plot for a single list or multiple lists of points with known *x* and *y* coordinates.

Optionally, we can pass a format parameter, for instance, to specify a dashed line style. The list of format options and parameters for the `plot()` function is pretty long, but easy to look up with the following commands:

```
$ ipython -pylab
In [1]: help(plot)
```

In this example, we will plot two lines: one with a solid line style (the default) and the other with a dashed line style.

The following demo code is in the `basic_plot.py` file in this book's code bundle:

```
import matplotlib.pyplot as plt
import numpy as np

x = np.linspace(0, 20)

plt.plot(x,   .5 + x)
plt.plot(x, 1 + 2 * x, '--')
plt.show()
```

Please follow the ensuing steps to plot the aforementioned lines:

1. First, we will specify the *x* coordinates with the NumPy `linspace()` function. Specify a start value of 0 and an end value of 20:

   ```
   x = np.linspace(0, 20)
   ```

2. Plot the lines as follows:

   ```
   plt.plot(x,   .5 + x)
   plt.plot(x, 1 + 2 * x, '--')
   ```

3. At this juncture, we can either save the plot to a file with the `savefig()` function or show the plot on the screen with the `show()` function. Show the plot on the screen as follows:

   ```
   plt.show()
   ```

Refer to the following plot for the end result:

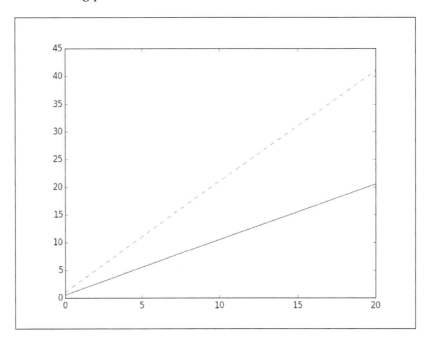

Logarithmic plots

Logarithmic plots (or log plots) are plots that use a logarithmic scale. A logarithmic scale shows the value of a variable which uses intervals that match orders of magnitude, instead of a regular linear scale. There are two types of logarithmic plots. The log-log plot employs logarithmic scaling on both axes and is represented in matplotlib by the `matplotlib.pyplot.loglog()` function. The semi-log plots use linear scaling on one axis and logarithmic scaling on the other axis. These plots are represented in the matplotlib API by the `semilogx()` and `semilogy()` functions. On log-log plots, power laws appear as straight lines. On semi-log plots, straight lines represent exponential laws.

Moore's law is such a law. It's not a physical, but more of an empirical observation. Gordon Moore discovered a trend of the number of transistors in integrated circuits doubling every two years. On `http://en.wikipedia.org/wiki/Transistor_count#Microprocessors`, a table can be found with transistor counts for various microprocessors and the corresponding year of introduction.

From the table, I have prepared a CSV file, `transcount.csv`, containing only the transistor count and year. We still need to average the transistor counts for each year. Averaging and loading can be done with pandas. If you need to, refer to *Chapter 4, pandas Primer*, for tips. Once we have the average transistor count for each year in the table, we can try to fit a straight line to the log of the counts versus the years. The NumPy `polyfit()` function allows to fit data to a polynomial.

Refer to the `log_plots.py` file in this book's code bundle for the following code:

```
import matplotlib.pyplot as plt
import numpy as np
import pandas as pd


df = pd.read_csv('transcount.csv')
df = df.groupby('year').aggregate(np.mean)
years = df.index.values
counts = df['trans_count'].values
poly = np.polyfit(years, np.log(counts), deg=1)
print "Poly", poly
plt.semilogy(years, counts, 'o')
plt.semilogy(years, np.exp(np.polyval(poly, years)))
plt.show()
```

The following steps will explain the preceding code:

1. Fit the data as follows:

    ```
    poly = np.polyfit(years, np.log(counts), deg=1)
    print "Poly", poly
    ```

2. The result of the fit is a `Polynomial` object (see `http://docs.scipy.org/doc/numpy/reference/generated/numpy.polynomial.polynomial.Polynomial.html#numpy.polynomial.polynomial.Polynomial`). The string representation of this object gives the polynomial coefficients with a descending order of degrees, so the highest degree coefficient comes first. For our data, we obtain the following polynomial coefficients:

    Poly [3.61559210e-01 -7.05783195e+02]

3. The NumPy `polyval()` function enables us to evaluate the polynomial we just obtained. Plot the data and fit with the `semilogy()` function:

    ```
    plt.semilogy(years, counts, 'o')
    plt.semilogy(years, np.exp(np.polyval(poly, years)))
    ```

The trend line is drawn as a solid line and the data points as filled circles. Refer to the following plot for the end result:

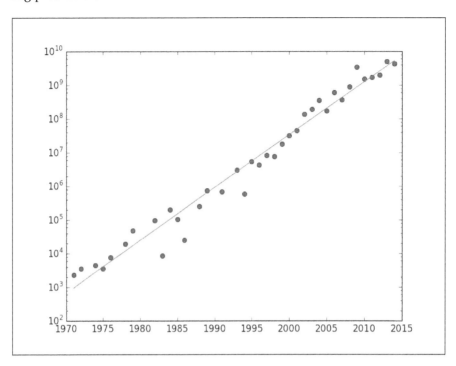

Scatter plots

A **scatter plot** shows the relationship between two variables in a Cartesian coordinate system. The position of each data point is determined by the values of these two variables. The scatter plot can provide hints for any correlation between the variables under study. An upward trending pattern suggests positive correlation. A **bubble chart** is an extension of the scatter plot. In a bubble chart, the value of a third variable is relatively represented by the size of the bubble surrounding a data point, hence the name.

On `http://en.wikipedia.org/wiki/Transistor_count#GPUs`, there is also a table with transistor counts for **Graphical Processor Units (GPUs)**.

GPUs are specialized circuits used to display graphics efficiently. Because of the way modern display hardware works, GPUs can process data with highly parallel operations. GPUs are a new development in computing. In the `gpu_transcount.csv` file in this book's code bundle, you will notice that we don't have many data points. Dealing with missing data is a recurring bubble chart issue. We will define a default bubble size for missing values. Again, we will load and average the data annually. Then, we will merge the transistor counts for the CPUs and GPUs `DataFrame` on the year indices with an outer join. The `NaN` values will be set to `0` (works for this example, but sometimes it's not a good idea to set `NaN` values to 0). All the functionality described in the preceding text was covered in *Chapter 4, pandas Primer*; therefore, please refer to that chapter if needed. The matplotlib API provides the `scatter()` function for scatter plots and bubble charts. We can view documentation for this function with the following commands:

```
$ ipython -pylab

In [1]: help(scatter)
```

In this example, we will specify the s parameter, which is related to the size of the bubble. The c parameter specifies colors. Unfortunately, you will not be able to see colors in this book, so you will have to run the examples yourself to see different colors. The `alpha` parameter determines how transparent the bubbles on the plot will be. This value varies between `0` (fully transparent) and `1` (opaque). Create a bubble chart as follows:

```
plt.scatter(years, cnt_log, c= 200 * years, s=20 + 200 *
gpu_counts/gpu_counts.max(), alpha=0.5)
```

The following code for this example can also be found in the `scatter_plot.py` file in this book's code bundle:

```python
import matplotlib.pyplot as plt
import numpy as np
import pandas as pd


df = pd.read_csv('transcount.csv')
df = df.groupby('year').aggregate(np.mean)

gpu = pd.read_csv('gpu_transcount.csv')
gpu = gpu.groupby('year').aggregate(np.mean)

df = pd.merge(df, gpu, how='outer', left_index=True, right_index=True)
df = df.replace(np.nan, 0)
```

```
print df
years = df.index.values
counts = df['trans_count'].values
gpu_counts = df['gpu_trans_count'].values
cnt_log = np.log(counts)
plt.scatter(years, cnt_log, c= 200 * years, s=20 + 200 * gpu_counts/
gpu_counts.max(), alpha=0.5)
plt.show()
```

Refer to the following plot for the end result:

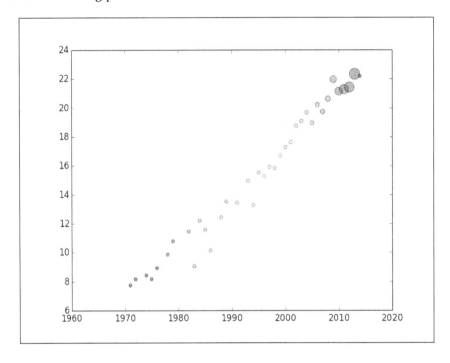

Legends and annotations

Legends and annotations are effective tools to display information required to comprehend a plot in a glance. A typical plot will have the following additional information elements:

- A legend describing the various data series in the plot. This is provided by invoking the matplotlib legend() function and supplying the labels for each data series.

- Annotations for important points in the plot. The matplotlib `annotate()` function can be used for this purpose. A matplotlib annotation consists of a label and an arrow. This function has many parameters describing the label and arrow style and position, so you may need to call `help(annotate)` for a detailed description.

- Labels on the horizontal and vertical axes. These labels can be drawn by the `xlabel()` and `ylabel()` functions. We need to give these functions the text of the labels as a string and optional parameters such as the font size of the label.

- A descriptive title for the graph with the matplotlib `title()` function. Typically, we will only give this function a string representing the title.

- A grid is also nice to have in order to localize points easily. The matplotlib `grid()` function turns the plot grid on and off.

We will modify the bubble chart code from the previous example and add the straight line fit from the second example in this chapter. In this setup, add a label to the data series as follows:

```
plt.plot(years, np.polyval(poly, years), label='Fit')
plt.scatter(years, cnt_log, c= 200 * years, s=20 + 200 *
gpu_counts/gpu_counts.max(), alpha=0.5, label="Scatter Plot")
```

Let's annotate the first GPU in our dataset. To do this, get a hold of the relevant point, define the label of the annotation, specify the style of the arrow (the `arrowprops` argument), and make sure that the annotation hovers above the point in question:

```
gpu_start = gpu.index.values.min()
y_ann = np.log(df.at[gpu_start, 'trans_count'])
ann_str = "First GPU\n %d" % gpu_start
plt.annotate(ann_str, xy=(gpu_start, y_ann),
arrowprops=dict(arrowstyle="->"), xytext=(-30, +70),
textcoords='offset points')
```

The complete code example is in the `legend_annotations.py` file in this book's code bundle:

```
import matplotlib.pyplot as plt
import numpy as np
import pandas as pd


df = pd.read_csv('transcount.csv')
df = df.groupby('year').aggregate(np.mean)
```

```
gpu = pd.read_csv('gpu_transcount.csv')
gpu = gpu.groupby('year').aggregate(np.mean)

df = pd.merge(df, gpu, how='outer', left_index=True, right_index=True)
df = df.replace(np.nan, 0)
years = df.index.values
counts = df['trans_count'].values
gpu_counts = df['gpu_trans_count'].values

poly = np.polyfit(years, np.log(counts), deg=1)
plt.plot(years, np.polyval(poly, years), label='Fit')

gpu_start = gpu.index.values.min()
y_ann = np.log(df.at[gpu_start, 'trans_count'])
ann_str = "First GPU\n %d" % gpu_start
plt.annotate(ann_str, xy=(gpu_start, y_ann), arrowprops=dict(arrowsty
le="->"), xytext=(-30, +70), textcoords='offset points')

cnt_log = np.log(counts)
plt.scatter(years, cnt_log, c= 200 * years, s=20 + 200 * gpu_counts/
gpu_counts.max(), alpha=0.5, label="Scatter Plot")
plt.legend(loc='upper left')
plt.grid()
plt.xlabel("Year")
plt.ylabel("Log Transistor Counts", fontsize=16)
plt.title("Moore's Law & Transistor Counts")
plt.show()
```

Refer to the following plot for the end result:

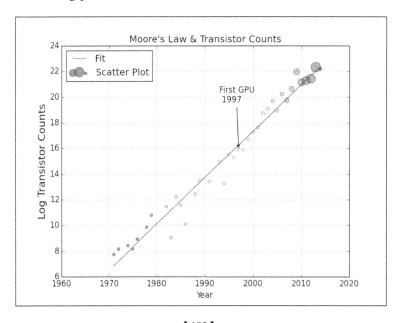

Three-dimensional plots

Two-dimensional plots are the bread and butter of data visualization. However, if you want to show off, nothing beats a good three-dimensional plot. I was in charge of a software package that could draw contour plots and three-dimensional plots. The software could even draw plots that when viewed with special glasses would pop right in front of you.

The matplotlib API has the `Axes3D` class for three-dimensional plots. By demonstrating how this class works, we will also show how the object-oriented matplotlib API works. The matplotlib `Figure` class is a top-level container for chart elements:

1. Create a `Figure` object as follows:

    ```
    fig = plt.figure()
    ```

2. Create an `Axes3D` object from the `Figure` object:

    ```
    ax = Axes3D(fig)
    ```

3. The years and CPU transistor counts will be our *x* and *y* axes. It is required to create coordinate matrices from the years and CPU transistor counts arrays. Create the coordinate matrices with the NumPy `meshgrid()` function:

    ```
    X, Y = np.meshgrid(X, Y)
    ```

4. Plot the data with the `plot_surface()` method of the `Axes3D` class:

    ```
    ax.plot_surface(X, Y, Z)
    ```

5. The naming convention of the object-oriented API methods is to start with `set_` and end with the procedural counterpart function name, as shown in the following code snippet:

    ```
    ax.set_xlabel('Year')
    ax.set_ylabel('Log CPU transistor counts')
    ax.set_zlabel('Log GPU transistor counts')
    ax.set_title("Moore's Law & Transistor Counts")
    ```

You can also have a look at the following code in the `three_dimensional.py` file in this book's code bundle:

```
from mpl_toolkits.mplot3d.axes3d import Axes3D
import matplotlib.pyplot as plt
import numpy as np
import pandas as pd


df = pd.read_csv('transcount.csv')
df = df.groupby('year').aggregate(np.mean)
```

```
gpu = pd.read_csv('gpu_transcount.csv')
gpu = gpu.groupby('year').aggregate(np.mean)

df = pd.merge(df, gpu, how='outer', left_index=True, right_index=True)
df = df.replace(np.nan, 0)

fig = plt.figure()
ax = Axes3D(fig)
X = df.index.values
Y = np.log(df['trans_count'].values)
X, Y = np.meshgrid(X, Y)
Z = np.log(df['gpu_trans_count'].values)
ax.plot_surface(X, Y, Z)
ax.set_xlabel('Year')
ax.set_ylabel('Log CPU transistor counts')
ax.set_zlabel('Log GPU transistor counts')
ax.set_title("Moore's Law & Transistor Counts")
plt.show()
```

Refer to the following plot for the end result:

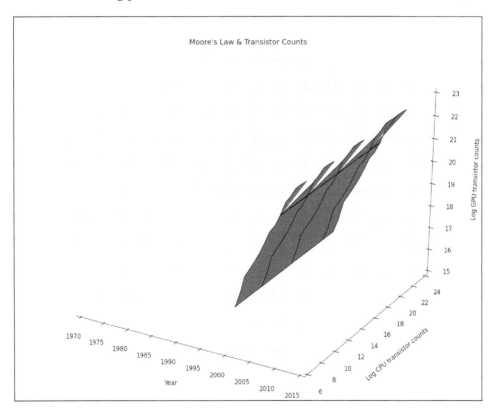

Plotting in pandas

The plot() method in the pandas Series and DataFrame classes wraps around the related matplotlib functions. In its most basic form without any arguments, the plot() method displays the following plot for the dataset we have been using throughout this chapter:

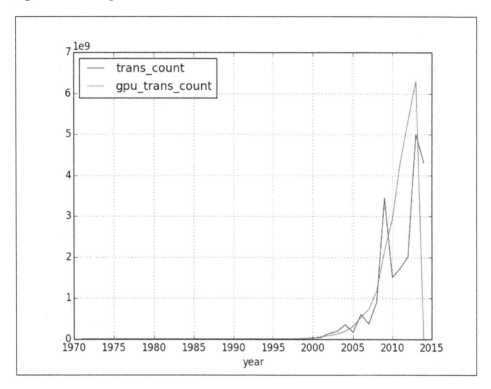

To create a semi-log plot, add the logy parameter:

```
df.plot(logy=True)
```

This results in the following plot for our data:

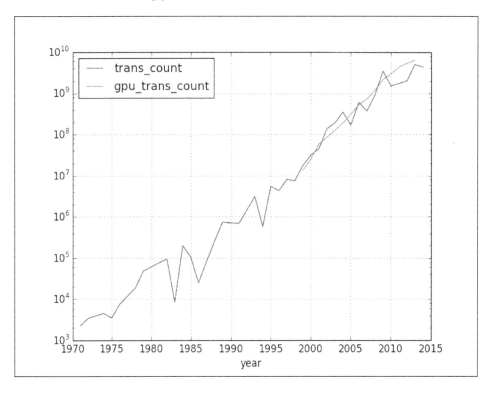

To create a scatter plot, specify the `kind` parameter to be `scatter`. We also need to specify two columns. Set the `loglog` parameter to `True` to produce a log-log graph (we need at least pandas 0.13.0 for this code):

```
df[df['gpu_trans_count'] > 0].plot(kind='scatter',
x='trans_count', y='gpu_trans_count', loglog=True)
```

Refer to the following plot for the end result:

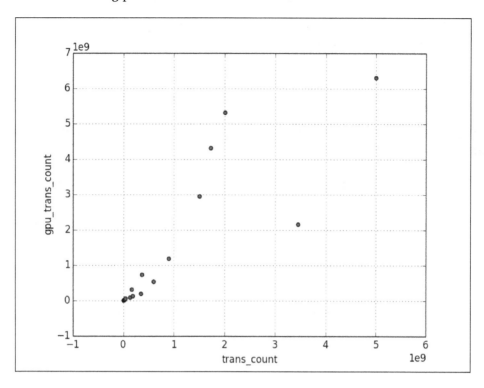

The following program is in the `pd_plotting.py` file in this book's code bundle:

```python
import matplotlib.pyplot as plt
import numpy as np
import pandas as pd


df = pd.read_csv('transcount.csv')
df = df.groupby('year').aggregate(np.mean)

gpu = pd.read_csv('gpu_transcount.csv')
gpu = gpu.groupby('year').aggregate(np.mean)

df = pd.merge(df, gpu, how='outer', left_index=True,
right_index=True)
df = df.replace(np.nan, 0)
```

```
df.plot()
df.plot(logy=True)
df[df['gpu_trans_count'] > 0].plot(kind='scatter',
x='trans_count', y='gpu_trans_count', loglog=True)
plt.show()
```

Lag plots

A **lag plot** is a scatter plot for a time series and the same data lagged. With such a plot, we can check whether there is a possible correlation between CPU transistor counts this year and the previous year, for instance. The `lag_plot()` pandas function in `pandas.tools.plotting` can draw a lag plot. Draw a lag plot with the default lag of 1 for the CPU transistor counts, as follows:

```
lag_plot(np.log(df['trans_count']))
```

Refer to the following plot for the end result:

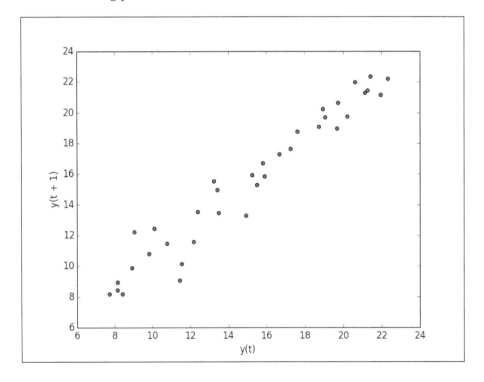

The following code for the lag plot example can also be found in the `lag_plot.py` file in this book's code bundle:

```
import matplotlib.pyplot as plt
import numpy as np
import pandas as pd
from pandas.tools.plotting import lag_plot


df = pd.read_csv('transcount.csv')
df = df.groupby('year').aggregate(np.mean)

gpu = pd.read_csv('gpu_transcount.csv')
gpu = gpu.groupby('year').aggregate(np.mean)

df = pd.merge(df, gpu, how='outer', left_index=True, right_index=True)
df = df.replace(np.nan, 0)
lag_plot(np.log(df['trans_count']))
plt.show()
```

Autocorrelation plots

Autocorrelation plots graph **autocorrelations** of time series data for different lags. Autocorrelation is the correlation of a time series with the same time series lagged. The `autocorrelation_plot()` pandas function in `pandas.tools.plotting` can draw an autocorrelation plot.

The following is the code from the `autocorr_plot.py` file in this book's code bundle:

```
import matplotlib.pyplot as plt
import numpy as np
import pandas as pd
from pandas.tools.plotting import autocorrelation_plot


df = pd.read_csv('transcount.csv')
df = df.groupby('year').aggregate(np.mean)

gpu = pd.read_csv('gpu_transcount.csv')
gpu = gpu.groupby('year').aggregate(np.mean)

df = pd.merge(df, gpu, how='outer', left_index=True, right_index=True)
df = df.replace(np.nan, 0)
autocorrelation_plot(np.log(df['trans_count']))
plt.show()
```

Draw an autocorrelation plot for the CPU transistor counts as follows:

```
autocorrelation_plot(np.log(df['trans_count']))
```

Refer to the following plot for the end result. As we can see in the following plot, more recent values (smaller lags) are stronger correlated with the current value than older values (larger lags), and at extremely large lags, the correlation decays to 0:

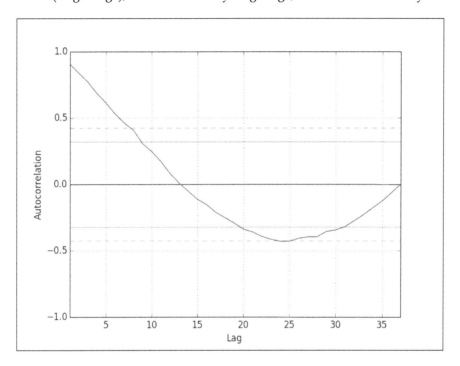

Plot.ly

Plot.ly is a website currently in the beta stage, which provides online data visualization tools and a related Python library to be used on a user's machine. We can import and analyze data via the web interface or work entirely in a local environment and publish the end result on the Plot.ly website. Plots can be easily shared on the website within a team, allowing for collaboration, which is really the point of the website in the first place. In this section, we will give an example of how to plot a box plot with the Python API.

A box plot is a special way of visualizing a dataset using quartiles. If we split a sorted dataset into four equal parts, the first quartile will be the largest value of the part with the smallest numbers. The second quartile will be the value in the middle of the dataset, which is also called the median. The third quartile will be the value in the middle between the median and the highest value. The bottom and the top of the box plot are formed by the first and third quartiles. The line through the box is the median. The whiskers on both ends of the box are usually the minimum and maximum of the dataset. At the end of this section, we will see an annotated box plot, which will clarify matters. Install the Plot.ly API with the following commands:

```
$ sudo pip install plotly
$ pip freeze|grep plotly
plotly==1.0.26
```

After installing the API, sign up to get an API key. The following code snippet signs you in after supplying a valid key:

```
api_key = getpass()

# Change the user to your own username
py.sign_in('username', api_key)
```

Create the box plots with the Plot.ly API as follows:

```
data = Data([Box(y=counts), Box(y=gpu_counts)])
plot_url = py.plot(data, filename='moore-law-scatter')
```

Please refer to the following code from the `plot_ly.py` file in this book's code bundle:

```
import plotly.plotly as py
from plotly.graph_objs import *
from getpass import getpass
import numpy as np
import pandas as pd

df = pd.read_csv('transcount.csv')
df = df.groupby('year').aggregate(np.mean)

gpu = pd.read_csv('gpu_transcount.csv')
gpu = gpu.groupby('year').aggregate(np.mean)
```

```
df = pd.merge(df, gpu, how='outer', left_index=True, right_index=True)
df = df.replace(np.nan, 0)

api_key = getpass()

# Change the user to your own username
py.sign_in('username', api_key)

counts = np.log(df['trans_count'].values)
gpu_counts = np.log(df['gpu_trans_count'].values)

data = Data([Box(y=counts), Box(y=gpu_counts)])
plot_url = py.plot(data, filename='moore-law-scatter')
print plot_url
```

Also, refer to the following plot for the end result:

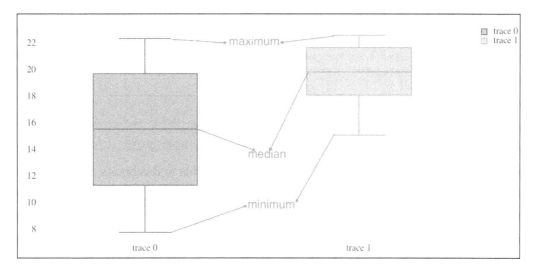

Summary

In this chapter, we discussed visualizing data with Python by plotting. We used matplotlib, pandas, and Plot.ly. We covered box plots, scatter plots, bubble charts, logarithmic plots, autocorrelation plots, lag plots, three-dimensional plots, legends, and annotations.

Logarithmic plots (or log plots) are plots that use a logarithmic scale. The semi-log plots use linear scaling on one axis and logarithmic scaling on the other axis. Scatter plots plot two variables against each other. A bubble chart is a special type of scatter plot. In a bubble chart, the value of a third variable is relatively represented by the size of the bubble surrounding a data point. Autocorrelation plots graph autocorrelations of time series data for different lags. A box plot visualizes data based on the data's quartiles.

The next chapter, *Chapter 7*, *Signal Processing and Time Series* is about a special type of data: time series. Time series are ordered data points that have been timestamped. A lot of the physical world data that we measure is in the form of a time series and can be considered a signal, for instance, sound, light, or electrical signals. You will learn how to filter signals and model time series.

7
Signal Processing and Time Series

Signal processing is a field of engineering and applied mathematics that analyzes analog and digital signals, corresponding to variables that vary with time. One of the categories of signal processing techniques is time series analysis. A **time series** is an ordered list of data points starting with the oldest measurements first. The data points are usually equidistant, for instance, consistent with daily or annual sampling. In time series analysis, the order of the values is important. It's common to try to derive a relation between a value and another data point or combination of data points a fixed number of periods in the past, in the same time series.

The time series examples in this chapter use annual sunspot cycles data. This data is provided by the statsmodels package (an open source Python project). The examples use NumPy/SciPy, pandas, and also statsmodels.

We will cover the following topics in this chapter:

- Moving averages
- Window functions
- Cointegration
- Autocorrelation
- Autoregressive models
- ARMA models
- Generating periodic signals
- Fourier analysis
- Spectral analysis
- Filtering

statsmodels subpackages

To install statsmodels, execute the following command:

```
$ pip install statsmodels
$ pip freeze|grep stat
statsmodels==0.6.0
```

Open the `pkg_check.py` file provided in the code bundle, and change the code to list the statsmodels subpackages to get the following result:

```
statmodels version 0.6.0.dev-3303360
```

```
statsmodels.base
```

```
statsmodels.compatnp
```

```
statsmodels.datasets
```

```
statsmodels.discrete
```

```
statsmodels.distributions
```

```
statsmodels.emplike
```

```
statsmodels.formula
```

```
statsmodels.genmod
```

```
statsmodels.graphics
```

```
statsmodels.interface
```

```
statsmodels.iolib
```

```
statsmodels.miscmodels
```

```
statsmodels.nonparametric DESCRIPTION For an overview of this module,
see docs/source/nonparametric.rst PACKAGE CONTENTS _kernel_base
_smoothers_lowess api bandwidths
```

```
statsmodels.regression
```

```
statsmodels.resampling
```

```
statsmodels.robust
```

```
statsmodels.sandbox
```

```
statsmodels.stats
```

```
statsmodels.tests
```

```
statsmodels.tools
```

```
statsmodels.tsa
```

Moving averages

Moving averages are frequently used to analyze time series. A moving average specifies a window of data that is previously seen, which is averaged each time the window slides forward by one period:

$$SMA = \frac{a_m + a_{m-1} + \cdots + a_{m-(n-1)}}{n}$$

The different types of moving averages differ essentially in the weights used for averaging. The **exponential moving average**, for instance, has exponentially decreasing weights with time:

$$EMA_n = EMA_{n-1} + \alpha \left(p_n - EMA_{n-1} \right)$$

This means that older values have less influence than newer values, which is sometimes desirable.

The following code from the moving_average.py file in this book's code bundle plots the simple moving average for the 11- and 22-year sunspots cycles:

```
import matplotlib.pyplot as plt
import statsmodels.api as sm
from pandas.stats.moments import rolling_mean

data_loader = sm.datasets.sunspots.load_pandas()
df = data_loader.data
year_range = df["YEAR"].values
plt.plot(year_range, df["SUNACTIVITY"].values, label="Original")
plt.plot(year_range, rolling_mean(df, 11)["SUNACTIVITY"].values,
label="SMA 11")
plt.plot(year_range, rolling_mean(df, 22)["SUNACTIVITY"].values,
label="SMA 22")
plt.legend()
plt.show()
```

We can express an exponential decreasing weight strategy for the exponential moving average, as shown in the following NumPy code:

```
weights = np.exp(np.linspace(-1., 0., N))
weights /= weights.sum()
```

A simple moving average uses equal weights, which in code looks as follows:

```
def sma(arr, n):
    weights = np.ones(n) / n

    return np.convolve(weights, arr)[n-1:-n+1]
```

Since we can load the data into a pandas `DataFrame`, it is more convenient to use the pandas `rolling_mean()` function. Load the data as follows using statsmodels:

```
data_loader = sm.datasets.sunspots.load_pandas()
df = data_loader.data
```

Refer to the following plot for the end result:

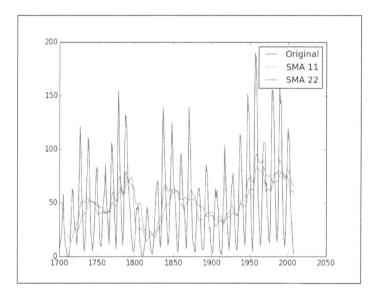

Window functions

NumPy has a number of window routines that can compute weights in a rolling window as we did in the previous section.

A **window function** is a function that is defined within an interval (the window) or is otherwise zero valued. We can use window functions for spectral analysis and filter design (for more background information, refer to http://en.wikipedia.org/wiki/Window_function). The **boxcar window** is a rectangular window with the following formula:

```
w(n) = 1
```

The **triangular window** is shaped like a triangle and has the following formula:

$$w(n) = 1 - \left| \frac{n - \frac{N-1}{2}}{\frac{L}{2}} \right|$$

In the preceding formula, `L` can be equal to `N`, `N+1`, or `N-1`. In the last case, the window function is called the **Bartlett window**. The **Blackman window** is bell shaped and defined as follows:

$$w(n) = a_0 - a_1 \cos\left(\frac{2\pi n}{N-1}\right) + a_2 \cos\left(\frac{4\pi n}{N-1}\right)$$

$$a_0 = \frac{1-\alpha}{2}; a_1 = \frac{1}{2}; a_2 = \frac{\alpha}{2}$$

The **Hanning window** is also bell shaped and defined as follows:

$$w(n) = 0.5\left(1 - \cos\left(\frac{2\pi n}{N-1}\right)\right)$$

In the pandas API, the `rolling_window()` function provides the same functionality with different values of the `win_type` string parameter corresponding to different window functions. The other parameter is the size of the window, which will be set to 22 for the middle cycle of the sunspots data (according to research, there are three cycles of 11, 22, and 100 years). The code is straightforward and given in the `window_functions.py` file in this book's code bundle (the data here is limited to the last 150 years only for easier comparison in the plots):

```
import matplotlib.pyplot as plt
import statsmodels.api as sm
from pandas.stats.moments import rolling_window
import pandas as pd

data_loader = sm.datasets.sunspots.load_pandas()
df = data_loader.data.tail(150)
df = pd.DataFrame({'SUNACTIVITY':df['SUNACTIVITY'].values},
index=df['YEAR'])
ax = df.plot()

def plot_window(win_type):
    df2 = rolling_window(df, 22, win_type)
```

```
        df2.columns = [win_type]
        df2.plot(ax=ax)

    plot_window('boxcar')
    plot_window('triang')
    plot_window('blackman')
    plot_window('hanning')
    plot_window('bartlett')
    plt.show()
```

Refer to the following plot for the end result:

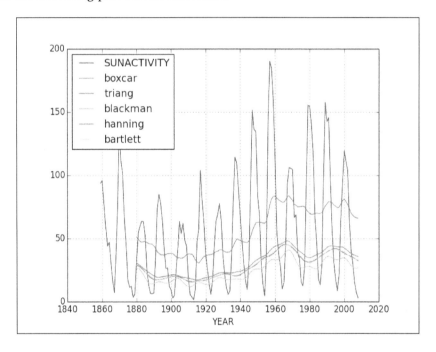

Defining cointegration

Cointegration is similar to correlation but is viewed by many as a superior metric to define the relatedness of two time series. Two time series `x(t)` and `y(t)` are cointegrated if a linear combination of them is stationary. In such a case, the following equation should be stationary:

```
y(t) - a x(t)
```

Consider a drunk man and his dog out on a walk. Correlation tells us whether they are going in the same direction. Cointegration tells us something about the distance over time between the man and his dog. We will show cointegration using randomly generated time series and real data. The **Augmented Dickey-Fuller (ADF)** test (see `http://en.wikipedia.org/wiki/Augmented_Dickey%E2%80%93Fuller_test`) tests for a unit root in a time series and can be used to determine the cointegration of time series.

For the following code, have a look at the `cointegration.py` file in this book's code bundle:

```
import statsmodels.api as sm
from pandas.stats.moments import rolling_window
import pandas as pd
import statsmodels.tsa.stattools as ts
import numpy as np

def calc_adf(x, y):
    result = sm.OLS(x, y).fit()
    return ts.adfuller(result.resid)

data_loader = sm.datasets.sunspots.load_pandas()
data = data_loader.data.values
N = len(data)

t = np.linspace(-2 * np.pi, 2 * np.pi, N)
sine = np.sin(np.sin(t))
print "Self ADF", calc_adf(sine, sine)

noise = np.random.normal(0, .01, N)
print "ADF sine with noise", calc_adf(sine, sine + noise)

cosine = 100 * np.cos(t) + 10
print "ADF sine vs cosine with noise", calc_adf(sine, cosine +
noise)

print "Sine vs sunspots", calc_adf(sine, data)
```

Let's get started with the cointegration demo:

1. Define the following function to calculate the ADF statistic:

```
def calc_adf(x, y):
    result = stat.OLS(x, y).fit()
    return ts.adfuller(result.resid)
```

2. Load the sunspots data into a NumPy array:

```
data_loader = sm.datasets.sunspots.load_pandas()
data = data_loader.data.values
N = len(data)
```

3. Generate a sine and calculate the cointegration of the sine with itself:

```
t = np.linspace(-2 * np.pi, 2 * np.pi, N)
sine = np.sin(np.sin(t))
print "Self ADF", calc_adf(sine, sine)
```

The code should print the following:

```
Self ADF (-5.0383000037165746e-16, 0.95853208606005591, 0,
308, {'5%': -2.8709700936076912, '1%': -3.4517611601803702,
'10%': -2.5717944160060719}, -21533.113655477719)
```

The first value in the printout is the ADF metric and the second value is the p-value. As you can see, the p-value is very high. The following values are the lag and sample size. The dictionary at the end gives the t-distribution values for this exact sample size.

4. Now, add noise to the sine to demonstrate how noise will influence the signal:

```
noise = np.random.normal(0, .01, N)
print "ADF sine with noise", calc_adf(sine, sine + noise)
```

With the noise, we get the following results:

```
ADF sine with noise (-7.4535502402193075,
5.5885761455106898e-11, 3, 305, {'5%': -2.8710633193086648,
'1%': -3.4519735736206991, '10%': -2.5718441306100512}, -
1855.0243977703672)
```

The p-value has gone down considerably. The ADF metric -7.45 here is lower than all the critical values in the dictionary. All these are strong arguments to reject cointegration.

5. Let's generate a cosine of a larger magnitude and offset. Again, let's add noise to it:

```
cosine = 100 * np.cos(t) + 10
print "ADF sine vs cosine with noise", calc_adf(sine,
cosine + noise)
```

The following values get printed:

```
ADF sine vs cosine with noise (-17.927224617871534,
2.8918612252729532e-30, 16, 292, {'5%': -2.8714895534256861,
'1%': -3.4529449243622383, '10%': -2.5720714378870331}, -
11017.837238220782)
```

Similarly, we have strong arguments to reject cointegration. Checking for cointegration between the sine and sunspots gives the following output:

```
Sine vs sunspots (-6.7242691810701016, 3.4210811915549028e-09, 16,
292, {'5%': -2.8714895534256861, '1%': -3.4529449243622383, '10%': -
2.5720714378870331}, -1102.5867415291168)
```

The confidence levels are roughly the same for the pairs used here because they are dependent on the number of data points, which don't vary much. The outcome is summarized in the following table:

Pair	Statistic	p-value	5%	1%	10%	Reject
Sine with self	-5.03E-16	0.95	-2.87	-3.45	-2.57	No
Sine versus sine with noise	-7.45	5.58E-11	-2.87	-3.45	-2.57	Yes
Sine versus cosine with noise	-17.92	2.89E-30	-2.87	-3.45	-2.57	Yes
Sine versus sunspots	-6.72	3.42E-09	-2.87	-3.45	-2.57	Yes

Autocorrelation

Autocorrelation is correlation within a dataset and can indicate a trend.

For a given time series, with known mean and standard deviations, we can define the autocorrelation for times s and t using the expected value operator as follows:

$$\frac{E\left[\left(x_t - \mu_t\right)\left(x_s - \mu_s\right)\right]}{\sigma_t \sigma_s}$$

This is, in essence, the formula for correlation applied to a time series and the same time series lagged.

For example, if we have a lag of one period, we can check if the previous value influences the current value. For that to be true, the autocorrelation value has to be pretty high.

In the previous chapter, *Chapter 6, Data Visualization*, we already used a pandas function that plots autocorrelation. In this example, we will use the NumPy `correlate()` function to calculate the actual autocorrelation values for the sunspots cycle. At the end, we need to normalize the values we receive. Apply the NumPy `correlate()` function as follows:

```
y = data - np.mean(data)
norm = np.sum(y ** 2)
correlated = np.correlate(y, y, mode='full')/norm
```

We are also interested in the indices corresponding to the highest correlations. These indices can be found with the NumPy `argsort()` function, which returns the indices that would sort an array:

```
print np.argsort(res)[-5:]
```

These are the indices found for the largest autocorrelations:

```
[ 9 11 10  1  0]
```

The largest autocorrelation is by definition for zero lag, that is, the correlation of a signal with itself. The next largest values are for a lag of one and ten years. Check the `autocorrelation.py` file in this book's code bundle:

```
import numpy as np
import pandas as pd
import statsmodels.api as sm
import matplotlib.pyplot as plt
from pandas.tools.plotting import autocorrelation_plot


data_loader = sm.datasets.sunspots.load_pandas()
data = data_loader.data["SUNACTIVITY"].values
y = data - np.mean(data)
norm = np.sum(y ** 2)
correlated = np.correlate(y, y, mode='full')/norm
res = correlated[len(correlated)/2:]

print np.argsort(res)[-5:]
plt.plot(res)
plt.grid(True)
plt.xlabel("Lag")
plt.ylabel("Autocorrelation")
plt.show()
autocorrelation_plot(data)
plt.show()
```

Refer to the following plot for the end result:

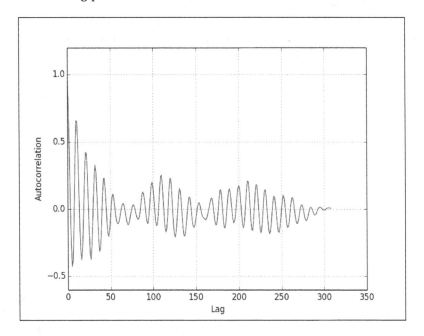

Compare the previous plot with the plot produced by pandas:

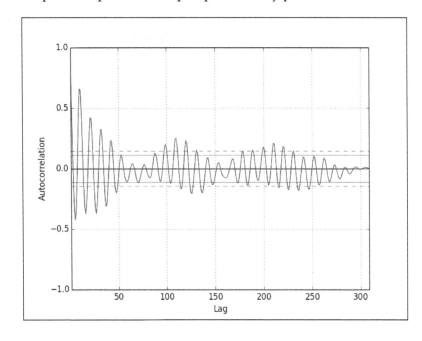

Autoregressive models

An **autoregressive model** can be used to represent a time series with the goal of forecasting future values. In such a model, a variable is assumed to depend on its previous values. The relation is also assumed to be linear and we are required to fit the data in order to find the parameters of the data.

The mathematical formula for the autoregressive model is as follows:

$$x_t = c + \sum_{i=1}^{p} a_i x_{t-i} + \epsilon_t$$

In the preceding formula, c is a constant and the last term is a random component also known as white noise.

This presents us with the very common problem of linear regression. For practical reasons, it's important to keep the model simple and only involve necessary lagged components. In machine learning jargon, these are called features. For regression problems, the Python machine learning scikit-learn library is a good, if not the best, choice. We will work with this API in *Chapter 10, Predictive Analytics and Machine Learning*.

In regression setups, we frequently encounter the problem of overfitting – this issue arises when we have a perfect fit for a sample, which performs poorly when we introduce new data points. The standard solution is to apply cross-validation (or use algorithms that avoid overfitting). In this method, we estimate model parameters on a part of the sample. The rest of the data is used to test and evaluate the model. This is actually a simplified explanation. There are more complex cross-validation schemes, a lot of which are supported by scikit-learn. To evaluate the model, we can compute appropriate evaluation metrics. As you can imagine, there are many metrics, and these metrics can have varying definitions due to constant tweaking by practitioners. We can look up these definitions in books or Wikipedia. The important thing to remember is that the evaluation of a forecast or fit is not an exact science. The fact that there are so many metrics only confirms that.

We will set up the model with the `scipy.optimize.leastsq()` function using the first two lagged components we found in the previous section. We could have chosen a linear algebra function instead. However, the `leastsq()` function is more flexible and lets us specify practically any type of model. Set up the model as follows:

```
def model(p, x1, x10):
    p1, p10 = p
    return p1 * x1 + p10 * x10

def error(p, data, x1, x10):
    return data - model(p, x1, x10)
```

To fit the model, initialize the parameter list and pass it to the `leastsq()` function as follows:

```
def fit(data):
    p0 = [.5, 0.5]
    params = leastsq(error, p0, args=(data[10:], data[9:-1], data[:-
10]))[0]
    return params
```

Train the model on a part of the data:

```
cutoff = .9 * len(sunspots)
params = fit(sunspots[:cutoff])
print "Params", params
```

The following are the parameters we get:

Params [0.67172672 0.33626295]

With these parameters, we will plot predicted values and compute various metrics. The following are the values we obtain for the metrics:

Root mean square error 22.8148122613

Mean absolute error 17.6515446503

Mean absolute percentage error 60.7817800736

Symmetric Mean absolute percentage error 34.9843386176

Coefficient of determination 0.799940292779

Refer to the following graph for the end result:

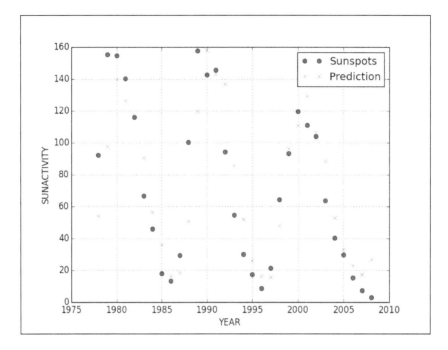

It seems that we have many predictions that are almost spot-on, but also a bunch of predictions that are pretty far off. Overall, we don't have a perfect fit; however, it's not a complete disaster. It's somewhere in the middle.

The following code is in the `ar.py` file in this book's code bundle:

```
from scipy.optimize import leastsq
import statsmodels.api as sm
import matplotlib.pyplot as plt
import numpy as np


def model(p, x1, x10):
    p1, p10 = p
    return p1 * x1 + p10 * x10

def error(p, data, x1, x10):
    return data - model(p, x1, x10)

def fit(data):
    p0 = [.5, 0.5]
```

```
      params = leastsq(error, p0, args=(data[10:], data[9:-1],
data[:-10]))[0]
      return params


data_loader = sm.datasets.sunspots.load_pandas()
sunspots = data_loader.data["SUNACTIVITY"].values

cutoff = .9 * len(sunspots)
params = fit(sunspots[:cutoff])
print "Params", params


pred = params[0] * sunspots[cutoff-1:-1] + params[1] *
sunspots[cutoff-10:-10]
actual = sunspots[cutoff:]
print "Root mean square error", np.sqrt(np.mean((actual - pred) **
2))
print "Mean absolute error", np.mean(np.abs(actual - pred))
print "Mean absolute percentage error", 100 *
np.mean(np.abs(actual - pred)/actual)
mid = (actual + pred)/2
print "Symmetric Mean absolute percentage error", 100 *
np.mean(np.abs(actual - pred)/mid)
print "Coefficient of determination", 1 - ((actual - pred) **
2).sum()/ ((actual - actual.mean()) ** 2).sum()
year_range = data_loader.data["YEAR"].values[cutoff:]
plt.plot(year_range, actual, 'o', label="Sunspots")
plt.plot(year_range, pred, 'x', label="Prediction")
plt.grid(True)
plt.xlabel("YEAR")
plt.ylabel("SUNACTIVITY")
plt.legend()
plt.show()
```

ARMA models

ARMA models are often used to forecast a time series. These models combine autoregressive and moving average models (see http://en.wikipedia.org/wiki/Autoregressive%E2%80%93moving-average_model). In moving average models, we assume that a variable is the sum of the mean of the time series and a linear combination of noise components.

> The autoregressive and moving average models can have different orders. In general, we can define an ARMA model with p autoregressive terms and q moving average terms as follows:
>
> $$x_t = c + \sum_{i=1}^{p} a_i x_{t-i} + \sum_{i=1}^{q} b_i \varepsilon_{t-i} + \in_t$$
>
> In the preceding formula, just like in the autoregressive model formula, we have a constant and a white noise component; however, we try to fit the lagged noise components as well.

Fortunately, it's possible to use the `statsmodelssm.tsa.ARMA()` routine for this analysis. Fit the data to an `ARMA(10,1)` model as follows:

```
model = sm.tsa.ARMA(df, (10,1)).fit()
```

Perform a forecast (statsmodels uses strings a lot):

```
prediction = model.predict('1975', str(years[-1]), dynamic=True)
```

Refer to the following plot for the end result:

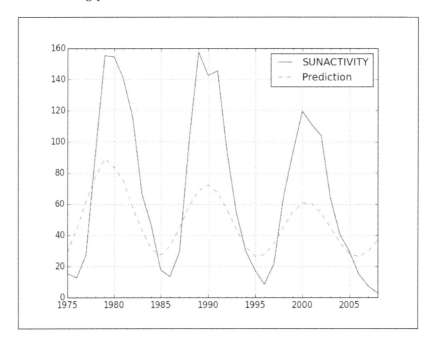

The fit is poor because frankly, we overfit the data. The simpler model in the previous section worked much better. The example code can be found in the `arma.py` file in this book's code bundle:

```
import pandas as pd
import matplotlib.pyplot as plt
import statsmodels.api as sm
import datetime

data_loader = sm.datasets.sunspots.load_pandas()
df = data_loader.data
years = df["YEAR"].values.astype(int)
df.index = pd.Index(sm.tsa.datetools.dates_from_range(str(years[0]),
str(years[-1])))
del df["YEAR"]

model = sm.tsa.ARMA(df, (10,1)).fit()
prediction = model.predict('1975', str(years[-1]), dynamic=True)

df['1975':].plot()
prediction.plot(style='--', label='Prediction')
plt.legend()
plt.show()
```

Generating periodic signals

Many natural phenomena are regular and trustworthy like an accurate clock. Some phenomena exhibit patterns that seem regular. A group of scientists found three cycles in the sunspot activity with the **Hilbert-Huang transform** (see http://en.wikipedia.org/wiki/Hilbert%E2%80%93Huang_transform). The cycles have a duration of 11, 22, and 100 years approximately. Normally, we would simulate a periodic signal using trigonometric functions such as a sine function. You probably remember a bit of trigonometry from high school. That's all we need for this example. Since we have three cycles, it seems reasonable to create a model, which is a linear combination of three sine functions. This just requires a tiny adjustment of the code for the autoregressive model. Refer to the `periodic.py` file in this book's code bundle for the following code:

```
from scipy.optimize import leastsq
import statsmodels.api as sm
import matplotlib.pyplot as plt
import numpy as np
```

```
def model(p, t):
    C, p1, f1, phi1 , p2, f2, phi2, p3, f3, phi3 = p
    return C + p1 * np.sin(f1 * t + phi1) + p2 * np.sin(f2 * t +
phi2) +p3 * np.sin(f3 * t + phi3)


def error(p, y, t):
    return y - model(p, t)

def fit(y, t):
    p0 = [y.mean(), 0, 2 * np.pi/11, 0, 0, 2 * np.pi/22, 0, 0, 2 *
np.pi/100, 0]
    params = leastsq(error, p0, args=(y, t))[0]
    return params

data_loader = sm.datasets.sunspots.load_pandas()
sunspots = data_loader.data["SUNACTIVITY"].values
years = data_loader.data["YEAR"].values

cutoff = .9 * len(sunspots)
params = fit(sunspots[:cutoff], years[:cutoff])
print "Params", params

pred = model(params, years[cutoff:])
actual = sunspots[cutoff:]
print "Root mean square error", np.sqrt(np.mean((actual - pred) **
2))
print "Mean absolute error", np.mean(np.abs(actual - pred))
print "Mean absolute percentage error", 100 *
np.mean(np.abs(actual - pred)/actual)
mid = (actual + pred)/2
print "Symmetric Mean absolute percentage error", 100 *
np.mean(np.abs(actual - pred)/mid)
print "Coefficient of determination", 1 - ((actual - pred) **
2).sum()/ ((actual - actual.mean()) ** 2).sum()
year_range = data_loader.data["YEAR"].values[cutoff:]
plt.plot(year_range, actual, 'o', label="Sunspots")
plt.plot(year_range, pred, 'x', label="Prediction")
plt.grid(True)
plt.xlabel("YEAR")
plt.ylabel("SUNACTIVITY")
plt.legend()
plt.show()
```

We get the following output:

```
Params [ 47.18800285  28.89947419    0.56827284    6.51168446
4.55214999
    0.29372077 -14.30926648 -18.16524041    0.06574835   -4.37789602]
Root mean square error 59.5619175499

Mean absolute error 44.5814573306

Mean absolute percentage error 65.1639657495

Symmetric Mean absolute percentage error 78.4477263927

Coefficient of determination -0.363525210982
```

The first line displays the coefficients of the model we attempted. We have a mean absolute error of 44, which means that we are off by that amount in either direction on average. We also want the coefficient of determination to be as close to one as possible to have a good fit. Instead, we get a negative value, which is undesirable. Refer to the following graph for the end result:

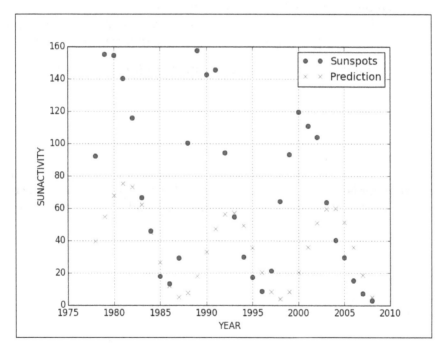

Fourier analysis

Fourier analysis is based on the **Fourier series** named after the mathematician Joseph Fourier. The Fourier series is a mathematical method used to represent functions as an infinite series of sine and cosine terms. The functions in question can be real or complex valued:

$$\sum_{t=-\infty}^{\infty} x[t] e^{-i\omega t}$$

The most efficient algorithm for Fourier analysis is the **Fast Fourier Transform (FFT)**. This algorithm is implemented in SciPy and NumPy. When applied to the time series data, the Fourier analysis transforms maps onto the frequency domain, producing a frequency spectrum. The frequency spectrum displays harmonics as distinct spikes at certain frequencies. Music, for example, is composed from different frequencies with the note A at 440 Hz. The note A can be produced by a pitch fork. We can produce this and other notes with musical instruments such as a piano. White noise is a signal consisting of many frequencies, which are represented equally. White light is a mix of all the visible frequencies of light, also represented equally.

In the following example, we will import two functions (refer to `fourier.py`):

```
from scipy.fftpack import rfft
from scipy.fftpack import fftshift
```

The `rfft()` function performs FFT on real-valued data. We could also have used the `fft()` function, but it gives a warning on this particular dataset. The `fftshift()` function shifts the zero-frequency component (the mean of the data) to the middle of the spectrum, for better visualization. We will also have a look at a sine wave because that is easy to understand. Create a sine wave and apply the FFT to it:

```
t = np.linspace(-2 * np.pi, 2 * np.pi, len(sunspots))
mid = np.ptp(sunspots)/2
sine = mid + mid * np.sin(np.sin(t))

sine_fft = np.abs(fftshift(rfft(sine)))
print "Index of max sine FFT", np.argsort(sine_fft)[-5:]
```

The following is the output that shows the indices corresponding to maximum amplitudes:

```
Index of max sine FFT [160 157 166 158 154]
```

Perform FFT on the sunspots data:

```
transformed = np.abs(fftshift(rfft(sunspots)))
print "Indices of max sunspots FFT", np.argsort(transformed)[-5:]
```

The five largest peaks in the spectrum can be found at the following indices:

Indices of max sunspots FFT [205 212 215 209 154]

The largest peak is situated at 154 too. Refer to the following plot for the end result:

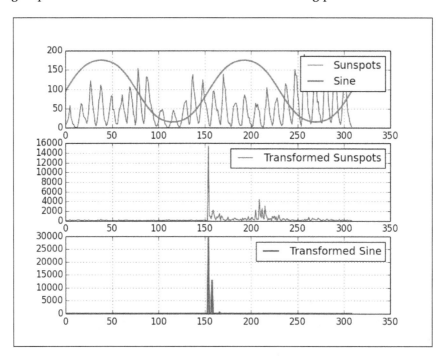

The complete code is located in the `fourier.py` file in this book's code bundle:

```
import numpy as np
import statsmodels.api as sm
import matplotlib.pyplot as plt
from scipy.fftpack import rfft
from scipy.fftpack import fftshift

data_loader = sm.datasets.sunspots.load_pandas()
sunspots = data_loader.data["SUNACTIVITY"].values

t = np.linspace(-2 * np.pi, 2 * np.pi, len(sunspots))
mid = np.ptp(sunspots)/2
```

```
sine = mid + mid * np.sin(np.sin(t))

sine_fft = np.abs(fftshift(rfft(sine)))
print "Index of max sine FFT", np.argsort(sine_fft)[-5:]


transformed = np.abs(fftshift(rfft(sunspots)))
print "Indices of max sunspots FFT", np.argsort(transformed)[-5:]

plt.subplot(311)
plt.plot(sunspots, label="Sunspots")
plt.plot(sine, lw=2, label="Sine")
plt.grid(True)
plt.legend()
plt.subplot(312)
plt.plot(transformed, label="Transformed Sunspots")
plt.grid(True)
plt.legend()
plt.subplot(313)
plt.plot(sine_fft, lw=2, label="Transformed Sine")
plt.grid(True)
plt.legend()
plt.show()
```

Spectral analysis

In the previous section, we charted the amplitude spectrum of the dataset. The **power spectrum** of a physical signal visualizes the energy distribution of the signal. We can modify the code easily to plot the power spectrum, just by squaring the values as follows:

```
plt.plot(transformed ** 2, label="Power Spectrum")
```

The **phase spectrum** visualizes the phase (the initial angle of a sine function) and can be plotted as follows:

```
plt.plot(np.angle(transformed), label="Phase Spectrum")
```

Refer to the following graph for the end result:

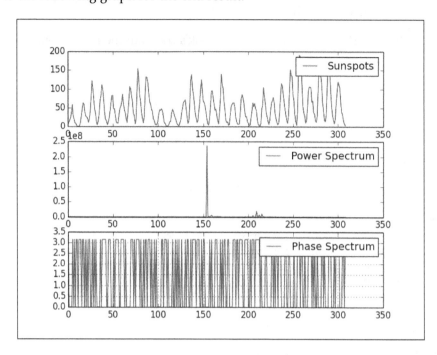

Please refer to the `spectrum.py` file in this book's code bundle for the complete code.

Filtering

Filtering is a type of signal processing, which involves removing or suppressing a part of the signal. After applying FFT, we can filter high or low frequencies, or we can try to remove the white noise. White noise is a random signal with a constant power spectrum and as such doesn't contain any useful information. The `scipy.signal` package has a number of utilities for filtering. In this example, we will demonstrate a small sample of these routines:

- The **median filter** calculates the median in a rolling window (see http://en.wikipedia.org/wiki/Median_filter). It's implemented by the `medfilt()` function, which has an optional window size parameter.

- The **Wiener filter** removes noise using statistics (see http://en.wikipedia.org/wiki/Wiener_filter). For a filter g(t) and signal s(t), the output is calculated with the convolution (g * [s + n])(t). It's implemented by the `wiener()` function. This function also has an optional window size parameter.

- The **detrend filter** removes a trend. This can be a linear or constant trend. It's implemented by the `detrend()` function.

Please refer to the `filtering.py` file in this book's code bundle for the following code:

```
import statsmodels.api as sm
import matplotlib.pyplot as plt
from scipy.signal import medfilt
from scipy.signal import wiener
from scipy.signal import detrend

data_loader = sm.datasets.sunspots.load_pandas()
sunspots = data_loader.data["SUNACTIVITY"].values
years = data_loader.data["YEAR"].values

plt.plot(years, sunspots, label="SUNACTIVITY")
plt.plot(years, medfilt(sunspots, 11), lw=2, label="Median")
plt.plot(years, wiener(sunspots, 11), '--', lw=2, label="Wiener")
plt.plot(years, detrend(sunspots), lw=3, label="Detrend")
plt.xlabel("YEAR")
plt.grid(True)
plt.legend()
plt.show()
```

Refer to the following graph for the end result:

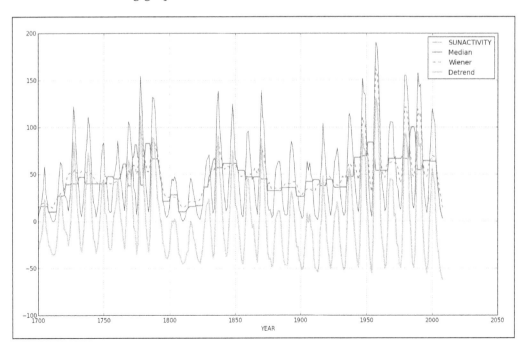

Summary

In this chapter, the time series examples used annual sunspot cycles data.

You learned that it's common to try to derive a relationship between a value and another data point or combination of data points a fixed number of periods in the past, in the same time series.

A moving average specifies a window of previously seen data, which is averaged each time the window slides forward by one period. In the pandas API, the `rolling_window()` function provides the window functions functionality with different values of the `win_type` string parameter corresponding to different window functions.

Cointegration is similar to correlation and is a metric to define the relatedness of two time series. In regression setups, we frequently encounter the problem of overfitting. This issue arises when we have a perfect fit for a sample, which performs poorly when we introduce new data points. To evaluate a model, we can compute appropriate evaluation metrics.

Databases are an important tool for data analysis. Relational databases have been around since the 1970s. Recently, NoSQL databases have become a viable alternative. The next chapter, *Chapter 8, Working with Databases*, contains information about the various databases (relational and NoSQL) and related APIs.

8
Working with Databases

If you work with data, sooner or later, you will come into contact with databases. This chapter introduces various databases (relational and NoSQL) and related APIs. A **relational database** is a database that has a collection of tables containing data organized by the relations between data items. A relationship can be set up between each row in the table and a row in another table. A relational database does not just pertain to relationships between tables; firstly, it has to do with the relationship between columns inside a table (obviously, columns within a table have to be related, for instance, a name column and an address column in a customer table); secondly, it relates to connections between tables.

NoSQL (Not Only SQL) databases are undergoing substantial growth in Big Data and web applications. NoSQL systems may in fact permit SQL-like query languages to be employed. The main theme of NoSQL databases is allowing data to be stored in a more flexible manner than the relational model permits. This may mean not having a database schema or a flexible database schema. Of course, the flexibility and speed may come at a price such as limited support for consistent transactions. NoSQL databases can store data using a dictionary style, in a column-oriented way, as documents, objects, graphs, tuples, or a combination thereof. The topics of this chapter are listed as follows:

- Lightweight access with sqlite3
- Accessing databases from pandas
- Installing and setting up SQLAlchemy
- Populating a database with SQLAlchemy
- Querying the database with SQLAlchemy
- Pony ORM
- Dataset—databases for lazy people
- PyMongo and MongoDB
- Storing data in Redis
- Apache Cassandra

Lightweight access with sqlite3

SQLite is a very popular relational database. It's very lightweight and used by many applications, for instance, web browsers such as Mozilla Firefox. The `sqlite3` module in the standard Python distribution can be used to work with a SQLite database. With `sqlite3`, we can either store the database in a file or keep it in RAM. For this example, we will do the latter. Import `sqlite3` as follows:

```
import sqlite3
```

A connection to the database is needed to proceed. If we wanted to store the database in a file, we would provide a filename. Instead, do the following:

```
with sqlite3.connect(":memory:") as con:
```

The `with` statement is standard Python and relies on the presence of a `__exit__()` method in a special context manager class. With this statement, we don't need to explicitly close the connection. The closing of the connection is done automatically by the context manager. After connecting to a database, we need a cursor. That's generally how it works with databases by the way. A **database cursor** is similar to a cursor in a text editor, in concept at least. We are required to close the cursor as well. Create the cursor as follows:

```
c = con.cursor()
```

We can now immediately create a table. Usually, you have to create a database first or have it created for you by a database specialist. In this chapter, you not only need to know Python, but SQL too. **SQL** is a specialized language for database querying and manipulating. We don't have enough space to describe SQL completely. However, basic SQL should be easy for you to pick up (for example, go through http://www.w3schools.com/sql/). To create a table, we pass a SQL string to the cursor as follows:

```
c.execute('''CREATE TABLE sensors
                (date text, city text, code text, sensor_id real,
temperature real)''')
```

This should create a table with several columns called `sensors`. In this string, `text` and `real` are data types corresponding to string and numerical values. We could trust the table creation to have worked properly. If something goes wrong, we will get an error. Listing the tables in a database is database dependent. There is usually a special table or set of tables containing metadata about user tables. List the SQLite tables as follows:

```
for table in c.execute("SELECT name FROM sqlite_master WHERE type
= 'table'"):
        print "Table", table[0]
```

As expected, we get the following output:

Table sensors

Let's insert and query some random data as follows:

```
c.execute("INSERT INTO sensors VALUES ('2016-11-
05','Utrecht','Red',42,15.14)")
c.execute("SELECT * FROM sensors")
print c.fetchone()
```

The record we inserted should be printed as follows:

(u'2016-11-05', u'Utrecht', u'Red', 42.0, 15.14)

When we don't need a table anymore, we can drop it. This is dangerous, so you have to be absolutely sure you don't need the table. Once a table is dropped, it cannot be recovered unless it was backed up. Drop the table and show the number of tables after dropping it as follows:

```
con.execute("DROP TABLE sensors")

print "# of tables", c.execute("SELECT COUNT(*) FROM sqlite_master
WHERE type = 'table'").fetchone()[0]
```

We get the following output:

# of tables 0

Refer to the `sqlite_demo.py` file in this book's code bundle for the following code:

```
import sqlite3

with sqlite3.connect(":memory:") as con:
    c = con.cursor()
    c.execute('''CREATE TABLE sensors
                (date text, city text, code text, sensor_id real,
temperature real)''')

    for table in c.execute("SELECT name FROM sqlite_master WHERE
type = 'table'"):
        print "Table", table[0]

    c.execute("INSERT INTO sensors VALUES ('2016-11-
05','Utrecht','Red',42,15.14)")
    c.execute("SELECT * FROM sensors")
    print c.fetchone()
```

```
con.execute("DROP TABLE sensors")

print "# of tables", c.execute("SELECT COUNT(*) FROM
sqlite_master WHERE type = 'table'").fetchone()[0]

c.close()
```

Accessing databases from pandas

We can give pandas a database connection such as the one in the previous example or a SQLAlchemy connection. We will cover the latter in the later sections of this chapter. We will load the statsmodels sunactivity data, just like in the previous chapter, *Chapter 7, Signal Processing and Time Series*:

1. Create a list of tuples to form the pandas `DataFrame`:

   ```
   rows = [tuple(x) for x in df.values]
   ```

   Contrary to the previous example, create a table without specifying data types:

   ```
   con.execute("CREATE TABLE sunspots(year, sunactivity)")
   ```

2. The `executemany()` method executes multiple statements; in this case, we will be inserting records from a list of tuples. Insert all the rows into the table and show the row count as follows:

   ```
   con.executemany("INSERT INTO sunspots(year, sunactivity)
   VALUES (?, ?)", rows)
   c.execute("SELECT COUNT(*) FROM sunspots")
   print c.fetchone()
   ```

   The number of rows in the table is printed as follows:

   ```
   (309,)
   ```

3. The `rowcount` attribute of the result of an `execute()` call gives the number of affected rows. This attribute is somewhat quirky and depends on your SQLite version. A SQL query, as shown in the previous code snippet, on the other hand is unambiguous. Delete the records where the number of events is more than 20:

   ```
   print "Deleted", con.execute("DELETE FROM sunspots where
   sunactivity > 20").rowcount, "rows"
   ```

   The following should be printed:

   ```
   Deleted 217 rows
   ```

4. If we hand the database connection to pandas, we can execute a query and return a pandas `DataFrame` with the `read_sql()` function. Select the records until 1732 as follows:

```
print read_sql("SELECT * FROM sunspots where year < 1732",
con)
```

The end result is the following pandas `DataFrame`:

	year	sunactivity
0	1700	5
1	1701	11
2	1702	16
3	1707	20
4	1708	10
5	1709	8
6	1710	3
7	1711	0
8	1712	0
9	1713	2
10	1714	11
11	1723	11

```
[12 rows x 2 columns]
```

Refer to the `panda_access.py` file in this book's code bundle for the following code:

```python
import statsmodels.api as sm
from pandas.io.sql import read_sql
import sqlite3

with sqlite3.connect(":memory:") as con:
    c = con.cursor()

    data_loader = sm.datasets.sunspots.load_pandas()
    df = data_loader.data
    rows = [tuple(x) for x in df.values]

    con.execute("CREATE TABLE sunspots(year, sunactivity)")
    con.executemany("INSERT INTO sunspots(year, sunactivity)
VALUES (?, ?)", rows)
    c.execute("SELECT COUNT(*) FROM sunspots")
```

```
    print c.fetchone()
    print "Deleted", con.execute("DELETE FROM sunspots where
sunactivity > 20").rowcount, "rows"

    print read_sql("SELECT * FROM sunspots where year < 1732",
con)
    con.execute("DROP TABLE sunspots")

    c.close()
```

SQLAlchemy

SQLAlchemy is renowned for its **object-relational mapping (ORM)** based on a design pattern, where Python classes are mapped to database tables. In practice, this means that an extra abstraction layer is added, so we use the SQLAlchemy API to talk to the database instead of issuing SQL commands. SQLAlchemy takes care of the details behind the scene. The drawback is that you have to learn the API and may have to pay a small performance penalty. In this section, you will learn how to set up SQLAlchemy, and populate and query databases with SQLAlchemy.

Installing and setting up SQLAlchemy

The following is the command to install SQLAlchemy:

```
$ pip install sqlalchemy
```

The latest version of SQLAlchemy at the time of writing was 0.9.6. The download page for SQLAlchemy is available at `http://www.sqlalchemy.org/download.html` with links to installers and code repositories.

SQLAlchemy also has a support page available at `http://www.sqlalchemy.org/support.html`. After modifying the `pkg_check.py` script, we can display the modules of SQLAlchemy:

```
sqlalchemy version 0.9.6

sqlalchemy.connectors DESCRIPTION # connectors/__init__.py #
Copyright (C) 2005-2014 the SQLAlchemy authors and contributors <see
AUTHORS file> # # This module is

sqlalchemy.databases DESCRIPTION Include imports from the
sqlalchemy.dialects package for backwards compatibility with pre 0.6
versions. PACKAGE CONTENTS DATA __

sqlalchemy.dialects DESCRIPTION # dialects/__init__.py # Copyright
(C) 2005-2014 the SQLAlchemy authors and contributors <see AUTHORS
file> # # This module is p
```

```
sqlalchemy.engine DESCRIPTION The engine package defines the basic
components used to interface DB-API modules with higher-level
statement construction, conne
```

```
sqlalchemy.event DESCRIPTION # event/__init__.py # Copyright (C)
2005-2014 the SQLAlchemy authors and contributors <see AUTHORS file>
# # This module is part
```

```
sqlalchemy.ext DESCRIPTION # ext/__init__.py # Copyright (C) 2005-
2014 the SQLAlchemy authors and contributors <see AUTHORS file> # #
This module is part o
```

```
sqlalchemy.orm DESCRIPTION See the SQLAlchemy object relational
tutorial and mapper configuration documentation for an overview of
how this module is used.
```

```
sqlalchemy.sql DESCRIPTION # sql/__init__.py # Copyright (C) 2005-
2014 the SQLAlchemy authors and contributors <see AUTHORS file> # #
This module is part o
```

```
sqlalchemy.testing DESCRIPTION # testing/__init__.py # Copyright (C)
2005-2014 the SQLAlchemy authors and contributors <see AUTHORS file>
# # This module is pa
```

```
sqlalchemy.util DESCRIPTION # util/__init__.py # Copyright (C) 2005-
2014 the SQLAlchemy authors and contributors <see AUTHORS file> # #
This module is part
```

SQLAlchemy requires us to define a superclass as follows:

```
from sqlalchemy.ext.declarative import declarative_base
Base = declarative_base()
```

In this and the following sections, we will make use of a small database with two tables. The first table defines an observation station. The second table represents sensors in the stations. Each station has zero, one, or many sensors. A station is identified by an integer ID, which is automatically generated by the database. Also, a station is identified by a name, which is unique and mandatory.

A sensor has an integer ID as well. We keep track of the last value measured by the sensor. This value can have a multiplier related to it. The setup described in this section is expressed in the `alchemy_entities.py` file in this book's code bundle (you don't have to run this script, but it is used by another script):

```
from sqlalchemy import Column, ForeignKey, Integer, String, Float
from sqlalchemy.ext.declarative import declarative_base
from sqlalchemy.orm import relationship
from sqlalchemy import create_engine
from sqlalchemy import UniqueConstraint

Base = declarative_base()
```

```
class Station(Base):
    __tablename__ = 'station'
    id = Column(Integer, primary_key=True)
    name = Column(String(14), nullable=False, unique=True)

    def __repr__(self):
        return "Id=%d name=%s" %(self.id, self.name)


class Sensor(Base):
    __tablename__ = 'sensor'
    id = Column(Integer, primary_key=True)
    last = Column(Integer)
    multiplier = Column(Float)
    station_id = Column(Integer, ForeignKey('station.id'))
    station = relationship(Station)

    def __repr__(self):
        return "Id=%d last=%d multiplier=%.1f station_id=%d"
%(self.id, self.last, self.multiplier, self.station_id)

if __name__ == "__main__":
    print "This script is used by another script. Run python
alchemy_query.py"
```

Populating a database with SQLAlchemy

Creating the tables will be deferred to the next section. In this section, we will
prepare a script, which will populate the database (you don't have to run this;
it is used by a script in a later section). With a DBSession object, we can insert
data into the tables. An engine is needed too, but creating the engine will also
be deferred until the next section.

1. Create the DBSession object as follows:

    ```
    Base.metadata.bind = engine

    DBSession = sessionmaker(bind=engine)
    session = DBSession()
    ```

2. Let's create two stations:

    ```
    de_bilt = Station(name='De Bilt')
    session.add(de_bilt)
    session.add(Station(name='Utrecht'))
    ```

```
session.commit()
print "Station", de_bilt
```

The rows are not inserted until we commit the session. The following is printed for the first station:

Station Id=1 name=De Bilt

3. Similarly, insert a sensor record as follows:

```
temp_sensor = Sensor(last=20, multiplier=.1,
station=de_bilt)
session.add(temp_sensor)
session.commit()
print "Sensor", temp_sensor
```

The sensor is in the first station; therefore, we get the following printout:

Sensor Id=1 last=20 multiplier=0.1 station_id=1

The database population code can be found in the populate_db.py file in this book's code bundle (again you don't need to run this code; it's used by another script):

```
from sqlalchemy import create_engine
from sqlalchemy.orm import sessionmaker

from alchemy_entities import Base, Sensor, Station

def populate(engine):
    Base.metadata.bind = engine

    DBSession = sessionmaker(bind=engine)
    session = DBSession()

    de_bilt = Station(name='De Bilt')
    session.add(de_bilt)
    session.add(Station(name='Utrecht'))
    session.commit()
    print "Station", de_bilt

    temp_sensor = Sensor(last=20, multiplier=.1, station=de_bilt)
    session.add(temp_sensor)
    session.commit()
    print "Sensor", temp_sensor

if __name__ == "__main__":
    print "This script is used by another script. Run python
alchemy_query.py"
```

Querying the database with SQLAlchemy

An engine is created from a URI as follows:

```
engine = create_engine('sqlite:///demo.db')
```

In this URI, we specified that we are using SQLite and the data is stored in the file demo.db. Create the station and sensor tables with the engine we just created:

```
Base.metadata.create_all(engine)
```

For SQLAlchemy queries, we need a DBSession object again, as shown in the previous section.

Select the first row in the station table:

```
station = session.query(Station).first()
```

Select all the stations as follows:

```
print "Query 1", session.query(Station).all()
```

The following will be the output:

Query 1 [Id=1 name=De Bilt, Id=2 name=Utrecht]

Select all the sensors as follows:

```
print "Query 2", session.query(Sensor).all()
```

The following will be the output:

Query 2 [Id=1 last=20 multiplier=0.1 station_id=1]

Select the first sensor, which belongs to the first station:

```
print "Query 3",
session.query(Sensor).filter(Sensor.station ==
station).one()
```

The following will be the output:

Query 3 Id=1 last=20 multiplier=0.1 station_id=1

We can again query with the pandas read_sql() method:

```
print read_sql("SELECT * FROM station",
engine.raw_connection())
```

You will get the following output:

```
    id     name
0   1   De Bilt
1   2   Utrecht
```

`[2 rows x 2 columns]`

Inspect the `alchemy_query.py` file in this book's code bundle:

```python
from alchemy_entities import Base, Sensor, Station
from populate_db import populate
from sqlalchemy import create_engine
from sqlalchemy.orm import sessionmaker
import os
from pandas.io.sql import read_sql


engine = create_engine('sqlite:///demo.db')
Base.metadata.create_all(engine)
populate(engine)
Base.metadata.bind = engine
DBSession = sessionmaker()
DBSession.bind = engine
session = DBSession()

station = session.query(Station).first()

print "Query 1", session.query(Station).all()
print "Query 2", session.query(Sensor).all()
print "Query 3", session.query(Sensor).filter(Sensor.station ==
station).one()
print read_sql("SELECT * FROM station", engine.raw_connection())

try:
    os.remove('demo.db')
    print "Deleted demo.db"
except OSError:
    pass
```

Pony ORM

Pony ORM is another Python ORM package. Pony ORM is written in pure Python and has automatic query optimization and a GUI database schema editor. It also supports automatic transaction management, automatic caching, and composite keys. Pony ORM uses Python generator expressions, which are translated in SQL. Install it as follows:

`$ sudo pip install pony`

```
$ pip freeze|grep pony
pony==0.5.1
```

Import the packages we will need in this example. Refer to the `pony_ride.py` file in this book's code bundle:

```
from pony.orm import Database, db_session
from pandas.io.sql import write_frame
import statsmodels.api as sm
```

Create an in-memory SQLite database:

```
db = Database('sqlite', ':memory:')
```

Load the sunspots data and write it to the database with the pandas `write_frame()` function:

```
with db_session:
    data_loader = sm.datasets.sunspots.load_pandas()
    df = data_loader.data
    write_frame(df, "sunspots", db.get_connection())
    print db.select("count(*) FROM sunspots")
```

The number of rows in the sunspots table is printed as follows:

```
[309]
```

Dataset – databases for lazy people

Dataset is a Python library, which is basically a wrapper around SQLAlchemy. It claims to be so easy to use that even lazy people like it.

Install `dataset` as follows:

```
$ sudo pip install dataset
$ pip freeze|grep dataset
dataset==0.5.4
```

Create a SQLite in-memory database and connect to it:

```
import dataset
db = dataset.connect('sqlite:///:memory:')
```

Create a table called `books`:

```
table = db["books"]
```

Actually, the table in the database isn't created yet, since we haven't specified any columns. We only created a related object. The table schema is created automatically from calls to the `insert()` method. Give the `insert()` method dictionaries with book titles:

```
table.insert(dict(title="NumPy Beginner's Guide",
author='Ivan Idris'))
table.insert(dict(title="NumPy Cookbook", author='Ivan
Idris'))
table.insert(dict(title="Learning NumPy", author='Ivan
Idris'))
```

These are all excellent books, of course! The `read_sql()` pandas function can query this table too:

```
print read_sql('SELECT * FROM books',
db.executable.raw_connection())
```

The following is the output:

```
   id       author                      title
0   1   Ivan Idris   NumPy Beginner's Guide
1   2   Ivan Idris           NumPy Cookbook
2   3   Ivan Idris           Learning NumPy

[3 rows x 3 columns]
```

Load the sunspots data and show the first five rows as follows:

```
write_frame(df, "sunspots", db.executable.raw_connection())
table = db['sunspots']

for row in table.find(_limit=5):
    print row
```

The following will be printed:

```
OrderedDict([(u'YEAR', 1700.0), (u'SUNACTIVITY', 5.0)])
OrderedDict([(u'YEAR', 1701.0), (u'SUNACTIVITY', 11.0)])
OrderedDict([(u'YEAR', 1702.0), (u'SUNACTIVITY', 16.0)])
OrderedDict([(u'YEAR', 1703.0), (u'SUNACTIVITY', 23.0)])
OrderedDict([(u'YEAR', 1704.0), (u'SUNACTIVITY', 36.0)])
```

We can easily show the tables in the database with the following line:

```
print "Tables", db.tables
```

The following is the output of the preceding code:

```
Tables [u'books', 'sunspots']
```

The following is the content of the `dataset_demo.py` file in this book's code bundle:

```
import dataset
from pandas.io.sql import read_sql
from pandas.io.sql import write_frame
import statsmodels.api as sm

db = dataset.connect('sqlite:///:memory:')
table = db["books"]
table.insert(dict(title="NumPy Beginner's Guide", author='Ivan
Idris'))
table.insert(dict(title="NumPy Cookbook", author='Ivan Idris'))
table.insert(dict(title="Learning NumPy", author='Ivan Idris'))
print read_sql('SELECT * FROM books', db.executable.raw_connection())

data_loader = sm.datasets.sunspots.load_pandas()
df = data_loader.data
write_frame(df, "sunspots", db.executable.raw_connection())
table = db['sunspots']

for row in table.find(_limit=5):
    print row

print "Tables", db.tables
```

PyMongo and MongoDB

MongoDB (*humongous*) is a NoSQL document-oriented database. The documents are stored in the BSON format, which is JSON like. You can download a MongoDB distribution from `http://www.mongodb.org/downloads`. Installing should be just a matter of unpacking a compressed archive. The version at the time of writing was 2.6.3. In the `bin` directory of the distribution, we will find the `mongod` file, which starts the server. MongoDB expects to find a `/data/db` directory. This is the directory where data is stored. We can specify another directory from the command line as follows:

`$ mkdir /tmp/db`

Start the database from the directory containing its binary executables:

```
./mongod --dbpath /tmp/db
```

We need to keep this process running to be able to query the database.

PyMongo is a Python driver for MongoDB. Install PyMongo as follows:

```
$ sudo pip install pymongo
$ pip freeze|grep pymongo
pymongo==2.7.1
```

Connect to the MongoDB test database:

```
from pymongo import MongoClient
client = MongoClient()
db = client.test_database
```

Recall that we can create JSON from a pandas `DataFrame`. Create the JSON and store it in MongoDB:

```
data_loader = sm.datasets.sunspots.load_pandas()
df = data_loader.data
rows = json.loads(df.T.to_json()).values()
db.sunspots.insert(rows)
```

Query the document we just created:

```
cursor = db['sunspots'].find({})
df =  pd.DataFrame(list(cursor))
print df
```

This prints the entire pandas `DataFrame`. Refer to the `mongo_demo.py` file in this book's code bundle:

```
from pymongo import MongoClient
import statsmodels.api as sm
import json
import pandas as pd


client = MongoClient()
db = client.test_database

data_loader = sm.datasets.sunspots.load_pandas()
df = data_loader.data
rows = json.loads(df.T.to_json()).values()
db.sunspots.insert(rows)

cursor = db['sunspots'].find({})
df =  pd.DataFrame(list(cursor))
print df

db.drop_collection('sunspots')
```

Storing data in Redis

Redis (REmote DIctionary Server) is an in-memory, key-value database, written in C. In the in-memory mode, Redis is extremely fast, with writing and reading being almost equally fast. Redis follows the publish/subscribe model and uses Lua scripts as stored procedures. Publish/subscribe makes use of channels to which a client can subscribe in order to receive messages. The most recent Redis version at the time of writing was 2.8.12. Redis can be downloaded from the home page at `http://redis.io/`. After unpacking the Redis distribution, issue the following command to compile the code and create all the binaries:

```
$ make
```

Run the server as follows:

```
$ src/redis-server
```

Now let's install a Python driver:

```
$ sudo pip install redis
$ pip freeze|grep redis
redis==2.10.1
```

It's pretty easy to use Redis when you realize it's a giant dictionary. However, Redis does have its limitations. Sometimes, it's just convenient to store a complex object as a JSON string (or other format). That's what we are going to do with a pandas `DataFrame`. Connect to Redis as follows:

```
    r = redis.StrictRedis()
```

Create a key-value pair with a JSON string:

```
    r.set('sunspots', data)
```

Retrieve the data with the following line:

```
    blob = r.get('sunspots')
```

The code is straightforward and given in the `redis_demo.py` file in this book's code bundle:

```
    import redis
    import statsmodels.api as sm
    import pandas as pd

    r = redis.StrictRedis()
    data_loader = sm.datasets.sunspots.load_pandas()
```

```
df = data_loader.data
data = df.T.to_json()
r.set('sunspots', data)
blob = r.get('sunspots')
print pd.read_json(blob)
```

Apache Cassandra

Apache Cassandra mixes features of key-value and traditional relational databases. In a conventional relational database, the columns of a table are fixed. In Cassandra, however, rows within the same table can have different columns. Cassandra is therefore column oriented, since it allows a flexible schema for each row. Columns are organized in so-called **column families**, which are equivalent to tables in relational databases. Joins and subqueries are not possible with Cassandra. Cassandra can be downloaded from `http://cassandra.apache.org/download/`. The latest version at the time of writing was 2.0.9. Please refer to `http://wiki.apache.org/cassandra/ GettingStarted` to get started.

Run the server from the command line as follows:

```
$ bin/cassandra -f
```

If you run the previous command, you may get the following error message:

```
Cassandra 2.0 and later require Java 7 or later.
```

Java in this context is a high-level programming language such as Python. Java 7 refers to version 1.7 (it's a marketing ploy). If you have Java installed, you can check its version as follows:

```
$ java -version
java version "1.7.0_60"
```

> For most operating systems, except Mac OS X, you can download Java from `http://www.oracle.com/technetwork/java/javase/ downloads/index.html`.
>
> Instructions for installing Java on Mac are given at `http://docs. oracle.com/javase/7/docs/webnotes/install/mac/mac- jdk.html`. Since this is a Python book, we will not dwell too long on the details of installing Java. A quick web search should give you more than enough information.

Create the directories listed in `conf/cassandra.yaml` or tweak them as follows:

```
data_file_directories:
/tmp/lib/cassandra/data
commitlog_directory: /tmp/lib/cassandra/commitlog
saved_caches_directory: /tmp/lib/cassandra/saved_caches
```

The following commands make sense if you don't want to keep the data:

```
$ mkdir -p /tmp/lib/cassandra/data
$ mkdir -p /tmp/lib/cassandra/commitlog
$ mkdir -p /tmp/lib/cassandra/saved_caches
```

Install a Python driver with the following command:

```
$ sudo pip install cassandra-driver
$ pip freeze|grep cassandra-driver
cassandra-driver==2.0.2
```

You might get the following error message:

```
The required version of setuptools (>=0.9.6) is not
available,
    and can't be installed while this script is running.
Please
    install a more recent version first, using
    'easy_install -U setuptools'.
```

This seems pretty self-explanatory.

Now it's time for the code. Connect to a cluster and create a session as follows:

```
cluster = Cluster()
session = cluster.connect()
```

Cassandra has the concept of **keyspace**. A keyspace holds tables. Cassandra has its own query language called **Cassandra Query Language** (CQL). CQL is very similar to SQL. Create the keyspace and set the session to use it:

```
session.execute("CREATE KEYSPACE IF NOT EXISTS mykeyspace
WITH REPLICATION = { 'class' : 'SimpleStrategy',
'replication_factor' : 1 };")
session.set_keyspace('mykeyspace')
```

Now, create a table for the sunspots data:

```
session.execute("CREATE TABLE IF NOT EXISTS sunspots (year
decimal PRIMARY KEY, sunactivity decimal);")
```

1. Create a statement that we will use in a loop to insert rows of the data as tuples:

```
query = SimpleStatement(
    "INSERT INTO sunspots (year, sunactivity) VALUES (%s,
%s)",
    consistency_level=ConsistencyLevel.QUORUM)
```

2. The following line inserts the data:

```
for row in rows:
    session.execute(query, row)
```

3. Get the count of the rows in the table:

```
print session.execute("SELECT COUNT(*) FROM sunspots")
```

This prints the row count as follows:

```
[Row(count=309)]
```

4. Drop the keyspace and shut down the cluster:

```
session.execute('DROP KEYSPACE mykeyspace')
cluster.shutdown()
```

Refer to the `cassandra_demo.py` file in this book's code bundle:

```
from cassandra import ConsistencyLevel
from cassandra.cluster import Cluster
from cassandra.query import SimpleStatement
import statsmodels.api as sm

cluster = Cluster()
session = cluster.connect()
session.execute("CREATE KEYSPACE IF NOT EXISTS mykeyspace WITH
REPLICATION = { 'class' : 'SimpleStrategy', 'replication_factor' :
1 };")
session.set_keyspace('mykeyspace')
session.execute("CREATE TABLE IF NOT EXISTS sunspots (year decimal
PRIMARY KEY, sunactivity decimal);")

query = SimpleStatement(
    "INSERT INTO sunspots (year, sunactivity) VALUES (%s, %s)",
    consistency_level=ConsistencyLevel.QUORUM)

data_loader = sm.datasets.sunspots.load_pandas()
df = data_loader.data
rows = [tuple(x) for x in df.values]
```

```
for row in rows:
    session.execute(query, row)

print session.execute("SELECT COUNT(*) FROM sunspots")

session.execute('DROP KEYSPACE mykeyspace')
cluster.shutdown()
```

Summary

We stored annual sunspots cycles data in different relational and NoSQL databases.

The term relational here does not just pertain to relationships between tables; firstly, it has to do with the relationship between columns inside a table; secondly, it relates to connections between tables.

The sqlite3 module in the standard Python distribution can be used to work with a SQLite database. We can give pandas a SQLite database connection or a SQLAlchemy connection.

SQLAlchemy is renowned for its ORM, based on a design pattern, where Python classes are mapped to database tables. The ORM pattern is a general architectural pattern applicable to other object-oriented programming languages. SQLAlchemy abstracts away the technical details of working with databases including writing SQL.

MongoDB is a document-based store, which can hold a huge amount of data.

In the in-memory mode, Redis is extremely fast, with writing and reading being almost equally fast. Redis is a key-value store that functions similarly to a Python dictionary.

Apache Cassandra mixes features of key-value and traditional relational databases. It is column oriented and its columns are organized into families, which are the equivalent of tables in relational databases. Rows in Apache Cassandra are not tied to a particular set of columns.

The next chapter, *Chapter 9, Analyzing Textual Data and Social Media*, describes analysis techniques for plain text data. Plain text data is found in many organizations and on the Internet. Generally, plain text data is very unstructured and requires a different approach than data that has been tabulated and cleaned. For the analysis, we will use NLTK—an open source Python package. NLTK is very comprehensive and comes with its own datasets.

9
Analyzing Textual Data and Social Media

In the previous chapters, we focused on the analysis of structured data, mostly in tabular format. In reality, plain text is the most predominant form of data available today. Text analysis applies analysis of word frequency distributions, pattern recognition, tagging, link and association analysis, sentiment analysis, and visualization. We will analyze text with the Python **Natural Language Toolkit (NLTK)** library. NLTK comes with a collection of sample texts called **corpora**. A small example of network analysis will also be covered. The following topics will be discussed in this chapter:

- Installing NLTK
- Filtering out stopwords, names, and numbers
- The bag-of-words model
- Analyzing word frequencies
- Naive Bayes classification
- Sentiment analysis
- Creating word clouds
- Social network analysis

Installing NLTK

NLTK is a Python API for the analysis of texts written in natural languages, such as English. NLTK was created in 2001 and was originally intended as a teaching tool. Install NLTK with the following command:

```
$ sudo pip install nltk
$ pip freeze|grep nltk
nltk==2.0.4
```

As usual, we will check the installation with a new version of the `pkg_check.py` file. The following import statement is required:

```
import nltk
```

If everything works, we should get a result similar to the following:

```
nltk version 2.0.4
```

nltk.app DESCRIPTION chartparser: Chart Parser chunkparser: Regular-Expression Chunk Parser collocations: Find collocations in text concordance: Part

nltk.ccg DESCRIPTION For more information see nltk/doc/contrib/ccg/ccg.pdf PACKAGE CONTENTS api chart combinator lexicon DATA BackwardApplication<n

nltk.chat DESCRIPTION A class for simple chatbots. These perform simple pattern matching on sentences typed by users, and respond with automatically g

nltk.chunk DESCRIPTION Classes and interfaces for identifying non-overlapping linguistic groups (such as base noun phrases) in unrestricted text. This

nltk.classify DESCRIPTION Classes and interfaces for labeling tokens with category labels (or "class labels"). Typically, labels are represented with stri

nltk.cluster DESCRIPTION This module contains a number of basic clustering algorithms. Clustering describes the task of discovering groups of similar ite

nltk.corpus

nltk.draw DESCRIPTION # Natural Language Toolkit: graphical representations package # # Copyright (C) 2001-2012 NLTK Project # Author: Edward Loper<e

nltk.examples

nltk.inference

nltk.metrics DESCRIPTION Classes and methods for scoring processing modules. PACKAGE CONTENTS agreement association confusionmatrix distance scores segme

nltk.misc DESCRIPTION # Natural Language Toolkit: Miscellaneous
modules # # Copyright (C) 2001-2012 NLTK Project # Author: Steven
Bird <sb@csse.unimel

nltk.model DESCRIPTION # Natural Language Toolkit: Language Models #
Copyright (C) 2001-2012 NLTK Project # Author: Steven Bird
<sb@csse.unimelb.edu.

nltk.parse DESCRIPTION Classes and interfaces for producing tree
structures that represent the internal organization of a text. This
task is known as "

nltk.sem DESCRIPTION This package contains classes for representing
semantic structure in formulas of first-order logic and for
evaluating such formu

nltk.stem DESCRIPTION Interfaces used to remove morphological affixes
from words, leaving only the word stem. Stemming algorithms aim to
remove those

nltk.tag DESCRIPTION This package contains classes and interfaces for
part-of-speech tagging, or simply "tagging". A "tag" is a case-
sensitive string

nltk.test DESCRIPTION Unit tests for the NLTK modules. These tests
are intended to ensure that changes that we make to NLTK's code don't
accidentally

nltk.tokenize DESCRIPTION Tokenizers divide strings into lists of
substrings. For example, tokenizers can be used to find the list of
sentences or words i

However, we are not done yet; we still need to download the NLTK corpora.
The download is relatively large (about 1.8 GB); however, we only have to
download it once. Unless you know exactly which corpora you require, it's
best to download all the available corpora. Download the corpora from the
Python shell as follows:

```
$ python
>>> import nltk
>>> nltk.download()
```

A GUI application should appear, where you can specify a destination and what
to download. If you are new to NLTK, it's most convenient to choose the default
options and download everything. In this chapter, we will need the **stopwords**,
movie reviews, names, and Gutenberg corpora.

Filtering out stopwords, names, and numbers

It's a common requirement in text analysis to get rid of stopwords (common words with low information value). NLTK has a stopwords corpora for a number of languages. Load the English stopwords corpus and print some of the words:

```
sw = set(nltk.corpus.stopwords.words('english'))
print "Stop words", list(sw)[:7]
```

The following common words are printed:

Stop words ['all', 'just', 'being', 'over', 'both', 'through', 'yourselves']

Notice that all the words in this corpus are in lowercase.

NLTK also has a **Gutenberg** corpus. The Gutenberg project is a digital library of books mostly with expired copyright, which are available for free on the Internet (see http://www.gutenberg.org/).

Load the Gutenberg corpus and print some of its filenames:

```
gb = nltk.corpus.gutenberg
print "Gutenberg files", gb.fileids()[-5:]
```

Some of the titles printed may be familiar to you:

Gutenberg files ['milton-paradise.txt', 'shakespeare-caesar.txt', 'shakespeare-hamlet.txt', 'shakespeare-macbeth.txt', 'whitman-leaves.txt']

Extract the first couple of sentences from the milton-paradise.txt file that we will filter later:

```
text_sent = gb.sents("milton-paradise.txt")[:2]
print "Unfiltered", text_sent
```

The following sentences are printed:

Unfiltered [['[', 'Paradise', 'Lost', 'by', 'John', 'Milton', '1667', ']'], ['Book', 'I']]

Now, filter out the stopwords as follows:

```
for sent in text_sent:
    filtered = [w for w in sent if w.lower() not in sw]
    print "Filtered", filtered
```

For the first sentence, we get the following output:

```
Filtered ['[', 'Paradise', 'Lost', 'John', 'Milton', '1667', ']']
```

If we compare with the previous snippet, we notice that the word by has been filtered out as it was found in the stopwords corpus. Sometimes, we want to remove numbers and names too. We can remove words based on **Part of Speech (POS)** tags. In this tagging scheme, numbers correspond to the **Cardinal Number (CD)** tag. Names correspond to the **proper noun singular (NNP)** tag. Tagging is an inexact process based on heuristics. It's a big topic that deserves an entire book (see the *Preface*). Tag the filtered text with the pos_tag() function:

```
tagged = nltk.pos_tag(filtered)
print "Tagged", tagged
```

For our text, we get the following tags:

```
Tagged [('[', 'NN'), ('Paradise', 'NNP'), ('Lost', 'NNP'), ('John',
'NNP'), ('Milton', 'NNP'), ('1667', 'CD'), (']', 'CD')]
```

The pos_tag() function returns a list of tuples, where the second element in each tuple is the tag. As you can see, some of the words are tagged as NNP, although they probably shouldn't be. The heuristic here is to tag words as NNP if the first character of a word is uppercase. If we set all the words to be lowercase, we will get a different result. This is left as an exercise for the reader. It's easy to remove the words in the list with the NNP and CD tags. Have a look at the filtering.py file in this book's code bundle:

```
import nltk

sw = set(nltk.corpus.stopwords.words('english'))
print "Stop words", list(sw)[:7]

gb = nltk.corpus.gutenberg
print "Gutenberg files", gb.fileids()[-5:]
text_sent = gb.sents("milton-paradise.txt")[:2]
print "Unfiltered", text_sent

for sent in text_sent:
    filtered = [w for w in sent if w.lower() not in sw]
    print "Filtered", filtered
    tagged = nltk.pos_tag(filtered)
    print "Tagged", tagged

    words= []
```

```
for word in tagged:
    if word[1] != 'NNP' and word[1] != 'CD':
        words.append(word[0])

print words
```

The bag-of-words model

In the **bag-of-words model**, we create from a document a bag containing words found in the document. In this model, we don't care about the word order. For each word in the document, we count the number of occurrences. With these word counts, we can do statistical analysis, for instance, to identify spam in e-mail messages.

If we have a group of documents, we can view each unique word in the corpus as a feature; here, "feature" means parameter or variable. Using all the word counts, we can build a feature vector for each document; "vector" is used here in the mathematical sense. If a word is present in the corpus but not in the document, the value of this feature will be 0. Surprisingly, NLTK doesn't have a handy utility currently to create a feature vector. However, the machine learning Python library, scikit-learn, does have a `CountVectorizer` class that we can use. In the next chapter, *Chapter 10, Predictive Analytics and Machine Learning*, we will do more with scikit-learn.

First, install scikit-learn as follows:

```
$ pip scikit-learn
$ pip freeze|grep learn
scikit-learn==0.15.0
```

Load two text documents from the NLTK Gutenberg corpus:

```
hamlet = gb.raw("shakespeare-hamlet.txt")
macbeth = gb.raw("shakespeare-macbeth.txt")
```

Create the feature vector by omitting English stopwords:

```
cv = CountVectorizer(stop_words='english')
print "Feature vector", cv.fit_transform([hamlet,
macbeth]).toarray()
```

These are the feature vectors for the two documents:

```
Feature vector [[ 1  0  1 ...,  14  0  1]
 [ 0  1  0 ...,  1  1  0]]
```

Print a small selection of the features (unique words) we found:

```
print "Features", cv.get_feature_names()[:5]
```

The features are given in alphabetical order:

Features [u'1599', u'1603', u'abhominably', u'abhorred', u'abide']

The code is contained in `bag_words.py` file in this book's code bundle:

```
import nltk
from sklearn.feature_extraction.text import CountVectorizer

gb = nltk.corpus.gutenberg
hamlet = gb.raw("shakespeare-hamlet.txt")
macbeth = gb.raw("shakespeare-macbeth.txt")

cv = CountVectorizer(stop_words='english')
print "Feature vector", cv.fit_transform([hamlet, macbeth]).toarray()
print "Features", cv.get_feature_names()[:5]
```

Analyzing word frequencies

The NLTK `FreqDist` class encapsulates a dictionary of words and counts for a given list of words. Load the Gutenberg text of Julius Caesar by William Shakespeare. Let's filter out stopwords and punctuation:

```
punctuation = set(string.punctuation)
filtered = [w.lower() for w in words if w.lower() not in sw and
w.lower() not in punctuation]
```

Create a `FreqDist` object and print associated keys and values with highest frequency:

```
fd = nltk.FreqDist(filtered)
print "Words", fd.keys()[:5]
print "Counts", fd.values()[:5]
```

The keys and values are printed as follows:

Words ['d', 'caesar', 'brutus', 'bru', 'haue']
Counts [215, 190, 161, 153, 148]

The first word in this list is of course not an English word, so we may need to add the heuristic that words have a minimum of two characters. The NLTK `FreqDist` class allows dictionary-like access, but it also has convenience methods. Get the word with the most frequent word and the related count:

```
print "Max", fd.max()
print "Count", fd['d']
```

The following result shouldn't be a surprise:

```
Max d
Count 215
```

The analysis until this point concerned single words, but we can extend the analysis to word pairs and triplets. These are also called bigrams and trigrams. We can find them with the `bigrams()` and `trigrams()` functions. Repeat the analysis, but this time for bigrams:

```
fd = nltk.FreqDist(nltk.bigrams(filtered))
print "Bigrams", fd.keys()[:5]
print "Counts", fd.values()[:5]
print "Bigram Max", fd.max()
print "Bigram count", fd[('let', 'vs')]
```

The following output should be printed:

```
Bigrams [('let', 'vs'), ('wee', 'l'), ('mark', 'antony'), ('marke',
'antony'), ('st', 'thou')]
Counts [16, 15, 13, 12, 12]
Bigram Max ('let', 'vs')
Bigram count 16
```

Have a peek at the `frequencies.py` file in this book's code bundle:

```
import nltk
import string


gb = nltk.corpus.gutenberg
words = gb.words("shakespeare-caesar.txt")

sw = set(nltk.corpus.stopwords.words('english'))
punctuation = set(string.punctuation)
filtered = [w.lower() for w in words if w.lower() not in sw and
w.lower() not in punctuation]
```

```
fd = nltk.FreqDist(filtered)
print "Words", fd.keys()[:5]
print "Counts", fd.values()[:5]
print "Max", fd.max()
print "Count", fd['d']

fd = nltk.FreqDist(nltk.bigrams(filtered))
print "Bigrams", fd.keys()[:5]
print "Counts", fd.values()[:5]
print "Bigram Max", fd.max()
print "Bigram count", fd[('let', 'vs')]
```

Naive Bayes classification

Classification algorithms are a type of machine learning algorithm that involve determining the class (category or type) of a given item. For instance, we could try to determine the genre of a movie based on some features. In this case, the genre is the class to be predicted. In the next chapter, *Chapter 10, Predictive Analytics and Machine Learning*, we will continue with an overview of machine learning. In the meantime, we will discuss a popular algorithm called **Naive Bayes classification**, which is frequently used to analyze text documents.

Naive Bayes classification is a probabilistic algorithm based on the Bayes theorem from probability theory and statistics. The Bayes theorem formulates how to discount the probability of an event based on new evidence. For example, imagine that we have a bag with pieces of chocolate and other items we can't see. We will call the probability of drawing a piece of dark chocolate P(D). We will denote the probability of drawing a piece of chocolate as P(C). Of course, the total probability is always 1, so P(D) and P(C) can be at most 1. The Bayes theorem states that the posterior probability is proportional to the prior probability times likelihood:

$$P(D|C) = \frac{P(D|C)P(D)}{P(C)}$$

P(D|C) in the preceding notation means the probability of event D given C. When we haven't drawn any items yet, P(D) = 0.5 because we don't have any information yet. To actually apply the formula, we need to know P(C|D) and P(C) or we have to determine those indirectly.

Naive Bayes Classification is called **naive** because it makes the simplifying assumption of independence between features. In practice, the results are usually pretty good, so this assumption is often warranted to a certain level. Recently, it was found that there are theoretical reasons why the assumption makes sense. However, since machine learning is a rapidly evolving field, algorithms have been invented with (slightly) better performance.

Let's try to classify words as stopwords or punctuation. As a feature, we will use the word length, since stopwords and punctuation tend to be short.

This setup leads us to define the following functions:

```
def word_features(word):
    return {'len': len(word)}

def isStopword(word):
    return word in sw or word in punctuation
```

Label the words in the Gutenberg `shakespeare-caesar.txt` as being a stopword or not:

```
labeled_words = ([(word.lower(), isStopword(word.lower())) for
word in words])
random.seed(42)
random.shuffle(labeled_words)
print labeled_words[:5]
```

Five labeled words will appear as follows:

```
[('was', True), ('greeke', False), ('cause', False), ('but', True),
('house', False)]
```

For each word, determine its length:

```
featuresets = [(word_features(n), word) for (n, word) in
labeled_words]
```

In previous chapters, we mentioned overfitting and how to avoid this with cross-validation by having a train and a test dataset. We will train a Naive Bayes classifier on 90 percent of the words and test on the remaining 10 percent. Create the train set and test set and train the data:

```
cutoff = int(.9 * len(featuresets))
train_set, test_set = featuresets[:cutoff], featuresets[cutoff:]
classifier = nltk.NaiveBayesClassifier.train(train_set)
```

We can now check what the classifier gives for some words:

```
classifier = nltk.NaiveBayesClassifier.train(train_set)
print "'behold' class",
classifier.classify(word_features('behold'))
print "'the' class", classifier.classify(word_features('the'))
```

Fortunately, the words are properly classified:

'behold' class False
'the' class True

Determine the classifier accuracy on the test set as follows:

```
print "Accuracy", nltk.classify.accuracy(classifier, test_set)
```

We get a high accuracy for this classifier of around 85 percent. Print an overview of the most informative features:

```
print classifier.show_most_informative_features(5)
```

The overview shows the word lengths that are most useful for the classification process:

len = 7	False : True	=	62.7 : 1.0
len = 6	False : True	=	49.1 : 1.0
len = 1	True : False	=	12.0 : 1.0
len = 2	True : False	=	10.7 : 1.0
len = 5	False : True	=	10.4 : 1.0

The code is in the naive_classification.py file in this book's code bundle:

```
import nltk
import string
import random


sw = set(nltk.corpus.stopwords.words('english'))
punctuation = set(string.punctuation)

def word_features(word):
    return {'len': len(word)}

def isStopword(word):
    return word in sw or word in punctuation
```

```
gb = nltk.corpus.gutenberg
words = gb.words("shakespeare-caesar.txt")

labeled_words = ([(word.lower(), isStopword(word.lower())) for
word in words])
random.seed(42)
random.shuffle(labeled_words)
print labeled_words[:5]

featuresets = [(word_features(n), word) for (n, word) in
labeled_words]
cutoff = int(.9 * len(featuresets))
train_set, test_set = featuresets[:cutoff], featuresets[cutoff:]
classifier = nltk.NaiveBayesClassifier.train(train_set)
print "'behold' class",
classifier.classify(word_features('behold'))
print "'the' class", classifier.classify(word_features('the'))

print "Accuracy", nltk.classify.accuracy(classifier, test_set)
print classifier.show_most_informative_features(5)
```

Sentiment analysis

Opinion mining or **sentiment analysis** is a hot, new research field dedicated to the automatic evaluation of opinions as expressed on social media, product review websites, or other forums. Often, we want to know whether an opinion is positive, neutral, or negative. This is, of course, a form of classification as seen in the previous section. As such, we can apply any number of classification algorithms. Another approach is to semiautomatically (with some manual editing) compose a list of words with an associated numerical sentiment score (the word "good" can have a score of 5 and the word "bad" a score of -5). If we have such a list, we can look up all words in a text document and, for example, sum up all the found sentiment scores. The number of classes can be more than three, like a five-star rating scheme.

We will apply Naive Bayes classification to the NLTK movie reviews corpus with the goal of classifying movie reviews as either positive or negative. First, we will load the corpus and filter out stopwords and punctuation. These steps will be omitted, since we have performed them before. You may consider more elaborate filtering schemes, but keep in mind that excessive filtering may hurt accuracy. Label the movie reviews documents using the `categories()` method:

```
labeled_docs = [(list(movie_reviews.words(fid)), cat)
        for cat in movie_reviews.categories()
        for fid in movie_reviews.fileids(cat)]
```

The complete corpus has tens of thousands of unique words that we can use as features. However, using all these words might be inefficient. Select the top five percent of the most frequent words:

```
words = FreqDist(filtered)
N = int(.05 * len(words.keys()))
word_features = words.keys()[:N]
```

For each document, we can extract features using a number of methods including the following:

- Check whether the given document has a word or not
- Determine the number of occurrences of a word for a given document
- Normalize word counts so that the maximum normalized word count will be less than or equal to 1
- Take the logarithm of counts plus one (to avoid taking the logarithm of zero)
- Combine all the previous points into one metric

As the saying goes, *all roads lead to Rome*. Of course, some roads are safer and will bring you to Rome faster. Define the following function, which uses raw word counts as a metric:

```
def doc_features(doc):
    doc_words = FreqDist(w for w in doc if not isStopWord(w))
    features = {}
    for word in word_features:
        features['count (%s)' % word] = (doc_words.get(word, 0))
    return features
```

We can now train our classifier just as we did in the previous example. An accuracy of 78 percent is reached, which is decent and comes close to what is possible with sentiment analysis. Research has found that even humans don't always agree on the sentiment of a given document (see http://mashable.com/2010/04/19/sentiment-analysis/). Therefore, we can't have a hundred percent perfect accuracy with sentiment analysis software.

The most informative features are printed as follows:

```
      count (wonderful) = 2        pos : neg   =    14.7 : 1.0
   count (outstanding) = 1        pos : neg   =    11.2 : 1.0
           count (bad) = 5        neg : pos   =    10.8 : 1.0
         count (stupid) = 2        neg : pos   =    10.8 : 1.0
         count (boring) = 2        neg : pos   =    10.4 : 1.0
         count (nature) = 2        pos : neg   =     8.5 : 1.0
      count (different) = 2        pos : neg   =     8.3 : 1.0
           count (bad) = 6        neg : pos   =     8.2 : 1.0
     count (apparently) = 2        neg : pos   =     8.0 : 1.0
           count (life) = 5        pos : neg   =     7.6 : 1.0
```

If we go through this list, we find obvious positive words such as "wonderful" and "outstanding". The words "bad", "stupid", and "boring" are the obvious negative words. It would be interesting to analyze the remaining features. This is left as an exercise for the reader. Refer to the sentiment.py file in this book's code bundle:

```
import random
from nltk.corpus import movie_reviews
from nltk.corpus import stopwords
from nltk import FreqDist
from nltk import NaiveBayesClassifier
from nltk.classify import accuracy
import string


labeled_docs = [(list(movie_reviews.words(fid)), cat)
        for cat in movie_reviews.categories()
        for fid in movie_reviews.fileids(cat)]
random.seed(42)
random.shuffle(labeled_docs)

review_words = movie_reviews.words()
print "# Review Words", len(review_words)

sw = set(stopwords.words('english'))
punctuation = set(string.punctuation)

def isStopWord(word):
    return word in sw or word in punctuation

filtered = [w.lower() for w in review_words if not isStopWord(w.
lower())]
print "# After filter", len(filtered)
```

```
words = FreqDist(filtered)
N = int(.05 * len(words.keys()))
word_features = words.keys()[:N]

def doc_features(doc):
    doc_words = FreqDist(w for w in doc if not isStopWord(w))
    features = {}
    for word in word_features:
        features['count (%s)' % word] = (doc_words.get(word, 0))
    return features

featuresets = [(doc_features(d), c) for (d,c) in labeled_docs]
train_set, test_set = featuresets[200:], featuresets[:200]
classifier = NaiveBayesClassifier.train(train_set)
print "Accuracy", accuracy(classifier, test_set)

print classifier.show_most_informative_features()
```

Creating word clouds

You may have seen word clouds produced by **Wordle** or others before. If not, you will see them soon enough in this chapter. A couple of Python libraries can create word clouds; however, these libraries don't seem to beat the quality produced by Wordle yet. We can create a word cloud via the Wordle web page on http://www.wordle.net/advanced. Wordle requires a list of words and weights in the following format:

```
Word1 : weight
Word2 : weight
```

Modify the code from the previous example to print the word list. As a metric, we will use the word frequency and select the top percent. We don't need anything new and the final code is in the cloud.py file in this book's code bundle:

```
from nltk.corpus import movie_reviews
from nltk.corpus import stopwords
from nltk import FreqDist
import string

sw = set(stopwords.words('english'))
punctuation = set(string.punctuation)

def isStopWord(word):
    return word in sw or word in punctuation
```

```
review_words = movie_reviews.words()
filtered = [w.lower() for w in review_words if not isStopWord(w.
lower())]

words = FreqDist(filtered)
N = int(.01 * len(words.keys()))
tags = words.keys()[:N]

for tag in tags:
    print tag, ':', words[tag]
```

Copy and paste the output into the Wordle web page and generate the following word cloud:

If we analyze the word cloud, it may occur to us that the result is far from perfect, so we may want to try something better. For instance, we can try to do the following things:

- **Filter more**: We should get rid of words that contain numeric characters and names. NLTK has a `names` corpus we can use. Also, words that only occur once in the whole corpus are good to ignore, since they probably don't add enough information value.

- **Use a better metric**: The term **frequency-inverse document frequency (tf-idf)** seems a good candidate.

The tf-idf metric can give us ranking weights for words in our corpus. Its value is proportional to the number of occurrences of a word (corresponds to term frequency) in a particular document. However, it's also inversely proportional to the number of documents in the corpus (corresponds to inverse document frequency), where the word occurs. The tf-idf value is the product of term frequency and inverse document frequency. If we need to implement tf-idf ourselves, we have to consider logarithmic scaling as well. Luckily, we don't have to concern ourselves with the implementation details, since scikit-learn has a `TfidfVectorizer` class with an efficient implementation. This class produces a sparse SciPy matrix. This is a term-document matrix with tf-idf values for each combination of available words and documents. So, for a corpus with 2,000 documents and 25,000 unique words, we get a 2,000 x 25,000 matrix. A lot of the matrix values will be zero, which is where the sparseness comes in handy. The final rank weights can be found by summing all the tf-idf values for each word.

Improve filtering by using the `isalpha()` method and `names` corpus:

```
all_names = set([name.lower() for name in names.words()])

def isStopWord(word):
    return (word in sw or word in punctuation) or not
word.isalpha() or word in all_names
```

We will again create a NLTK `FreqDist` to be able to ignore words that occur only once. The `TfidfVectorizer` class needs a list of strings representing each document in the corpus.

Create the list as follows:

```
for fid in movie_reviews.fileids():
    texts.append(" ".join([w.lower() for w in movie_reviews.words(fid)
if not isStopWord(w.lower()) and words[w.lower()] > 1]))
```

Create the vectorizer; to be safe, let it ignore stopwords:

```
vectorizer = TfidfVectorizer(stop_words='english')
```

Create the sparse term-document matrix:

```
matrix = vectorizer.fit_transform(texts)
```

Sum the tf-idf values for each word and store it in a NumPy array:

```
sums = np.array(matrix.sum(axis=0)).ravel()
```

Now, create a pandas DataFrame with the word rank weights and sort it:

```
ranks = []

for word, val in itertools.izip(vectorizer.get_feature_names(), sums):
    ranks.append((word, val))

    df = pd.DataFrame(ranks, columns=["term", "tfidf"])
    df = df.sort(['tfidf'])
    print df.head()
```

The lowest ranking values are printed as follows and can be considered for filtering:

```
term       tfidf
8742             greys    0.03035
2793        cannibalize    0.03035
2408            briefer    0.03035
19977    superintendent    0.03035
14022             ology    0.03035
```

Now, it's a matter of printing the top ranking words and presenting them to Wordle in order to create the following cloud:

Unfortunately, you have to run the code yourself to see the difference in color with the previous word cloud. The tf-idf metric allows for more variation than the mere word frequency, so we get more varied colors. Also, the words in the cloud seem more relevant. Refer to `cloud2.py` file in this book's code bundle:

```python
from nltk.corpus import movie_reviews
from nltk.corpus import stopwords
from nltk.corpus import names
from nltk import FreqDist
from sklearn.feature_extraction.text import TfidfVectorizer
import itertools
import pandas as pd
import numpy as np
import string

sw = set(stopwords.words('english'))
punctuation = set(string.punctuation)
all_names = set([name.lower() for name in names.words()])

def isStopWord(word):
    return (word in sw or word in punctuation) or not word.isalpha() or word in all_names

review_words = movie_reviews.words()
filtered = [w.lower() for w in review_words if not isStopWord(w.lower())]

words = FreqDist(filtered)

texts = []

for fid in movie_reviews.fileids():
    texts.append(" ".join([w.lower() for w in movie_reviews.words(fid) if not isStopWord(w.lower()) and words[w.lower()] > 1]))

vectorizer = TfidfVectorizer(stop_words='english')
matrix = vectorizer.fit_transform(texts)
sums = np.array(matrix.sum(axis=0)).ravel()
```

```
ranks = []

for word, val in itertools.izip(vectorizer.get_feature_names(), sums):
    ranks.append((word, val))

df = pd.DataFrame(ranks, columns=["term", "tfidf"])
df = df.sort(['tfidf'])
print df.head()

N = int(.01 * len(df))
df = df.tail(N)

for term, tfidf in itertools.izip(df["term"].values, df["tfidf"].
values):
    print term, ":", tfidf
```

Social network analysis

Social network analysis studies social relations using network theory. Nodes represent participants in a network. Lines between nodes represent relationships. Formally, this is called a graph. Due to the constraints of this book, we will only have a quick look at a simple graph that comes with the popular NetworkX Python library. matplotlib will help with the visualization of the graph.

Install NetworkX with the following commands:

```
$ pip install networkx
$ pip freeze|grep networkx
networkx==1.9
```

The import convention for NetworkX is as follows:

```
import networkx as nx
```

NetworkX provides a number of sample graphs, which can be listed as follows:

```
print [s for s in dir(nx) if s.endswith('graph')]
```

Load the Davis Southern women graph and plot a histogram of the degree of connections:

```
G = nx.davis_southern_women_graph()
plt.figure(1)
plt.hist(nx.degree(G).values())
```

The resulting histogram is shown as follows:

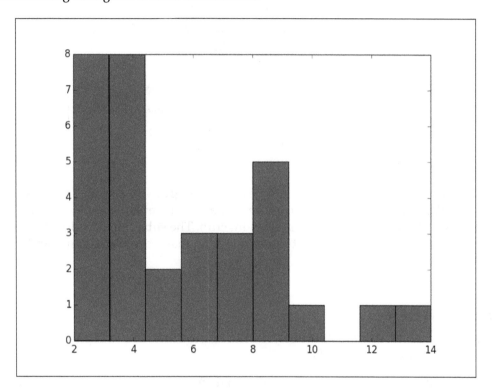

Draw the graph with node labels as follows:

```
plt.figure(2)
pos = nx.spring_layout(G)
nx.draw(G, node_size=9)
nx.draw_networkx_labels(G, pos)
plt.show()
```

We get the following graph:

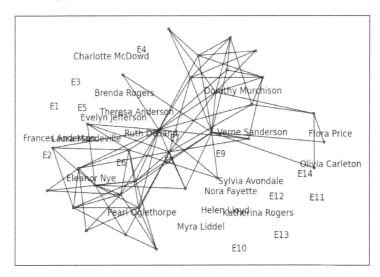

This was a short example, but it should be enough to give you a taste of what is possible. We can use NetworkX to explore, visualize, and analyze social media networks such as Twitter, Facebook, and LinkedIn. The subject matter doesn't even have to be a social network, it can be anything that resembles a graph and NetworkX understands.

Summary

This was a chapter about textual analysis. We learned that it's a best practice in text analysis to get rid of stopwords.

In the bag-of-words model, we created from a document a bag containing words found in the document. Using all the word counts, we can build a feature vector for each document.

Classification algorithms are a type of machine learning algorithm, which involve determining the class of a given item. Naive Bayes classification is a probabilistic algorithm based on the Bayes theorem from probability theory and statistics. The Bayes theorem states that the posterior probability is proportional to the prior probability multiplied by the likelihood.

The next chapter will describe machine learning in more detail. Machine learning is a research field that shows a lot of promise. One day, it may even replace human labor completely. We will explore what we can do with scikit-learn, the Python machine learning package, using weather data as an example.

10
Predictive Analytics and Machine Learning

Predictive analytics and **machine learning** are hot, new research fields. They are new compared to other fields and, without a doubt, we can expect a lot of rapid growth. It is even predicted that machine learning will accelerate so fast that within mere decades human labor will be replaced by intelligent machines (see http://en.wikipedia.org/wiki/Technological_singularity). The current state of art is far from that utopia. A lot of computing power and data is still needed to make even simple decisions, such as determining whether pictures on the Internet contain dogs or cats. Predictive analytics uses a variety of techniques, including machine learning to make useful predictions, for instance, to determine whether a customer can repay his or her loans or identify female customers who are pregnant (see http://www.forbes.com/sites/kashmirhill/2012/02/16/how-target-figured-out-a-teen-girl-was-pregnant-before-her-father-did/).

To make these predictions, features are extracted from huge volumes of data. We mentioned features before—they are also called predictors. Features are input variables that can be used to make predictions. In essence, we have features found in our data and we are looking for a function that maps the features to a target, which may or may not be known. Finding the appropriate function can be hard; often, different algorithms and models are grouped together in so called *ensembles*. The output of an ensemble can be a majority vote or an average of a group of models, but we can also use a more advanced algorithm to produce the final result. We will not be using ensembles in this chapter, but it is something to keep in mind.

In the previous chapter, we got a taste of machine learning algorithms—the Naive Bayes classification algorithm. We can divide machine learning into the following categories:

- **Supervised learning**: This requires us to label training data. For instance, if we want to classify spam, we need to provide examples of spam and normal e-mail messages.

- **Unsupervised learning**: This doesn't require human input. This type of learning can discover patterns such as clusters in large datasets.

- **Reinforcement learning**: This is learning without a tutor, but with some sort of feedback. For example, a computer can play chess against itself or if you remember the *War Games* movie from 1983 (see `http://en.wikipedia.org/wiki/WarGames`), think of tic-tac-toe and thermonuclear warfare.

We will use weather prediction as a running example. In this chapter, we will mostly use the Python scikit-learn library. This library has clustering, regression, and classification algorithms. However, some machine learning algorithms are not covered by scikit-learn so, for those, we will be using other APIs. The topics of this chapter are as follows:

- A tour of scikit-learn
- Preprocessing
- Classification with logistic regression
- Classification with support vector machines
- Regression with ElasticNetCV
- Support vector regression
- Clustering with affinity propagation
- Mean Shift
- Genetic algorithms
- Neural networks
- Decision trees

A tour of scikit-learn

In the previous chapter, *Chapter 9, Analyzing Textual Data and Social Media*, we installed scikit-learn. With the `pkg_check.py` file in this book's code bundle, we can print the following scikit-learn module descriptions:

```
sklearn version 0.15.0
sklearn.__check_build DESCRIPTION Module to give helpful messages to the
user that did not compile the scikit properly. PACKAGE CONTENTS _check_
build setup FUNCTI
sklearn.cluster DESCRIPTION The :mod:`sklearn.cluster` module gathers
popular unsupervised clustering algorithms. PACKAGE CONTENTS _feature_
agglomeration _h
sklearn.covariance DESCRIPTION The :mod:`sklearn.covariance` module
includes methods and algorithms to robustly estimate the covariance of
features given a set
sklearn.cross_decomposition
sklearn.datasets DESCRIPTION The :mod:`sklearn.datasets` module includes
utilities to load datasets, including methods to load and fetch popular
reference da
sklearn.decomposition DESCRIPTION The :mod:`sklearn.decomposition` module
includes matrix decomposition algorithms, including among others PCA, NMF
or ICA. Most o
sklearn.ensemble DESCRIPTION The :mod:`sklearn.ensemble` module includes
ensemble-based methods for classification and regression. PACKAGE
CONTENTS _gradient
sklearn.externals
sklearn.feature_extraction DESCRIPTION The :mod:`sklearn.feature_
extraction` module deals with feature extraction from raw data. It
currently includes methods to extra
sklearn.feature_selection DESCRIPTION The :mod:`sklearn.feature_
selection` module implements feature selection algorithms. It currently
includes univariate filter sel
sklearn.gaussian_process DESCRIPTION The :mod:`sklearn.gaussian_process`
module implements scalar Gaussian Process based predictions. PACKAGE
CONTENTS correlation_mo
sklearn.linear_model DESCRIPTION The :mod:`sklearn.linear_model` module
implements generalized linear models. It includes Ridge regression,
Bayesian Regression,
sklearn.manifold
sklearn.metrics DESCRIPTION The :mod:`sklearn.metrics` module includes
score functions, performance metrics and pairwise metrics and distance
computations.
sklearn.mixture
sklearn.neighbors DESCRIPTION The :mod:`sklearn.neighbors` module
implements the k-nearest neighbors algorithm. PACKAGE CONTENTS ball_tree
base classification
```

```
sklearn.neural_network DESCRIPTION The :mod:`sklearn.neural_network`
module includes models based on neural networks. PACKAGE CONTENTS rbm
CLASSES sklearn.base.Bas
sklearn.preprocessing DESCRIPTION The :mod:`sklearn.preprocessing` module
includes scaling, centering, normalization, binarization and imputation
methods. PACKAGE
sklearn.semi_supervised DESCRIPTION The :mod:`sklearn.semi_supervised`
module implements semi-supervised learning algorithms. These algorithms
utilized small amount
sklearn.svm
sklearn.tests
sklearn.tree DESCRIPTION The :mod:`sklearn.tree` module includes decision
tree-based models for classification and regression. PACKAGE CONTENTS
_tree _ut
sklearn.utils
```

The neural networks module is not very well supported at this moment, so it is recommended to use another library for neural networks. Note that there is a preprocessing module, which is the topic of the next section.

Preprocessing

In the previous chapter, we did a form of data preprocessing by filtering out stopwords. Some machine learning algorithms have trouble with data that is not distributed as a Gaussian with a mean of 0 and variance of 1. The `sklearn.preprocessing` module takes care of this issue. We will be demonstrating it in this section. We will preprocess the meteorological data from the Dutch KNMI institute (original data for De Bilt weather station from `http://www.knmi.nl/climatology/daily_data/datafiles3/260/etmgeg_260.zip`). The data is just one column of the original datafile and contains daily rainfall values. It is stored in the `.npy` format discussed in *Chapter 5*, *Retrieving, Processing, and Storing Data*. We can load the data into a NumPy array. The values are integers that we have to multiply by 0.1 to get the daily precipitation amounts in mm.

The data has the somewhat quirky feature that values below 0.05 mm are quoted as -1. We will set those values equal to 0.025 (0.05 divided by 2). Values are missing for some days in the original data. We will completely ignore the missing data. We can do that because we have a lot of data points as it is. Data is missing for about a year at the beginning of the century and for a couple of days later in the century. The `preprocessing` module has an `Imputer` class with default strategies to deal with missing values. Those strategies, however, seem inappropriate in this case. Data analysis is about looking through data as if it is a window — window to knowledge. Data cleaning and imputing are activities that can make our window nicer to look at. However, we should be careful not to distort the original data too much.

The main feature for the machine learning examples will be an array of day-of-the-year values (1 to 366). This should help explain any seasonal effects.

The mean, variance, and output from the **Anderson-Darling test** (see *Chapter 3, Statistics and Linear Algebra*) are printed as follows:

```
Rain mean 2.17919594267
Rain variance 18.803443919
Anderson rain (inf, array([ 0.576,  0.656,  0.787,  0.918,  1.092]),
array([ 15. ,  10. ,   5. ,   2.5,   1. ]))
```

We can safely conclude that the data doesn't have a 0 mean and variance of 1, and it does not conform to a normal distribution. The data has a large percentage of 0 values corresponding to days on which it didn't rain. Large amounts of rain are increasingly rare (which is a good thing). However, the data distribution is completely asymmetric and therefore not Gaussian. We can easily arrange for a 0 mean and variance of 1. Scale the data with the `scale()` function:

```
scaled = preprocessing.scale(rain)
```

We now get the required values for the mean and variance, but the data distribution remains asymmetric:

```
Scaled mean 3.41301602808e-17
Scaled variance 1.0
Anderson scaled (inf, array([ 0.576,  0.656,  0.787,  0.918,
1.092]), array([ 15. ,  10. ,   5. ,   2.5,   1. ]))
```

Sometimes, we want to convert numerical feature values into Boolean values. This is often used in text analysis in order to simplify computation. Perform the conversion with the `binarize()` function:

```
binarized = preprocessing.binarize(rain)
print np.unique(binarized), binarized.sum()
```

By default, a new array is created; we could have also chosen to perform the operation in-place. The default threshold is at zero, meaning that positive values are replaced by 1 and negative values by 0:

```
[ 0.  1.] 24594.0
```

The `LabelBinarizer` class can label integers as classes (in the context of classification):

```
lb = preprocessing.LabelBinarizer()
lb.fit(rain.astype(int))
print lb.classes_
```

The output is a list of integers from 0 to 62. Refer to the `preproc.py` file in this book's code bundle:

```
import numpy as np
from sklearn import preprocessing
from scipy.stats import anderson


rain = np.load('rain.npy')
rain = .1 * rain
rain[rain < 0] = .05/2
print "Rain mean", rain.mean()
print "Rain variance", rain.var()
print "Anderson rain", anderson(rain)

scaled = preprocessing.scale(rain)
print "Scaled mean", scaled.mean()
print "Scaled variance", scaled.var()
print "Anderson scaled", anderson(scaled)

binarized = preprocessing.binarize(rain)
print np.unique(binarized), binarized.sum()

lb = preprocessing.LabelBinarizer()
lb.fit(rain.astype(int))
print lb.classes_
```

Classification with logistic regression

Logistic regression is a type of a classification algorithm (see http://en.wikipedia.org/wiki/Logistic_regression). This algorithm can be used to predict probabilities associated with a class or an event occurring. A classification problem with multiple classes can be reduced to a binary classification problem. In this simplest case, a high probability for one class, means a low probability for another class. Logistic regression is based on the **logistic function**, which has values in the range between 0 and 1—just like for probabilities. The logistic function can therefore be used to transform arbitrary values into probabilities.

We can define a function that performs classification with logistic regression. Create a classifier object as follows:

```
clf = LogisticRegression(random_state=12)
```

The `random_state` parameter acts like a seed for a pseudorandom generator. We touched upon the importance of cross-validation earlier in this book as a technique to avoid overfitting. The **k-fold cross-validation** is a form of cross-validation involving *k* (a small integer number) random data partitions called **folds**. In *k* iterations, each fold is used once for validation and the rest of the data is used for training. The classes in scikit-learn have a default *k* value of 3, but typically we may want to set it to a higher value such as 5 or 10. The results of the iterations can be combined at the end. The scikit-learn has a utility `KFold` class for k-fold cross-validation. Create a `KFold` object with 10 folds as follows:

```
kf = KFold(len(y), n_folds=10)
```

Train the data with the `fit()` method, as follows:

```
clf.fit(x[train], y[train])
```

The `score()` method measures classification accuracy:

```
scores.append(clf.score(x[test], y[test]))
```

In this example, we will use the day-of-the-year and previous day rain amount as features. Construct an array with features, as follows:

```
x = np.vstack((dates[:-1], rain[:-1]))
```

As classes, define first rainless days with 0 amount of rain; second, low amount of rain corresponding to -1 in our data and third, rainy days. These three classes can be linked to the sign of values in our data:

```
y = np.sign(rain[1:])
```

Using this setup, we get an average accuracy of 57 percent. For the scikit-learn sample iris dataset, we get an average accuracy of 41 percent (refer to `log_regress.py` file in this book's code bundle):

```
from sklearn.linear_model import LogisticRegression
from sklearn.cross_validation import KFold
from sklearn import datasets
import numpy as np


def classify(x, y):
    clf = LogisticRegression(random_state=12)
    scores = []
    kf = KFold(len(y), n_folds=10)
```

```
      for train,test in kf:
        clf.fit(x[train], y[train])
        scores.append(clf.score(x[test], y[test]))

      print np.mean(scores)

rain = np.load('rain.npy')
dates = np.load('doy.npy')

x = np.vstack((dates[:-1], rain[:-1]))
y = np.sign(rain[1:])
classify(x.T, y)

#iris example
iris = datasets.load_iris()
x = iris.data[:, :2]
y = iris.target
classify(x, y)
```

Classification with support vector machines

Support vector machines (SVM) can be used for regression—**support vector regression (SVR)**—and classification (SVC). The algorithm was invented by Vladimir Vapnik in 1993 (see `http://en.wikipedia.org/wiki/Support_vector_machine`). SVM maps data points to points in multidimensional space. The mapping is performed by a so-called **kernel function**. The kernel function can be linear or nonlinear. The classification problem is then reduced to finding a hyperplane or hyperplanes that best separate the points into classes. It can be hard to perform the separation with hyperplanes, which lead to the emergence of the concept of **soft margin**. The soft margin measures the tolerance for misclassification and is governed by a constant commonly denoted with C. Another important parameter is the type of the kernel function, which can be:

- A linear function
- A polynomial function
- A radial basis function
- A sigmoid function

A **grid search** can find the proper parameters for a problem. This is a systematic method that tries all possible parameter combinations. We will perform a grid search with the scikit-learn `GridSearchCV` class. We give this class a classifier or regressor type object with a dictionary. The keys of the dictionary are parameters we want to tweak. The values of the dictionary are the corresponding lists of parameter values to try. The scikit-learn API has a number of classes that add cross-validation functionality to a counterpart class. Cross-validation is turned off by default. Create a `GridSearchCV` object as follows:

```
clf = GridSearchCV(SVC(random_state=42, max_iter=100), {'kernel':
['linear', 'poly', 'rbf'], 'C':[1, 10]})
```

In this line, we specified the number of maximum iterations to not test our patience too much. Cross-validation was turned off also to speed up the process. Furthermore, we varied the types of kernels and the soft margin parameter.

The preceding code snippet created a grid of two by three for the possible parameter variations. If we had more time, we could have created a bigger grid with more possible values. We would also set the `cv` parameter of `GridSearchCV` to the number of folds we want, such as 5 or 10. The maximum iterations should be set to a higher value as well. The different kernels can vary wildly in time required to fit. We can print more information such as execution time for each combination of parameter values with the verbose parameter set to a non-zero integer value. Typically, we want to vary the soft-margin parameter by orders of magnitude, for instance, from 1 to 10,000. We can achieve this with the NumPy `logspace()` function.

Applying this classifier, we obtain an accuracy of 56 percent for the weather data and an accuracy of 82 percent for the iris sample dataset. The `grid_scores_` field of `GridSearchCV` contains scores resulting from the grid search. For the weather data, the scores are as follows:

```
[mean: 0.42879, std: 0.11308, params: {'kernel': 'linear', 'C': 1},
mean: 0.55570, std: 0.00559, params: {'kernel': 'poly', 'C': 1},
mean: 0.36939, std: 0.00169, params: {'kernel': 'rbf', 'C': 1},
mean: 0.30658, std: 0.03034, params: {'kernel': 'linear', 'C': 10},
mean: 0.41673, std: 0.20214, params: {'kernel': 'poly', 'C': 10},
mean: 0.49195, std: 0.08911, params: {'kernel': 'rbf', 'C': 10}]
```

For the iris sample data, we get the following scores:

```
[mean: 0.80000, std: 0.03949, params: {'kernel': 'linear', 'C': 1},
mean: 0.58667, std: 0.12603, params: {'kernel': 'poly', 'C': 1},
mean: 0.80000, std: 0.03254, params: {'kernel': 'rbf', 'C': 1},
mean: 0.74667, std: 0.07391, params: {'kernel': 'linear', 'C': 10},
mean: 0.56667, std: 0.13132, params: {'kernel': 'poly', 'C': 10},
mean: 0.79333, std: 0.03467, params: {'kernel': 'rbf', 'C': 10}]
```

Refer to the `svm_class.py` file in this book's code bundle:

```
from sklearn.svm import SVC
from sklearn.grid_search import GridSearchCV
from sklearn import datasets
import numpy as np
from pprint import PrettyPrinter

def classify(x, y):
    clf = GridSearchCV(SVC(random_state=42, max_iter=100), {'kernel':
['linear', 'poly', 'rbf'], 'C':[1, 10]})

    clf.fit(x, y)
    print "Score", clf.score(x, y)
    PrettyPrinter().pprint(clf.grid_scores_)

rain = np.load('rain.npy')
dates = np.load('doy.npy')

x = np.vstack((dates[:-1], rain[:-1]))
y = np.sign(rain[1:])
classify(x.T, y)

#iris example
iris = datasets.load_iris()
x = iris.data[:, :2]
y = iris.target
classify(x, y)
```

Regression with ElasticNetCV

Elastic net regularization is a method that reduces the danger of overfitting in the context of regression (see `http://en.wikipedia.org/wiki/Elastic_net_regularization`). The elastic net regularization combines linearly the **least absolute shrinkage and selection operator** (**LASSO**) and **ridge** methods. LASSO limits the so-called L1 norm or Manhattan distance. This norm measures for a points pair the sum of absolute coordinates differences. The ridge method uses a penalty, which is the L1 norm squared. For regression problems, the goodness-of-fit is often determined with the **coefficient of determination** also called **R squared** (see `http://en.wikipedia.org/wiki/Coefficient_of_determination`). Unfortunately, there are several definitions of R squared. Also, the name is a bit misleading, since negative values are possible. A perfect fit would have a coefficient of determination of one. Since the definitions allow for a wide range of acceptable values, we should aim for a score that is as close to one as possible.

Let's use a 10-fold cross-validation. Define an `ElasticNetCV` object, as follows:

```
clf = ElasticNetCV(max_iter=200, cv=10, l1_ratio = [.1, .5, .7,
.9, .95, .99, 1])
```

The `ElasticNetCV` class has an `l1_ratio` argument with values between 0 and 1. If the value is 0, we have only ridge regression; if it is one, we have only LASSO regression. Otherwise, we have a mixture. We can either specify a single number or a list of numbers to choose from. For the rain data, we get the following score:

Score 0.0527838760942

This score suggests that we are *underfitting* the data. This can occur for several reasons, such as we are not using enough features or the model is wrong. For the Boston house price data, with all the present features we get:

Score 0.683143903455

The `predict()` method gives prediction for new data. We will visualize the quality of the predictions with a scatter plot. For the rain data, we obtain the following plot:

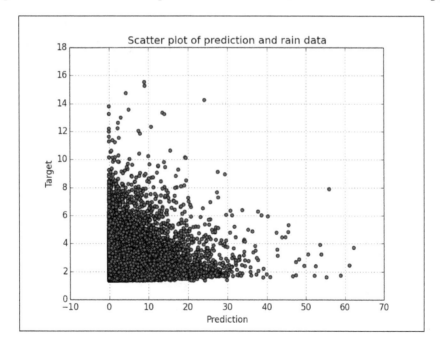

The plot in the previous figure confirms that we have a bad fit (underfitting). A straight diagonal line through the origin would indicate a perfect fit. That's almost what we get for the Boston house price data:

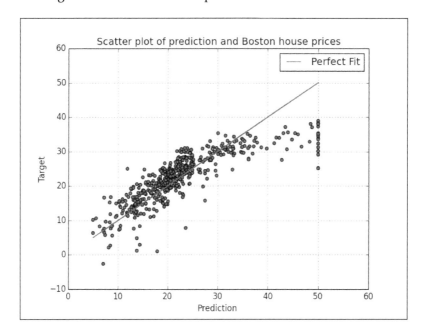

Refer to the `encv.py` file in this book's code bundle:

```
from sklearn.linear_model import ElasticNetCV
import numpy as np
from sklearn import datasets
import matplotlib.pyplot as plt



def regress(x, y, title):
    clf = ElasticNetCV(max_iter=200, cv=10, l1_ratio = [.1, .5,
.7, .9, .95, .99, 1])

    clf.fit(x, y)
    print "Score", clf.score(x, y)

    pred = clf.predict(x)
    plt.title("Scatter plot of prediction and " + title)
    plt.xlabel("Prediction")
    plt.ylabel("Target")
    plt.scatter(y, pred)
```

```
    # Show perfect fit line
    if "Boston" in title:
        plt.plot(y, y, label="Perfect Fit")
        plt.legend()

    plt.grid(True)
    plt.show()

rain = .1 * np.load('rain.npy')
rain[rain < 0] = .05/2
dates = np.load('doy.npy')

x = np.vstack((dates[:-1], rain[:-1]))
y = rain[1:]
regress(x.T, y, "rain data")

boston = datasets.load_boston()
x = boston.data
y = boston.target
regress(x, y, "Boston house prices")
```

Support vector regression

As mentioned before, support vector machines can be used for regression. In the case of regression, we are using a hyperplane not to separate points, but for a fit. A **learning curve** is a way to visualize the behavior of a learning algorithm. It is a plot of training and test scores for a range of train data sizes. Creating a learning curve forces us to train the estimator multiple times and is therefore on aggregate slow. We can compensate for this by creating multiple concurrent estimator jobs. Support vector regression is one of the algorithms that may require scaling. We get the following top scores:

Max test score Rain 0.0161004084576

Max test score Boston 0.662188537037

This is similar to the results obtained with the `ElasticNetCV` class. Many scikit-learn classes have an `n_jobs` parameter for that purpose. As a rule of thumb, we often create as many jobs as there are CPUs in our system. The jobs are created using the standard Python multiprocessing API. Call the `learning_curve()` function to perform training and testing:

```
train_sizes, train_scores, test_scores = learning_curve(clf, X, Y,
n_jobs=ncpus)
```

Plot scores by averaging them:

```
plt.plot(train_sizes, train_scores.mean(axis=1), label="Train
score")
plt.plot(train_sizes, test_scores.mean(axis=1), '--', label="Test
score")
```

The rain data learning curve looks like this:

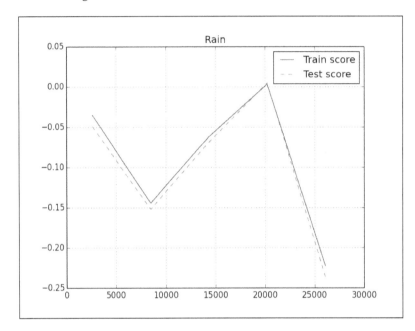

A learning curve is something we are familiar with in our daily lives. The more experience we have, the more we should have learned. In data analysis terms, we should have a better score if we add more data. If we have a good training score, but a poor test score, this means that we are overfitting. Our model only works on the training data. The Boston house price data learning curve looks much better:

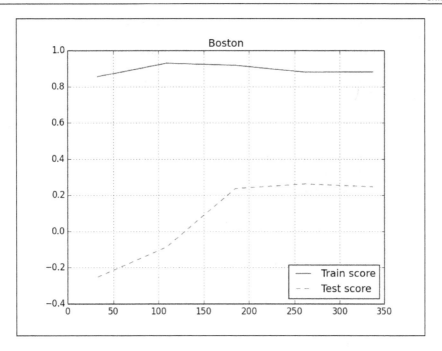

The code is in the sv_regress.py file in this book's code bundle:

```
import numpy as np
from sklearn import datasets
from sklearn.learning_curve import learning_curve
from sklearn.svm import SVR
from sklearn import preprocessing
import multiprocessing
import matplotlib.pyplot as plt


def regress(x, y, ncpus, title):
    X = preprocessing.scale(x)
    Y = preprocessing.scale(y)
    clf = SVR(max_iter=ncpus * 200)

    train_sizes, train_scores, test_scores = learning_curve(clf,
X, Y, n_jobs=ncpus)

    plt.figure()
    plt.title(title)
```

```
    plt.plot(train_sizes, train_scores.mean(axis=1), label="Train
score")
    plt.plot(train_sizes, test_scores.mean(axis=1), '--',
label="Test score")
    print "Max test score " + title, test_scores.max()
    plt.grid(True)
    plt.legend(loc='best')
    plt.show()

rain = .1 * np.load('rain.npy')
rain[rain < 0] = .05/2
dates = np.load('doy.npy')

x = np.vstack((dates[:-1], rain[:-1]))
y = rain[1:]
ncpus = multiprocessing.cpu_count()
regress(x.T, y, ncpus, "Rain")

boston = datasets.load_boston()
x = boston.data
y = boston.target
regress(x, y, ncpus, "Boston")
```

Clustering with affinity propagation

Clustering aims to partition data into groups called clusters. Clustering is usually unsupervised in the sense that no examples are given. Some clustering algorithms require a guess for the number of clusters, while other algorithms don't. Affinity propagation falls in the latter category. Each item in a dataset can be mapped into Euclidean space using feature values. Affinity propagation depends on a matrix containing Euclidean distances between data points. Since the matrix can quickly become quite large, we should be careful not to take up too much memory. The scikit-learn library has utilities to generate structured data. Create three data blobs, as follows:

```
x, _ = datasets.make_blobs(n_samples=100, centers=3, n_features=2,
random_state=10)
```

Call the `euclidean_distances()` function to create the aforementioned matrix:

```
S = euclidean_distances(x)
```

Cluster using the matrix in order to label the data with the corresponding cluster:

```
aff_pro = cluster.AffinityPropagation().fit(S)
labels = aff_pro.labels_
```

If we plot the cluster, we get the following figure:

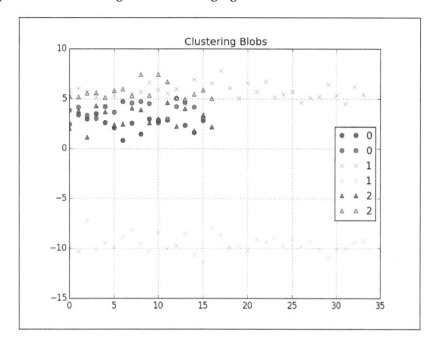

Refer to the `aff_prop.py` file in this book's code bundle:

```
from sklearn import datasets
from sklearn import cluster
import numpy as np
import matplotlib.pyplot as plt
from sklearn.metrics import euclidean_distances


x, _ = datasets.make_blobs(n_samples=100, centers=3, n_features=2,
random_state=10)
S = euclidean_distances(x)

aff_pro = cluster.AffinityPropagation().fit(S)
labels = aff_pro.labels_

styles = ['o', 'x', '^']

for style, label in zip(styles, np.unique(labels)):
    print label
    plt.plot(x[labels == label], style, label=label)
```

```
plt.title("Clustering Blobs")
plt.grid(True)
plt.legend(loc='best')
plt.show()
```

Mean Shift

Mean Shift is another clustering algorithm that doesn't require an estimate for the number of clusters. It has been successfully applied to image processing. The algorithm tries to iteratively find the maxima of a density function. Before demonstrating mean shift, we will average the rain data on a day-of-the-year basis using a pandas `DataFrame`. Create the `DataFrame` and average its data as follows:

```
df = pd.DataFrame.from_records(x.T, columns=['dates', 'rain'])
df = df.groupby('dates').mean()

df.plot()
```

The following plot is the result:

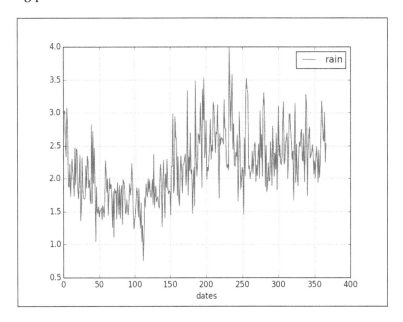

Cluster the data with the mean shift algorithm as follows:

```
x = np.vstack((np.arange(1, len(df) + 1) ,
df.as_matrix().ravel()))
x = x.T
```

```
ms = cluster.MeanShift()
ms.fit(x)
labels = ms.predict(x)
```

If we visualize the data with different line widths and shading for the three resulting clusters, the following figure is obtained:

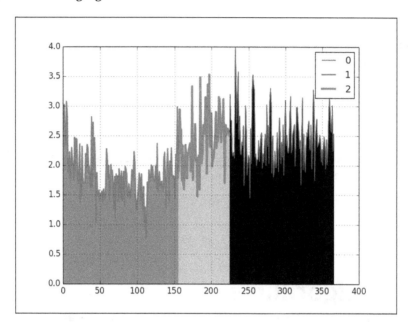

As you can see, we have three clusters based on the average rainfall in mm on the day of year (1-366). The complete code is in the `mean_shift.py` file in this book's code bundle:

```
import numpy as np
from sklearn import cluster
import matplotlib.pyplot as plt
import pandas as pd


rain = .1 * np.load('rain.npy')
rain[rain < 0] = .05/2
dates = np.load('doy.npy')
x = np.vstack((dates, rain))
df = pd.DataFrame.from_records(x.T, columns=['dates', 'rain'])
df = df.groupby('dates').mean()
```

```
df.plot()
x = np.vstack((np.arange(1, len(df) + 1) ,
df.as_matrix().ravel()))
x = x.T
ms = cluster.MeanShift()
ms.fit(x)
labels = ms.predict(x)

plt.figure()
grays = ['0', '0.5', '0.75']

for gray, label in zip(grays, np.unique(labels)):
    match = labels == label
    x0 = x[:, 0]
    x1 = x[:, 1]
    plt.plot(x0[match], x1[match], lw=label+1, label=label)
    plt.fill_between(x0, x1, where=match, color=gray)

plt.grid(True)
plt.legend()
plt.show()
```

Genetic algorithms

This is the most controversial section in the book so far. **Genetic algorithms** are based on the biological theory of evolution (see `http://en.wikipedia.org/wiki/Evolutionary_algorithm`). This type of algorithm is useful for searching and optimization. For instance, we can use it to find the optimal parameters for a regression or classification problem.

Humans and other life forms on Earth carry genetic information in chromosomes. Chromosomes are frequently modeled as strings. A similar representation is used in genetic algorithms. The first step is to initialize the population with random individuals and related representation of genetic information. We can also initialize with already-known candidate solutions for the problem. After that, we go through many iterations called **generations**. During each generation, individuals are selected for mating based on a predefined **fitness function**. The fitness function evaluates how close an individual is to the desired solution.

Two **genetic operators** generate new genetic information:

- **Crossover**: This occurs via mating and creates new children. We will explain **one-point crossover** here. This process takes a piece of genetic information from one parent and a complementary piece from the other parent. For example, if the information is represented by 100 list elements, crossover may take the first 80 element of the first parent and the last 20 from the other parent. It is possible in genetic algorithms to produce children from more than two parents. This is an area under research (refer to Eiben, A. E. et al. *Genetic algorithms with multi-parent recombination, Proceedings of the International Conference on Evolutionary Computation – PPSN III*. The Third Conference on Parallel Problem Solving from Nature: 78–87. ISBN 3-540-58484-6, 1994).

- **Mutation**: This is controlled by a fixed mutation rate. This concept is explained in several Hollywood movies and popular culture. Mutation is rare and often detrimental or even fatal. However, sometimes mutants can acquire desirable traits. In certain cases, the trait can be passed on to future generations.

Eventually, the new individuals replace the old population and we can start a new iteration. In this example, we will use the Python DEAP library. Install DEAP as follows:

```
$ sudo pip install deap
$ pip freeze|grep deap
deap==1.0.1
```

Start by defining a `Fitness` subclass that maximizes fitness:

```
creator.create("FitnessMax", base.Fitness, weights=(1.0,))
```

Then, define a template for each individual in the population:

```
creator.create("Individual", array.array, typecode='d',
fitness=creator.FitnessMax)
```

DEAP has the concept of a toolbox, which is a registry of necessary functions. Create a toolbox and register the initialization functions, as follows:

```
toolbox = base.Toolbox()
toolbox.register("attr_float", random.random)
toolbox.register("individual", tools.initRepeat,
creator.Individual, toolbox.attr_float, 200)
toolbox.register("populate", tools.initRepeat, list,
toolbox.individual)
```

The first function generates floating-point numbers between 0 and 1. The second function creates an individual with a list of 200 floating point numbers. The third function creates a list of individuals. This list represents the population of possible solutions for a search or optimization problem.

In a society, we want "normal" individuals, but also people like Einstein. In *Chapter 3, Statistics and Linear Algebra*, we were introduced to the `shapiro()` function, which performs a normality test. For an individual to be normal, we require that the normality test p-value of his or her list to be as high as possible. The following code defines the fitness function:

```
def eval(individual):
    return shapiro(individual)[1],
```

Let's define the genetic operators:

```
toolbox.register("evaluate", eval)
toolbox.register("mate", tools.cxTwoPoint)
toolbox.register("mutate", tools.mutFlipBit, indpb=0.1)
toolbox.register("select", tools.selTournament, tournsize=4)
```

The following list will give you an explanation about the preceding genetic operators:

- `evaluate`: This operator measures the fitness of each individual. In this example, the p-value of a normality test is used as a fitness score.
- `mate`: This operator produces children. In this example, it uses two-point crossover.
- `mutate`: This operator changes an individual at random. For a list of Boolean values, this means that some values are flipped from `True` to `False` and vice versa.
- `select`: This operator selects the individuals that are allowed to mate.

In the preceding code snippet, we specified that we are going to use two-point crossover and the probability of an attribute to be flipped. Generate 400 individuals as the initial population:

```
pop = toolbox.populate(n=400)
```

Now start the evolution process, as follows:

```
hof = tools.HallOfFame(1)
stats = tools.Statistics(key=lambda ind: ind.fitness.values)
stats.register("max", np.max)

algorithms.eaSimple(pop, toolbox, cxpb=0.5, mutpb=0.2, ngen=80,
stats=stats, halloffame=hof)
```

The program reports statistics including the maximum fitness for each generation. We specified the crossover probability, mutation rate, and maximum generations after which to stop. The following is an extract of the displayed statistics report:

```
gen         nevals         max
0           400            0.000484774
1           245            0.000776807
2           248            0.00135569
...
79          250            0.99826
80          248            0.99826
```

As you can see, we start out with distributions that are far from normal, but eventually we get an individual with the following histogram:

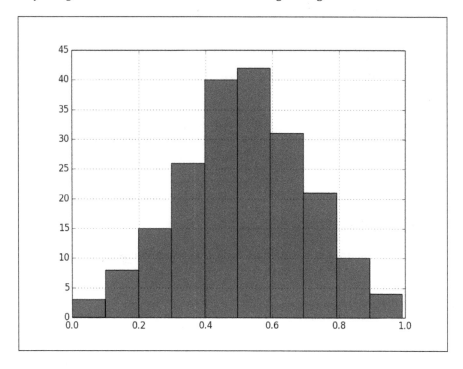

Refer to the gen_algo.py file in this book's code bundle:

```
import array
import random
import numpy as np
from deap import algorithms
from deap import base
```

```
from deap import creator
from deap import tools
from scipy.stats import shapiro
import matplotlib.pyplot as plt


creator.create("FitnessMax", base.Fitness, weights=(1.0,))
creator.create("Individual", array.array, typecode='d',
fitness=creator.FitnessMax)

toolbox = base.Toolbox()
toolbox.register("attr_float", random.random)
toolbox.register("individual", tools.initRepeat,
creator.Individual, toolbox.attr_float, 200)
toolbox.register("populate", tools.initRepeat, list,
toolbox.individual)

def eval(individual):
    return shapiro(individual)[1],

toolbox.register("evaluate", eval)
toolbox.register("mate", tools.cxTwoPoint)
toolbox.register("mutate", tools.mutFlipBit, indpb=0.1)
toolbox.register("select", tools.selTournament, tournsize=4)

random.seed(42)

pop = toolbox.populate(n=400)
hof = tools.HallOfFame(1)
stats = tools.Statistics(key=lambda ind: ind.fitness.values)
stats.register("max", np.max)

algorithms.eaSimple(pop, toolbox, cxpb=0.5, mutpb=0.2, ngen=80,
stats=stats, halloffame=hof)

print shapiro(hof[0])[1]
plt.hist(hof[0])
plt.grid(True)
plt.show()
```

Neural networks

Artificial Neural Networks (ANN) are models inspired by the animal brain (highly evolved animals). A neural network is a network of neurons—units with inputs and outputs. For example, the input can be a value related to the pixel of an image and the output of a neuron can be passed to another neuron and so on, thus creating a multilayered network. Neural networks contain adaptive elements making them suitable to deal with nonlinear models and pattern recognition problems. We will again try to predict whether it is going to rain based on day-of-the-year and previous day values. Let's use the theanets Python library, which can be installed as follows:

```
$ sudo pip install theanets
$ pip freeze|grep theanets
theanets==0.2.0
```

One of the technical reviewers encountered an error, which was resolved by updating NumPy and SciPy. We first create an `Experiment` corresponding to a neural network and then train the network. Create a network with two input neurons and one output neuron:

```
e = theanets.Experiment(theanets.Regressor,
                        layers=(2, 3, 1),
                        learning_rate=0.1,
                        momentum=0.5,
                        patience=300,
                        train_batches=multiprocessing.cpu_count(),
                        num_updates=500)
```

The network has a hidden layer with three neurons and uses the standard Python multiprocessing API to speed up computations. Train using a training and validation dataset:

```
train = [x[:N], y[:N]]
valid = [x[N:], y[N:]]
e.run(train, valid)
```

Get predictions for the validation data, as follows:

```
pred = e.network(x[N:]).ravel()
```

The scikit-learn library has a utility function, which computes the accuracy of a classifier. Compute the accuracy as follows:

```
print "Pred Min", pred.min(), "Max", pred.max()
print "Y Min", y.min(), "Max", y.max()
print "Accuracy", accuracy_score(y[N:], pred >= .5)
```

Due to the nature of neural nets, the output values can vary. The output may look like the following:

```
Pred Min 0.303503170562 Max 0.737862165479
Y Min 0.0 Max 1.0
Accuracy 0.632345426673
```

Refer to the `neural_net.py` file in this book's code bundle:

```python
import numpy as np
import theanets
import multiprocessing
from sklearn import datasets
from sklearn.metrics import accuracy_score


rain = .1 * np.load('rain.npy')
rain[rain < 0] = .05/2
dates = np.load('doy.npy')
x = np.vstack((dates[:-1], np.sign(rain[:-1])))
x = x.T

y = np.vstack(np.sign(rain[1:]),)
N = int(.9 * len(x))

e = theanets.Experiment(theanets.Regressor,
                        layers=(2, 3, 1),
                        learning_rate=0.1,
                        momentum=0.5,
                        patience=300,
                        train_batches=multiprocessing.cpu_count(),
                        num_updates=500)

train = [x[:N], y[:N]]
valid = [x[N:], y[N:]]
e.run(train, valid)

pred = e.network(x[N:]).ravel()
print "Pred Min", pred.min(), "Max", pred.max()
print "Y Min", y.min(), "Max", y.max()
print "Accuracy", accuracy_score(y[N:], pred >= .5)
```

Decision trees

The `if a: else b` statement is one of the most common statements in Python programming. By nesting and combining such statements, we can build a so-called **decision tree**. This is similar to an old-fashioned flowchart, although flowcharts also allow loops. The application of decision trees in machine learning is called **decision tree learning**. The end nodes of the trees in decision tree learning, also known as **leaves**, contain the class labels of a classification problem. Each non-leaf node is associated with a Boolean condition involving feature values. The scikit-learn implementation uses Gini impurity and entropy as information metrics. These metrics measure the probability that an item is misclassified (see `http://en.wikipedia.org/wiki/Decision_tree_learning`). Decision trees are easy to understand, use, visualize, and verify. To visualize the tree, we will make use of Graphviz, which can be downloaded from `http://graphviz.org/`. Also, we need to install pydot2, as follows:

```
$ pip install pydot2
$ pip freeze|grep pydot2
pydot 2==1.0.33
```

Split the rain data into a training and test set as follows, with the scikit-learn `train_test_split()` function:

```
x_train, x_test, y_train, y_test = train_test_split(x, y,
random_state=37)
```

Create `DecisionTreeClassifier` as follows:

```
clf = tree.DecisionTreeClassifier(random_state=37)
```

We will use the scikit-learn `RandomSearchCV` class to try out a range of parameters. Use the class as follows:

```
params = {"max_depth": [2, None],
            "min_samples_leaf": sp_randint(1, 5),
            "criterion": ["gini", "entropy"]}
rscv = RandomizedSearchCV(clf, params)
rscv.fit(x_train,y_train)
```

We get the following best score and parameters from the search:

```
Best Train Score 0.703164923517
Test Score 0.705058763413
Best params {'criterion': 'gini', 'max_depth': 2, 'min_samples_leaf':
2}
```

It's good to visualize the decision tree even if it's only to verify our assumptions. Create a decision tree figure with the following code:

```
sio = StringIO.StringIO()
tree.export_graphviz(rscv.best_estimator_, out_file=sio,
feature_names=['day-of-year','yest'])
dec_tree = pydot.graph_from_dot_data(sio.getvalue())

with NamedTemporaryFile(prefix='rain', suffix='.png',
delete=False) as f:
    dec_tree.write_png(f.name)
    print "Written figure to", f.name
```

Refer to the following plot for the end result:

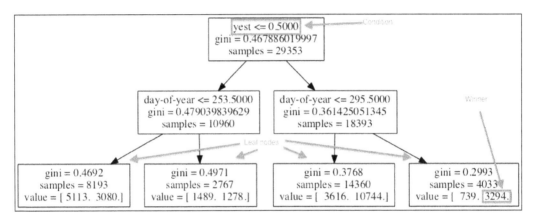

In the non-leaf nodes, we see conditions printed as the top line. If the condition is true, we go to the left child; otherwise, we go to the right. When we reach a leaf node, the class with highest value, as given in the bottom line, wins. Inspect the dec_tree. py file in this book's code bundle:

```
from sklearn.cross_validation import train_test_split
from sklearn import tree
from sklearn.grid_search import RandomizedSearchCV
from scipy.stats import randint as sp_randint
import pydot
import StringIO
import numpy as np
from tempfile import NamedTemporaryFile

rain = .1 * np.load('rain.npy')
rain[rain < 0] = .05/2
```

```
dates = np.load('doy.npy').astype(int)
x = np.vstack((dates[:-1], np.sign(rain[:-1])))
x = x.T


y = np.sign(rain[1:])


x_train, x_test, y_train, y_test = train_test_split(x, y,
random_state=37)


clf = tree.DecisionTreeClassifier(random_state=37)
params = {"max_depth": [2, None],
            "min_samples_leaf": sp_randint(1, 5),
            "criterion": ["gini", "entropy"]}
rscv = RandomizedSearchCV(clf, params)
rscv.fit(x_train,y_train)


sio = StringIO.StringIO()
tree.export_graphviz(rscv.best_estimator_, out_file=sio,
feature_names=['day-of-year','yest'])
dec_tree = pydot.graph_from_dot_data(sio.getvalue())


with NamedTemporaryFile(prefix='rain', suffix='.png',
delete=False) as f:
    dec_tree.write_png(f.name)
    print "Written figure to", f.name


print "Best Train Score", rscv.best_score_
print "Test Score", rscv.score(x_test, y_test)
print "Best params", rscv.best_params_
```

Summary

This chapter was devoted to predictive modeling and machine learning. These are very large fields to cover in one chapter, so you may want to have a look at some of the books mentioned in the *Preface*. Predictive analytics uses a variety of techniques, including machine learning, to make useful predictions for instance to determine whether it is going to rain tomorrow.

SVM maps the data points to points in multidimensional space. The classification problem is then reduced to finding a hyperplane or hyperplanes that best separate the points into classes.

The elastic net regularization combines linearly the LASSO and ridge methods. For regression problems, goodness-of-fit is often determined with the coefficient of determination also called R squared. Some clustering algorithms require a guess for the number of clusters, while other algorithms don't.

The first step in genetic algorithms is to initialize the population with random individuals and related representation of genetic information. During each generation, individuals are selected for mating based on a predefined fitness function. The application of decision trees in machine learning is called decision tree learning.

The next chapter, *Chapter 11, Environments Outside the Python Ecosystem and Cloud Computing*, describes interoperability and Cloud possibilities.

11
Environments Outside the Python Ecosystem and Cloud Computing

Outside the Python ecosystem, programming languages such as R, C, Java, and Fortran are fairly popular. In this chapter, we will delve into the particulars of exchanging information with these environments.

Cloud computing aims to deliver computing power as a utility over the Internet. This means that we don't need to have a lot of powerful hardware locally. Instead, we pay as we go—depending on our current needs. We will also talk about how to get our Python code in the Cloud. This is a rapidly evolving industry in a fast-paced world. We have many options available, of which we will cover Google App Engine and PythonAnywhere. **Amazon Web Services** (**AWS**) is deliberately not discussed in this book, since other books such as *Building Machine Learning Systems with Python*, *Willi Richert and Luis Pedro Coelho, Packt Publishing*, mentioned in the *Preface*, cover the topic in great detail. We should also be aware of the Data Science Toolbox at `http://datasciencetoolbox.org/`. This is a virtual environment for data analysis based on Linux, which can be run locally or on AWS. The instructions given on the Data Science Toolbox website are very clear and should help you set up an environment with lots of Python packages that we have already installed.

The topics that will be covered in this chapter are as follows:

- Exchanging information with MATLAB/Octave
- Installing rpy2
- Interfacing with R

- Sending NumPy arrays to Java
- Integrating SWIG and NumPy
- Integrating Boost and Python
- Using Fortran code through f2py
- Setting up Google App Engine
- Running programs on PythonAnywhere
- Working with Wakari

Exchanging information with MATLAB/Octave

MATLAB and its open source alternative **Octave** are popular numerical programs and programming languages. Octave and MATLAB have syntax very similar to Python's. In fact, you can find websites that compare their syntax (for instance, see `http://wiki.scipy.org/NumPy_for_Matlab_Users`).

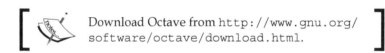

Download Octave from `http://www.gnu.org/software/octave/download.html`.

The most recent Octave version at the time of writing was 3.8.0. The `scipy.io.savemat()` function saves an array in a file compliant to the Octave and MATLAB format. The function accepts as parameters the name of the file and a dictionary with a name for the array and the values. Refer to the `octave_demo.py` file in this book's code bundle:

```
import statsmodels.api as sm
from scipy.io import savemat

data_loader = sm.datasets.sunspots.load_pandas()
df = data_loader.data
savemat("sunspots", {"sunspots": df.values})
```

The preceding code stores sunspots data in a file called `sunspots.mat`. The extension is added automatically. Start the Octave Graphical User Interface or command-line interface. Load the file we created and view the data as follows:

```
octave:1> load sunspots.mat
octave:2> sunspots
sunspots =
```

```
1.7000e+03    5.0000e+00
1.7010e+03    1.1000e+01
1.7020e+03    1.6000e+01
...
```

Installing rpy2

The **R programming language** is popular among statisticians. It is written in C and Fortran and is available under the GNU General Public License. R has support for modeling, statistical tests, time-series analysis, classification, visualization, and clustering. The **Comprehensive R Archive Network (CRAN)** and other repository websites offer thousands of R packages for various tasks.

Download R from http://www.r-project.org/.

The latest R version as of August 2014 was 3.1.1. The rpy2 package facilitates interfacing with R from Python. Install rpy2 as follows with `pip`:

```
$ pip install rpy2
$ pip freeze|grep rpy2
rpy2==2.4.2
```

If you already have rpy2 installed, follow the instructions on http://rpy.sourceforge.net/rpy2/doc-dev/html/overview.html as upgrading is not a straightforward process.

Interfacing with R

R provides a `datasets` package that contains sample datasets. The `morley` dataset has data from measurements of the speed of light made in 1879. The speed of light is a fundamental physical constant and its value is currently known very precisely. The data is described at http://stat.ethz.ch/R-manual/R-devel/library/datasets/html/morley.html. The speed of light value can be found in the `scipy.constants` module. The R data is stored in an R dataframe with three columns:

- The experiment number from one to five
- The run number with twenty runs per experiment, bringing the total measurements to 100
- The measured speed of light in kilometers per second with 299,000 subtracted

The `rpy2.robjects.r()` function executes R code in a Python environment. Load the data as follows:

```
ro.r('data(morley)')
```

The pandas library provides an R interface via the `pandas.rpy.common` module. Load the data into a pandas `DataFrame` as follows:

```
df = com.load_data('morley')
```

Let's group the data by experiment with the following code, which creates a five by two NumPy array:

```
samples = dict(list(df.groupby('Expt')))
samples = np.array([samples[i]['Speed'].values for i in samples.keys()])
```

When we have data from different experiments, it's interesting to know whether the data points of these experiments come from the same distribution. The **Kruskal-Wallis one-way analysis of variance** (refer to `http://en.wikipedia.org/wiki/Kruskal%E2%80%93Wallis_one-way_analysis_of_variance`) is a statistical method, which analyzes samples without making assumptions about their distributions. The null hypothesis for this test is that all the medians of the samples are equal. The test is implemented in the `scipy.stats.kruskal()` function. Perform the test as follows:

```
print "Kruskal", kruskal(samples[0], samples[1], samples[2], samples[3], samples[4])
```

The test statistic and p-value are printed in the following line:

Kruskal (15.022124661246552, 0.0046555484175328015)

We can reject the null hypothesis, but this doesn't tell us which experiment or experiments have a deviating median. Further analysis is left as an exercise for the reader. If we plot the minimum, maximum, and means for each experiment, we get the following figure:

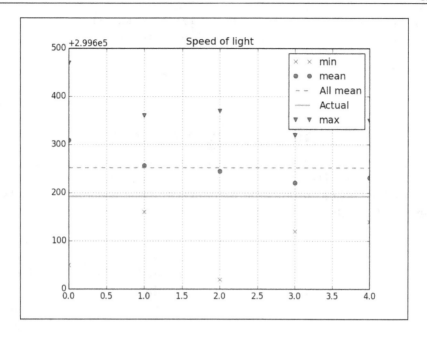

Check out the `r_demo.py` file in this book's code bundle:

```
import pandas.rpy.common as com
import rpy2.robjects as ro
from scipy.stats import kruskal
import matplotlib.pyplot as plt
import numpy as np
from scipy.constants import c


ro.r('data(morley)')
df = com.load_data('morley')
df['Speed'] = df['Speed'] + 299000

samples = dict(list(df.groupby('Expt')))
samples = np.array([samples[i]['Speed'].values for i in
samples.keys()])
print "Kruskal", kruskal(samples[0], samples[1], samples[2],
samples[3], samples[4])

plt.title('Speed of light')
plt.plot(samples.min(axis=1), 'x', label='min')
plt.plot(samples.mean(axis=1), 'o', label='mean')
plt.plot(np.ones(5) * samples.mean(), '--', label='All mean')
```

```
plt.plot(np.ones(5) * c/1000, lw=2, label='Actual')
plt.plot(samples.max(axis=1), 'v', label='max')
plt.grid(True)
plt.legend()
plt.show()
```

Sending NumPy arrays to Java

Like Python, Java is a very popular programming language. We installed Java in *Chapter 8*, *Working with Databases*, as a prerequisite to using Cassandra. To run Java code, we need the **Java Runtime Environment** (JRE). For development, the **Java Development Kit** (JDK) is required.

Jython is an implementation of Python written in Java. Jython code can use any Java class. However, Python modules written in C cannot be imported in Jython. This is an issue, because many numerical and data analysis Python libraries have modules written in C. The JPype package offers a solution and can be downloaded from `http://pypi.python.org/pypi/JPype1` or `http://github.com/originell/jpype`. The most current JPype version at the time of writing was 0.5.5.2. Once you have downloaded and unpacked JPype, run the following command:

```
$ python setup.py install
```

Start the **Java Virtual Machine** (JVM) with the following line:

```
jpype.startJVM(jpype.getDefaultJVMPath())
```

Create a JPype array `JArray` with some random values:

```
values = np.random.randn(7)
java_array = jpype.JArray(jpype.JDouble, 1)(values.tolist())
```

Print each array element as follows:

```
for item in java_array:
    jpype.java.lang.System.out.println(item)
```

At the end, we should shut down the JVM with the following line:

```
jpype.shutdownJVM()
```

The following is the code listing from the `java_demo.py` file in this book's code bundle:

```
import jpype
import numpy as np
from numpy import random
```

```
jpype.startJVM(jpype.getDefaultJVMPath())

random.seed(44)
values = np.random.randn(7)
java_array = jpype.JArray(jpype.JDouble, 1)(values.tolist())

for item in java_array:
    jpype.java.lang.System.out.println(item)

jpype.shutdownJVM()
```

Integrating SWIG and NumPy

C is a widespread programming language developed around 1970. Various C dialects exist and C has influenced other programming languages. C is not object-oriented. This led to the creation of C++, which is an object-oriented language with C features, since C is a subset of C++. C and C++ are compiled languages. We need to compile source code to create so-called object files. After that, we must link the object files to create dynamically shared libraries.

The good thing about integrating C and Python is that a lot of options are available to us. The first option is **Simplified Wrapper and Interface Generator (SWIG)**. SWIG adds an additional step in the development process, which is the generation of glue code between Python and C (or C++). Download SWIG from http://www.swig.org/download.html. At the time of writing, the most current SWIG version was 3.0.2. A prerequisite to installing SWIG is to install **Perl Compatible Regular Expressions (PCRE)**. PCRE is a C regular expressions library. Download PCRE from http://www.pcre.org/. The most current PCRE version at the time of writing was 8.35. After unpacking PCRE, run the following commands:

```
$ ./configure
$ make
$ make install
```

The last command in the preceding snippet requires root or sudo access. We can install SWIG with the same commands. We start by writing a header file containing function definitions. Write a header file, which defines the following function:

```
double sum_rain(int* rain, int len);
```

We will use the preceding function to sum the `rain` amount values we analyzed in the previous chapter. Please refer to the `sum_rain.h` file in this book's code bundle. The function is implemented in the `sum_rain.cpp` file in this book's code bundle:

```cpp
double sum_rain(int* rain, int len) {

   double sum = 0.;

   for (int i = 0; i < len; i++){
     if(rain[i] == -1) {
        sum += 0.025;
     } else {
        sum += 0.1 * rain[i];
     }
   }

   return sum;
}
```

Define the following SWIG interface file (refer to the `sum_rain.i` file in this book's code bundle):

```
%module sum_rain

%{
  #define SWIG_FILE_WITH_INIT
  #include "sum_rain.h"
%}

%include "/tmp/numpy.i"

%init %{
  import_array();
%}

%apply (int* IN_ARRAY1, int DIM1) {(int* rain, int len)};

%include "sum_rain.h"
```

The preceding code depends on the `numpy.i` interface file, which can be found at `https://github.com/numpy/numpy/blob/master/tools/swig/numpy.i`. In this example, the file was placed in the `/tmp` directory, but we can put this file almost anywhere. Generate the SWIG glue code with the following command:

```
$ swig -c++ -python sum_rain.i
```

The preceding step creates a sum_rain_wrap.cxx file. Compile the sum_rain.cpp file as follows:

```
$ g++ -O2 -fPIC -c sum_rain.cpp -I<Python headers dir>
```

In the previous command, we need to specify the actual Python C headers directory. We can find it with the following command:

```
$ python-config -includes
```

Therefore, we could have also compiled with the following command:

```
$ g++ -O2 -fPIC -c sum_rain.cpp -I $(python-config -includes)
```

The location of this directory will differ depending on Python version and operating system (it would be something like /usr/include/python2.7). Compile the generated SWIG wrapper file as follows:

```
$ g++ -O2 -fPIC -c sum_rain_wrap.cxx -I<Python headers dir>  -
I<numpy-dir>/core/include/
```

The preceding command depends on the location of the installed NumPy. Locate it from the Python shell as follows:

```
$ python
>>> import numpy as np
>>> np.__file__
```

The string printed on the screen should contain the Python version, site-packages, and end in __init__.pyc. If we strip the last part, we should have the NumPy directory. Alternatively, we can use the following code:

```
>>> from imp import find_module
>>> find_module('numpy')
```

The final step is to link the object files created by compiling:

```
$ g++ -lpython -dynamiclib sum_rain.o sum_rain_wrap.o -o _sum_rain.so
```

The preceding steps will work differently on other operating systems, such as Windows, unless we use Cygwin. It is recommended to ask for help on the SWIG user mailing lists (http://www.swig.org/mail.html) or StackOverflow, if required.

Test the created library with the swig_demo.py file in this book's code bundle:

```
from _sum_rain import *
import numpy as np

rain = np.load('rain.npy')
```

```
print "Swig", sum_rain(rain)
rain = .1 * rain
rain[rain < 0] = .025
print "Numpy", rain.sum()
```

If everything went fine and we didn't confuse Python installations, the following lines will be printed:

```
Swig 85291.55
Numpy 85291.55
```

Integrating Boost and Python

Boost is a C++ library that can interface with Python. Download it from `http://www.boost.org/users/download/`. The latest Boost version at the time of writing was 1.56.0. The easiest but also slowest installation method involves the following commands:

```
$ ./bootstrap.sh --prefix=/path/to/boost
$ ./b2 install
```

The `prefix` argument specifies the installation directory. In this example, we will assume that Boost was installed under the user's `home` directory in a directory called Boost (such as `~/Boost`). In this directory, a `lib` and `include` directory will be created. For Unix and Linux, it is useful to run the following command:

```
export LD_LIBRARY_PATH=$HOME/Boost/lib:${LD_LIBRARY_PATH}
```

On Mac OS X, set the following environment variable:

```
export DYLD_LIBRARY_PATH=$HOME/Boost/lib
```

Redefine a rain summation function as given in the `boost_rain.cpp` file in this book's code bundle:

```cpp
#include <boost/python.hpp>

double sum_rain(boost::python::list rain, int len) {

  double sum = 0.;

  for (int i = 0; i < len; i++){
    int val = boost::python::extract<int>(rain[i]);
    if(val == -1) {
      sum += 0.025;
```

```
        } else {
            sum += 0.1 * val;
        }
    }

    return sum;
}

BOOST_PYTHON_MODULE(rain) {
    using namespace boost::python;

    def("sum_rain", sum_rain);
}
```

The function accepts a Python list and the size of the list. Call the function from Python, as given in the rain_demo.py file in this book's code bundle:

```
import numpy as np
from rain import sum_rain

rain = np.load('../rain.npy')
print "Boost", sum_rain(rain.astype(int).tolist(), len(rain))
rain = .1 * rain
rain[rain < 0] = .025
print "Numpy", rain.sum()
```

We will automate the development process with the Makefile file in this book's code bundle:

```
CC = g++
PYLIBPATH = $(shell python-config --exec-prefix)/lib
LIB = -L$(PYLIBPATH) $(shell python-config --libs) -L ${HOME}/Boost/
lib -lboost_python
OPTS = $(shell python-config --include) -O2 -I${HOME}/Boost/include

default: rain.so
    @python ./rain_demo.py

rain.so: rain.o
    $(CC) $(LIB)  -Wl,-rpath,$(PYLIBPATH) -shared $< -o $@

rain.o: boost_rain.cpp Makefile
    $(CC) $(OPTS) -c $< -o $@

clean:
    rm -rf *.so *.o

.PHONY: default clean
```

From the command line, run the following commands:

```
$ make clean;make
```

The results are identical as expected:

```
Boost 85291.55
Numpy 85291.55
```

Using Fortran code through f2py

Fortran (from **Formula Translation System**) is a mature programming language mostly used for scientific computing. It was developed in the 1950s with newer versions emerging such as Fortran 77, Fortran 90, Fortran 95, Fortran 2003, and Fortran 2008 (refer to http://en.wikipedia.org/wiki/Fortran). Each version added features and new programming paradigms. We will need a Fortran compiler for this example. The **gfortran** compiler is a GNU Fortran compiler, which can be downloaded from http://gcc.gnu.org/wiki/GFortranBinaries.

The NumPy f2py module serves as an interface between Fortran and Python. If a Fortran compiler is present, we can create a shared library from Fortran code using this module. We will write a Fortran subroutine that is intended to sum rain amount values as given in the previous examples. Define the subroutine and store it in a Python string. After that, we can call the f2py.compile() function to produce a shared library from the Fortran code. The end product is in the fort_src.py file in this book's code bundle:

```
from numpy import f2py
fsource = '''
       subroutine sumarray(A, N)
       REAL, DIMENSION(N) :: A
       INTEGER :: N
       RES = 0.1 * SUM(A, MASK = A .GT. 0)
       RES2 = -0.025 * SUM(A, MASK = A .LT. 0)
       print*, RES + RES2
       end
  '''
f2py.compile(fsource,modulename='fort_sum',verbose=0)
```

Call the subroutine as given in the fort_demo.py file in this book's code bundle:

```
import fort_sum
import numpy as np
```

```
rain = np.load('rain.npy')
fort_sum.sumarray(rain, len(rain))
rain = .1 * rain
rain[rain < 0] = .025
print "Numpy", rain.sum()
```

The results of Fortran and NumPy agree as expected (we can ignore the last two digits printed by the Fortran subroutine):

```
85291.5547
Numpy 85291.55
```

Setting up Google App Engine

Cloud computing was briefly mentioned in the introduction to this chapter. **Google App Engine (GAE)** is one of the offerings in that area. GAE puts each application made by users in separate sandboxes located somewhere in the Google data centers (Google Cloud). GAE automatically scales application resources according to the number of requests. GAE supports several Python web frameworks and numerical software such as NumPy.

To use GAE, we need a Google account, which is free. Download the GAE tools and libraries for various operating systems from `https://developers.google.com/appengine/downloads`. From this web page, we can download documentation and the GAE Eclipse plugin as well. For developers who use the Eclipse IDE, the plugin is recommended. The GAE **Standard Development Kit (SDK)** provides a development environment, which mimics the Google Cloud. GAE at the moment supports Python 2.7 only. We can manage GAE apps either with Python scripts or using a GUI, which are part of the SDK.

Create a new application with the launcher (navigate to **File | New Application**). We will give the project the name `gaedemo`. In the corresponding folder, GAE creates configuration files and the `main.py` file, which serves as an entry point for the application. If we check `https://developers.google.com/appengine/docs/python/tools/libraries27`, we will see that NumPy and matplotlib are supported in GAE, although not the most recent versions. The matplotlib functionality is limited in GAE; for instance, we can't run the `show()` function. Add NumPy support as given in the `app.yaml` file in this book's code bundle:

```
application: gaedemo
version: 1
runtime: python27
```

```
api_version: 1
threadsafe: yes

handlers:
- url: /favicon\.ico
  static_files: favicon.ico
  upload: favicon\.ico

- url: .*
  script: main.app

libraries:
- name: webapp2
  version: "2.5.1"
- name: numpy
  version: "1.6.1"
```

Add some code that uses NumPy as given in the `main.py` file in this book's code bundle:

```
import webapp2
import numpy as np

class MainHandler(webapp2.RequestHandler):
    def get(self):
        self.response.out.write('Hello world!<br/>')
        np.random.seed(42)
        self.response.out.write('NumPy sum = ' + str(np.random.randn(7).sum()))

app = webapp2.WSGIApplication([('/', MainHandler)],
                                 debug=True)
```

If we click on the **Run** button and then click on the **Browse** button in the GAE launcher, we should see a web page with the following output in our web browser:

Hello world!
NumPy sum = 3.64009073018

Running programs on PythonAnywhere

PythonAnywhere is a Cloud service for Python development. The interface is completely web-based and simulates the Bash, Python, and IPython consoles. The support of Python versions and libraries is more varied compared to GAE. The preinstalled Python libraries are listed at `https://www.pythonanywhere.com/batteries_included/`.

The software version may lag a little behind the latest stable versions available, but not as much as GAE. At the time of writing, installing Python software from the PythonAnywhere Bash console appears a bit problematic and is not recommended.

It is recommended to upload Python source files instead of using the PythonAnywhere environment, as it is less responsive than our local environment. Upload files by clicking on the **Files** tab in the web application. Since rpy2 is supported, upload the r_demo.py file from this chapter. To execute the program, click on the **Consoles** tab and then click on the **Bash** link. Refer to the following screenshot for the end result:

```
18:18 ~ $ python r_demo.py
Kruskal (15.022124661246552, 0.0046555484175328015)
18:19 ~ $
```

Unfortunately, PythonAnywhere is not able to process the matplotlib show() function, so we can only print values on the console.

Working with Wakari

The Cloud service on https://wakari.io/ is similar to the PythonAnywhere website. The team behind **Wakari** has people on board who have actively contributed to SciPy and NumPy in the past. Once we have logged in, we are presented with the Wakari workspace. On the left in this workspace, we have a file browser that can also be used to upload files. On the right, we can open the Bash, Python, or IPython consoles.

You can clearly see the file browser in the following screenshot. Use the file browser to upload the r_demo.py file again.

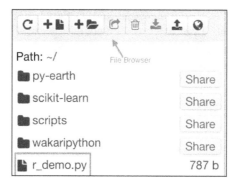

Run the program in a Python 2.7 console. Refer to the following screenshot for the end result:

```
[~]$ python r_demo.py
Kruskal (15.0221246661246552, 0.0046555484175328015)
Traceback (most recent call last):
  File "r_demo.py", line 17, in <module>
    plt.title('Speed of light')
  File "/opt/anaconda/envs/np18py27-1.9/lib/python2.7/site-packages/matplotlib/pyplot.py", line 1311, in title
    l =  gca().set_title(s, *args, **kwargs)
  File "/opt/anaconda/envs/np18py27-1.9/lib/python2.7/site-packages/matplotlib/pyplot.py", line 803, in gca
    ax =  gcf().gca(**kwargs)
  File "/opt/anaconda/envs/np18py27-1.9/lib/python2.7/site-packages/matplotlib/pyplot.py", line 450, in gcf
    return figure()
  File "/opt/anaconda/envs/np18py27-1.9/lib/python2.7/site-packages/matplotlib/pyplot.py", line 423, in figure
    **kwargs)
  File "/opt/anaconda/envs/np18py27-1.9/lib/python2.7/site-packages/matplotlib/backends/backend_qt4agg.py", line 31, in new_figure_manager
    return new_figure_manager_given_figure(num, thisFig)
  File "/opt/anaconda/envs/np18py27-1.9/lib/python2.7/site-packages/matplotlib/backends/backend_qt4agg.py", line 38, in new_figure_manager_given_figure
    canvas = FigureCanvasQTAgg(figure)
  File "/opt/anaconda/envs/np18py27-1.9/lib/python2.7/site-packages/matplotlib/backends/backend_qt4agg.py", line 70, in __init__
    FigureCanvasQT.__init__( self, figure )
  File "/opt/anaconda/envs/np18py27-1.9/lib/python2.7/site-packages/matplotlib/backends/backend_qt4.py", line 207, in __init__
    _create_qApp()
  File "/opt/anaconda/envs/np18py27-1.9/lib/python2.7/site-packages/matplotlib/backends/backend_qt4.py", line 62, in _create_qApp
    raise RuntimeError('Invalid DISPLAY variable')
RuntimeError: Invalid DISPLAY variable
```

As we can see, the matplotlib show() function causes an exception to be thrown this time.

Summary

We looked over the borders of Python in this chapter. Outside the Python ecosystem, programming languages such as R, C, Java, and Fortran are fairly popular. We checked out libraries that provide glue to connect Python with external code—rpy2 for R, SWIG and Boost for C, JPype for Java, and f2py for Fortran. Cloud computing aims to deliver computing power as a utility over the Internet. A brief overview of current Cloud computing services specialized in Python, including Google App Engine, PythonAnywhere, and Wakari was also given.

The next chapter, *Chapter 12, Performance Tuning, Profiling, and Concurrency*, gives hints on improving performance. Typically, we can speed up Python code by optimizing our code by using parallelization or rewriting parts of our code in C. We will discuss several profiling tools and concurrency APIs.

12
Performance Tuning, Profiling, and Concurrency

"Premature optimization is the root of all evil"

– Donald Knuth, a renowned computer scientist and mathematician

In the real world, there are more important things than performance, such as features, robustness, maintainability, testability, and usability. That's one of the reasons that we delayed discussing the topic of performance until the last chapter of the book. We will give hints on improving performance with profiling as the key technique. For multicore, distributed systems, we will discuss the relevant frameworks too. We will discuss the following topics in this chapter:

- Profiling the code
- Installing Cython
- Calling the C code
- Creating a pool process with multiprocessing
- Speeding up embarrassingly parallel for loops with Joblib
- Comparing Bottleneck to NumPy functions
- Performing MapReduce with Jug
- Installing MPI for Python
- IPython Parallel

Profiling the code

Profiling is about identifying parts of the code that are slow or use a lot of memory. We will profile a modified version of the `sentiment.py` code from *Chapter 9, Analyzing Textual Data and Social Media*. The code is refactored to comply with multiprocessing programming guidelines. You will learn about multiprocessing later in this chapter. Also, we simplified the stopwords filtering. The third change is to have fewer word features as the reduction doesn't impact accuracy. This last change has the most impact. The original code ran for about 20 seconds. The new code runs faster than that and will serve as the baseline in this chapter. Some changes have to do with profiling and will be explained later in this section. Please refer to the `prof_demo.py` file in this book's code bundle:

```python
import random
from nltk.corpus import movie_reviews
from nltk.corpus import stopwords
from nltk import FreqDist
from nltk import NaiveBayesClassifier
from nltk.classify import accuracy
from lprof_hack import profile


@profile
def label_docs():
    docs = [(list(movie_reviews.words(fid)), cat)
            for cat in movie_reviews.categories()
            for fid in movie_reviews.fileids(cat)]
    random.seed(42)
    random.shuffle(docs)

    return docs


@profile
def isStopWord(word):
    return word in sw or len(word) == 1


@profile
def filter_corpus():
    review_words = movie_reviews.words()
    print "# Review Words", len(review_words)
    res = [w.lower() for w in review_words if not
isStopWord(w.lower())]
    print "# After filter", len(res)

    return res
```

```
@profile
def select_word_features(corpus):
    words = FreqDist(corpus)
    N = int(.02 * len(words.keys()))
    return words.keys()[:N]

@profile
def doc_features(doc):
    doc_words = FreqDist(w for w in doc if not isStopWord(w))
    features = {}
    for word in word_features:
        features['count (%s)' % word] = (doc_words.get(word, 0))
    return features

@profile
def make_features(docs):
    return [(doc_features(d), c) for (d,c) in docs]

@profile
def split_data(sets):
    return sets[200:], sets[:200]

if __name__ == "__main__":
    labeled_docs = label_docs()

    sw = set(stopwords.words('english'))
    filtered = filter_corpus()
    word_features = select_word_features(filtered)
    featuresets = make_features(labeled_docs)
    train_set, test_set = split_data(featuresets)
    classifier = NaiveBayesClassifier.train(train_set)
    print "Accuracy", accuracy(classifier, test_set)
    print classifier.show_most_informative_features()
```

When we measure time, it helps to have as few processes running as possible. However, we can't be sure that nothing is running in the background, so we will take the lowest time measured from three measurements with the `time` command. This is a command available on various operating systems and Cygwin. Run the command as follows:

```
$ time python prof_demo.py
```

We get a *real* time, which is the time we would measure using a clock. The *user* and *sys* times measure the CPU time used by the program. The sys time is the time spent in the kernel. On my machine, the following times in seconds were obtained (the lowest values were placed between brackets):

Types of time	Run 1	Run 2	Run 3
real	(13.753)	14.090	13.916
user	(13.374)	13.732	13.583
sys	0.424	0.416	(0.373)

Profile the code with the standard Python profiler as follows:

```
$ python -m cProfile -o /tmp/stat.prof prof_demo.py
```

The -o switch specifies an output file. We can visualize the profiler output with the gprof2dot PyPi package. Install it as follows:

```
$ pip install gprof2dot
$ pip freeze|grep gprof2dot
gprof2dot==2014.08.05
```

Create a PNG visualization with the following command:

```
$ gprof2dot -f pstats /tmp/stat.prof |dot -Tpng -o /tmp/cprof.png
```

 If you get the error dot: command not found, it means that you don't have Graphviz installed. You can download Graphviz from http://www.graphviz.org/Download.php.

The full image is too large to display here; here is a small excerpt of it:

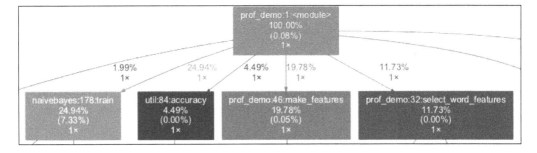

Query the profiler output as follows:

```
$ python -m pstats /tmp/stat.prof
```

With this command, we enter the profile statistics browser. Strip the filenames from the output, sort by time, and show the top 10 times:

```
/tmp/stat.prof% strip
/tmp/stat.prof% sort time
/tmp/stat.prof% stats 10
```

Refer to the following screenshot for the end result:

```
   ncalls  tottime  percall  cumtime  percall filename:lineno(function)
  2853946    3.140    0.000    4.186    0.000 probability.py:122(__setitem__)
   319975    2.528    0.000    2.528    0.000 {method 'findall' of '_sre.SRE_Pat
tern' objects}
  2855528    2.106    0.000    6.673    0.000 probability.py:107(inc)
        1    1.499    1.499    5.099    5.099 naivebayes.py:178(train)
     2001    0.962    0.000    5.440    0.003 probability.py:422(update)
        1    0.873    0.873    4.879    4.879 prof_demo.py:23(filter_corpus)
  3167640    0.847    0.000    0.979    0.000 prof_demo.py:19(isStopWord)
  7621042    0.803    0.000    0.803    0.000 {method 'get' of 'dict' objects}
  2857530    0.797    0.000    0.797    0.000 probability.py:452(_reset_caches)
  6343280    0.776    0.000    4.467    0.000 util.py:268(iterate_from)
```

The following is a description of the headers:

Headers	Description
ncalls	This is the number of calls.
tottime	This is the total time spent in the given function (excluding time made in calls to subfunctions).
percall	This is the quotient of tottime divided by ncalls.
cumtime	This is the total time spent in this and all subfunctions (from invocation till exit). This figure is accurate even for recursive functions.
percall (second)	This is the quotient of cumtime divided by primitive calls.

The line_profiler is another profiler we can use. This profiler is still in beta, but it can display statistics for each line in functions, which have been decorated with the @profile decorator. Also, it requires a workaround, which has been included in the lprof_hack.py file in this book's code bundle. The workaround is from an Internet forum (refer to https://stackoverflow.com/questions/18229628/ python-profiling-using-line-profiler-clever-way-to-remove-profile- statements). Install and run this profiler with the following commands:

```
$ pip install --pre line_profiler
$ kernprof.py -l -v prof_demo.py
```

The full report is too long to reproduce here; instead, the following is a per-function summary (there is some overlap):

```
Function: label_docs at line 9 Total time: 6.19904 s
Function: isStopWord at line 19 Total time: 2.16542 s
File: prof_demo.py Function: filter_corpus at line 23
Function: select_word_features at line 32 Total time: 4.05266 s
Function: doc_features at line 38 Total time: 12.5919 s
Function: make_features at line 46 Total time: 14.566 s
Function: split_data at line 50 Total time: 3.6e-05 s
```

Installing Cython

The **Cython** programming language acts as glue between Python and C/C++. With the Cython tools, we can compile plain Python code, which is closer to the machine level. The following command will install Cython:

```
$ pip install cython
```

The cytoolz package contains utilities created by Cythonizing the handy Python toolz package. Install cytoolz as follows:

```
$ pip install cytoolz
$ pip freeze|grep cytoolz
cytoolz==0.7.0
```

Just as in cooking shows, we will show the results of Cythonizing before going through the process involved (deferred to the next section). The `timeit` Python module measures time. We will use this module to measure different functions. Define the following function, which accepts as arguments a short code snippet, a function call, and the number of times the code will run:

```
def time(code, n):
    times = min(timeit.Timer(code, setup=setup).repeat(3, n))

    return round(1000* np.array(times)/n, 3)
```

We predefine a large setup string containing all the code. The code is in the `timeits.py` file in this book's code bundle (the code uses `cython_module` built on your machine):

```
import timeit
import numpy as np

setup = '''
```

```python
import nltk
import cython_module as cm
import collections
from nltk.corpus import stopwords
from nltk.corpus import movie_reviews
from nltk.corpus import names
import string
import pandas as pd
import cytoolz


sw = set(stopwords.words('english'))
punctuation = set(string.punctuation)
all_names = set([name.lower() for name in names.words()])
txt = movie_reviews.words(movie_reviews.fileids()[0])

def isStopWord(w):
    return w in sw or w in punctuation

def isStopWord2(w):
    return w in sw or w in punctuation or not w.isalpha()

def isStopWord3(w):
    return w in sw or len(w) == 1 or not w.isalpha() or w in
all_names

def isStopWord4(w):
    return w in sw or len(w) == 1

def freq_dict(words):
    dd = collections.defaultdict(int)

    for word in words:
        dd[word] += 1

    return dd

def zero_init():
    features = {}

    for word in set(txt):
        features['count (%s)' % word] = (0)

def zero_init2():
    features = {}
```

```
        for word in set(txt):
            features[word] = (0)

    keys = list(set(txt))

    def zero_init3():
        features = dict.fromkeys(keys, 0)

    zero_dict = dict.fromkeys(keys, 0)

    def dict_copy():
        features = zero_dict.copy()
    '''

    def time(code, n):
        times = min(timeit.Timer(code, setup=setup).repeat(3, n))

        return round(1000* np.array(times)/n, 3)

if __name__ == '__main__':
    print "Best of 3 times per loop in milliseconds"
    n = 10
    print "zero_init ", time("zero_init()", n)
    print "zero_init2", time("zero_init2()", n)
    print "zero_init3", time("zero_init3()", n)
    print "dict_copy ", time("dict_copy()", n)
    print

    n = 10**2
    print "isStopWord ", time('[w.lower() for w in txt if not
isStopWord(w.lower())]', n)
    print "isStopWord2", time('[w.lower() for w in txt if not
isStopWord2(w.lower())]', n)
    print "isStopWord3", time('[w.lower() for w in txt if not
isStopWord3(w.lower())]', n)
    print "isStopWord4", time('[w.lower() for w in txt if not
isStopWord4(w.lower())]', n)
    print "Cythonized isStopWord", time('[w.lower() for w in txt
if not cm.isStopWord(w.lower())]', n)
    print "Cythonized filter_sw()", time('cm.filter_sw(txt)', n)
    print
```

```
print "FreqDist", time("nltk.FreqDist(txt)", n)
print "Default dict", time('freq_dict(txt)', n)
print "Counter", time('collections.Counter(txt)', n)
print "Series", time('pd.Series(txt).value_counts()', n)
print "Cytoolz", time('cytoolz.frequencies(txt)', n)
print "Cythonized freq_dict", time('cm.freq_dict(txt)', n)
```

So, we have several `isStopword()` function versions with the following running times in milliseconds:

```
isStopWord   0.843
isStopWord2  0.902
isStopWord3  0.963
isStopWord4  0.869
Cythonized isStopWord 0.924
Cythonized filter_sw()  0.887
```

For comparison, we also have the time the running time of a plain `pass` statement. The Cythonized `isStopWord()` is based on the `isStopWord3()` function (the most elaborate filter). If we look at the `doc_features()` function in `prof_demo.py`, it becomes obvious that we shouldn't go over each word feature. Instead, we should just intersect the set of words in a document and the words chosen as features. All the other word counts can be safely set to zero. In fact, it's best if we initialize all the values to zero once and copy this dictionary. For the corresponding functions, we get the following execution times:

```
zero_init   0.61
zero_init2  0.555
zero_init3  0.017
dict_copy   0.011
```

Another improvement is to use the Python `defaultdict` class instead of the NLTK `FreqDist` class. The related routines have the following run times:

```
FreqDist 2.206
Default dict 0.674
Counter 0.79
Series 7.006
Cytoolz 0.542
Cythonized freq_dict 0.616
```

As we can see, the Cythonized versions are consistently faster, although not by much.

Calling C code

We can call C functions from Cython. The C string `strlen()` function is the equivalent of the Python `len()` function. Call this function from a Cython `.pyx` file by importing it as follows:

```
from libc.string cimport strlen
```

We can then call `strlen()` from somewhere else in the `.pyx` file. The `.pyx` file can contain any Python code. Have a look at the `cython_module.pyx` file in this book's code bundle:

```
from collections import defaultdict
from nltk.corpus import stopwords
from nltk.corpus import names
from libc.string cimport strlen

sw = set(stopwords.words('english'))
all_names = set([name.lower() for name in names.words()])

def isStopWord(w):
    return w in sw or strlen(w) == 1 or not w.isalpha() or w in
all_names

def filter_sw(words):
    return [w.lower() for w in words if not isStopWord(w.lower())]

def freq_dict(words):
    dd = defaultdict(int)

    for word in words:
        dd[word] += 1

    return dd
```

To compile this code we need a `setup.py` file with the following contents:

```
from distutils.core import setup
from Cython.Build import cythonize

setup(
    ext_modules = cythonize("cython_module.pyx")
)
```

Compile the code with the following command:

```
$ python setup.py build_ext -inplace
```

We can now modify the sentiment analysis program to call the Cython functions. We will also add the improvements mentioned in the previous section. As we are going to use some of the functions over and over again, these functions were extracted into the `core.py` file in this book's code bundle. Check out the `cython_demo.py` file in this book's code bundle (the code uses `cython_module` built on your machine):

```python
... NLTK imports omitted ...
import cython_module as cm
import cytoolz
from core import label_docs
from core import filter_corpus
from core import split_data


def select_word_features(corpus):
    words = cytoolz.frequencies(filtered)
    sorted_words = sorted(words, key=words.get)
    N = int(.02 * len(sorted_words))

    return sorted_words[-N:]

def match(a, b):
    return set(a.keys()).intersection(b)

def doc_features(doc):
    doc_words = cytoolz.frequencies(cm.filter_sw(doc))

    # initialize to 0
    features = zero_features.copy()

    word_matches = match(doc_words, word_features)

    for word in word_matches:
        features[word] = (doc_words[word])

    return features

def make_features(docs):
    return [(doc_features(d), c) for (d,c) in docs]

if __name__ == "__main__":
    labeled_docs = label_docs()
```

```
filtered = filter_corpus()
word_features = select_word_features(filtered)
zero_features = dict.fromkeys(word_features, 0)
featuresets = make_features(labeled_docs)
train_set, test_set = split_data(featuresets)
classifier = NaiveBayesClassifier.train(train_set)
print "Accuracy", accuracy(classifier, test_set)
print classifier.show_most_informative_features()
```

The following table summarizes the results of the `time` command (lowest values were placed between brackets):

Types of time	Run 1	Run 2	Run 3
real	(9.974)	9.995	10.024
user	(9.618)	9.682	9.713
sys	0.404	0.365	(0.36)

Creating a process pool with multiprocessing

Multiprocessing is a standard Python module that targets machines with multiple processors. Multiprocessing works around the **Global Interpreter Lock (GIL)** by creating multiple processes.

 The GIL locks Python bytecode so that only one thread can access it.

Multiprocessing supports process pools, queues, and pipes. A process pool is a pool of system processes that can execute a function in parallel. Queues are data structures that are usually used to store tasks. Pipes connect different processes in such a way that the output of one process becomes the input of another.

 Windows doesn't have an `os.fork()` function, so we need to make sure that outside the `if __name__ == "__main__"` block only imports and `def` blocks are defined.

Create a pool and register a function as follows:

```
p = mp.Pool(nprocs)
```

The pool has a `map()` method that is the parallel equivalent of the Python `map()` function:

```
p.map(simulate, [i for i in xrange(10, 50)])
```

We will simulate the movement of a particle in one dimension. The particle performs a random walk and we are interested in computing the average end position of the particle. We repeat this simulation for different walk lengths. The calculation itself is not important. The important part is to compare the speedup with multiple processes versus a single process. We will plot the speedup with matplotlib. The full code is in the `multiprocessing_sim.py` file in this book's code bundle:

```
from numpy.random import random_integers
from numpy.random import randn
import numpy as np
import timeit
import argparse
import multiprocessing as mp
import matplotlib.pyplot as plt


def simulate(size):
    n = 0
    mean = 0
    M2 = 0

    speed = randn(10000)

    for i in xrange(1000):
        n = n + 1
        indices = random_integers(0, len(speed)-1, size=size)
        x = (1 + speed[indices]).prod()
        delta = x - mean
        mean = mean + delta/n
        M2 = M2 + delta*(x - mean)

    return mean

def serial():
    start = timeit.default_timer()

    for i in xrange(10, 50):
        simulate(i)

    end = timeit.default_timer() - start
    print "Serial time", end

    return end
```

```
def parallel(nprocs):
    start = timeit.default_timer()
    p = mp.Pool(nprocs)
    print nprocs, "Pool creation time", timeit.default_timer() -
start

    p.map(simulate, [i for i in xrange(10, 50)])
    p.close()
    p.join()

    end = timeit.default_timer() - start
    print nprocs, "Parallel time", end
    return end

if __name__ == "__main__":
    ratios = []
    baseline = serial()

    for i in xrange(1, mp.cpu_count()):
        ratios.append(baseline/parallel(i))

    plt.xlabel('# processes')
    plt.ylabel('Serial/Parallel')
    plt.plot(np.arange(1, mp.cpu_count()), ratios)
    plt.grid(True)
    plt.show()
```

If we take the speedup values for process pool sizes ranging from 1 to 8 (the number of processors is hardware dependent), we get the following figure:

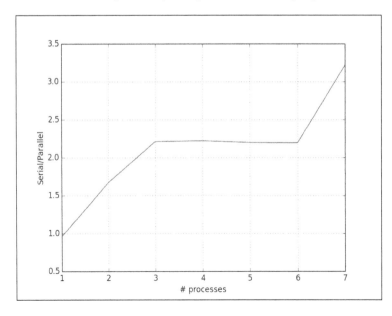

Amdahl's law (see http://en.wikipedia.org/wiki/Amdahl%27s_law) best describes the speedups due to parallelization. This law predicts the maximum possible speedup. The number of processes limits the absolute maximum speedup. However, as we can see in the preceding plot, we don't get a doubling of speed with two processes nor does using three processes triple the speed, but we come close. Some parts of any given Python code may be impossible to parallelize. For example, we may need to wait for a resource to become available or we may be performing a calculation that has to be performed sequentially. We also have to take into account overhead from parallelization setup and related interprocess communication. Amdahl's law states that there is a linear relationship between the inverse of the speedup, the inverse of the number of processes, and the portion of the code, which cannot be parallelized.

Speeding up embarrassingly parallel for loops with Joblib

Joblib is a Python library created by the developers of scikit-learn. Its main mission is to improve the performance of long-running Python functions. Joblib achieves the improvements through caching and parallelization using multiprocessing or threading under the hood. Install Joblib as follows:

```
$ pip install joblib
$ pip freeze|grep joblib
joblib==0.8.2
```

We will reuse the code from the previous example only changing the `parallel()` function. Refer to the `joblib_demo.py` file in this book's code bundle:

```
def parallel(nprocs):
    start = timeit.default_timer()
    Parallel(nprocs)(delayed(simulate)(i) for i in xrange(10, 50))

    end = timeit.default_timer() - start
    print nprocs, "Parallel time", end
    return end
```

Refer to the following plot for the end result (the number of processors is hardware-dependent):

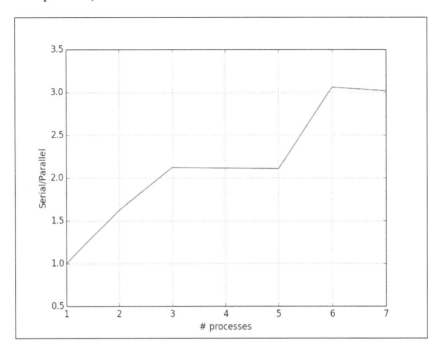

Comparing Bottleneck to NumPy functions

Bottleneck is a set of functions inspired by NumPy and SciPy, but written in Cython with high performance in mind. Bottleneck provides separate Cython functions for each combination of array dimensions, axis, and data type. This is not shown to the end user and the limiting factor for Bottleneck is to determine which Cython function to execute. Install Bottleneck as follows:

```
$ pip install bottleneck
```

We will compare the execution times for the `numpy.median()` and `scipy.stats.rankdata()` functions in relation to their Bottleneck counterparts. It can be useful to determine the Cython function manually before using it in a tight loop or frequently called function. Print the name of the Bottleneck `median()` function as follows:

```
func, _ = bn.func.median_selector(a, axis=0)
print "Bottleneck median func name", func
```

For the `rankdata()` function, we can do the following:

```
func, _ = bn.func.rankdata_selector(a, axis=0)
print "Bottleneck rankdata func name", func
```

This program is given in the `bn_demo.py` file in this book's code bundle:

```
import bottleneck as bn
import numpy as np
import timeit


setup = '''
import numpy as np
import bottleneck as bn
from scipy.stats import rankdata

np.random.seed(42)
a = np.random.randn(30)
'''
def time(code, setup, n):
    return timeit.Timer(code, setup=setup).repeat(3, n)

if __name__ == '__main__':
    n = 10**3
    print n, "pass", max(time("pass", "", n))
    print n, "min np.median", min(time('np.median(a)', setup, n))
    print n, "min bn.median", min(time('bn.median(a)', setup, n))
    a = np.arange(7)
    print "Median diff", np.median(a) - bn.median(a)
    func, _ = bn.func.median_selector(a, axis=0)
    print "Bottleneck median func name", func

    print n, "min scipy.stats.rankdata", min(time('rankdata(a)',
setup, n))
    print n, "min bn.rankdata", min(time('bn.rankdata(a)', setup,
n))
    func, _ = bn.func.rankdata_selector(a, axis=0)
    print "Bottleneck rankdata func name", func
```

The following is the output with running times and function names:

```
1000 pass 1.4066696167e-05
1000 min np.median 0.0271320343018
1000 min bn.median 0.00440287590027
Median diff 0.0
Bottleneck median func name <built-in function median_1d_int64_axis0>
1000 min scipy.stats.rankdata 0.0171868801117
```

```
1000 min bn.rankdata 0.00528407096863
Bottleneck rankdata func name <built-in function
rankdata_1d_int64_axis0>
```

Clearly, Bottleneck is very fast; unfortunately, due to its setup, Bottleneck doesn't have that many functions yet. The following table lists the implemented functions from `http://pypi.python.org/pypi/Bottleneck`:

Category	Functions
NumPy/SciPy	median, nanmedian, rankdata, ss, nansum, nanmin, nanmax, nanmean, nanstd, nanargmin, and nanargmax
Functions	nanrankdata, nanvar, partsort, argpartsort, replace, nn, anynan, and allnan
Moving window	move_sum, move_nansum, move_mean, move_nanmean, move_median, move_std, move_nanstd, move_min, move_nanmin, move_max, and move_nanmax

Performing MapReduce with Jug

Jug is a distributed computing framework that uses tasks as central parallelization units. As backends, Jug uses filesystems or the Redis server. The Redis server was discussed in *Chapter 8, Working with Databases*. Install Jug with the following command:

```
$ pip install jug
```

MapReduce (see `http://en.wikipedia.org/wiki/MapReduce`) is a distributed algorithm used to process large datasets with a cluster of computers. The algorithm consists of a **Map** and a **Reduce** phase. During the Map phase, data is processed in a parallel fashion. The data is split up in parts and on each part, filtering or other operations are performed. In the Reduce phase, the results from the Map phase are aggregated, for instance, to create a statistics report.

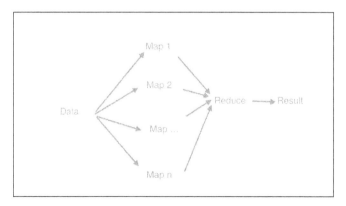

If we have a list of text files, we can compute word counts for each file. This can be done during the Map phase. At the end, we can combine individual word counts into a corpus word frequency dictionary. Jug has MapReduce functionality, which is demonstrated in the `jug_demo.py` file in this book's code bundle (the code depends on the `cython_module` artifact):

```python
import jug.mapreduce
from jug.compound import CompoundTask
import cython_module as cm
import cytoolz
import cPickle


def get_txts():
    return [(1, 'Lorem ipsum dolor sit amet, consectetur
adipiscing elit.'), (2, 'Donec a elit pharetra, malesuada massa
vitae, elementum dolor.'), (3, 'Integer a tortor ac mi vehicula
tempor at a nunc.')]


def freq_dict(file_words):
    filtered = cm.filter_sw(file_words[1].split())

    fd = cytoolz.frequencies(filtered)

    return fd


def merge(left, right):
    return cytoolz.merge_with(sum, left, right)


merged_counts = CompoundTask(jug.mapreduce.mapreduce, merge, freq_
dict, get_txts(), map_step=1)
```

In the preceding code, the `merge()` function is called during the Reduce phase and the `freq_dict()` function is called during the Map phase. We define a Jug `CompoundTask` consisting of multiple subtasks. Before we run this code, we need to start a Redis server. Perform MapReduce by issuing the following command:

```
$ jug execute jug_demo.py --jugdir=redis://127.0.0.1/&
```

The ampersand (&) at the end means that this command runs in the background. We can issue the command from multiple computers in this manner, if the Redis server is accessible in the network. In this example, Redis only runs on the local machine (127.0.0.1 is the IP address of the localhost). However, we can still run the command multiple times locally. We can check the status of the Jug command as follows:

```
$ jug status jug_demo.py
```

By default, Jug stores data in the current working directory if we don't specify the `jugdir` option. Clean the Jug directory with the following command:

```
$ jug cleanup jug_demo.py
```

To query Redis and perform the rest of the analysis, we will use another program. In this program, initialize Jug as follows:

```
jug.init('jug_demo.py', 'redis://127.0.0.1/')
import jug_demo
```

The following line gets the results from the Reduce phase:

```
words = jug.task.value(jug_demo.merged_counts)
```

The rest of the code is given in the `jug_redis.py` file in this book's code bundle:

```
import jug


def main():
    jug.init('jug_demo.py', 'redis://127.0.0.1/')
    import jug_demo
    print "Merged counts", jug.task.value(jug_demo.merged_counts)

if __name__ == "__main__":
    main()
```

Installing MPI for Python

The **Message Passing Interface** (**MPI**) (see `http://en.wikipedia.org/wiki/Message_Passing_Interface`) is a standard protocol developed by experts to work on a broad assortment of distributed machines. Originally, in the '90s, MPI was used to write programs in Fortran and C. MPI is independent of hardware and programming languages. MPI functions include the send and receive operations, MapReduce functionality, and synchronization. MPI has point-to-point functions involving two processors and operations involving all processors. MPI has bindings for several programming languages, including Python. Download MPI from `http://www.open-mpi.org/software/ompi/v1.8/` `1.8.1`. MPI 1.8.1 was the latest MPI version at the time of writing. We can check on the website whether there is a newer version available. Installing MPI can take a while (nearly 30 minutes). The following are the commands involved, assuming that we install it in the `/usr/local` directory:

```
$ ./configure --prefix=/usr/local
$ make all
$ sudo make install
```

Install Python bindings for MPI as follows:

```
$ pip install mpi4py
$ pip freeze|grep mpi4py
mpi4py==1.3.1
```

IPython Parallel

IPython Parallel is the IPython API for parallel computing. We will set it up to use MPI for message passing. We may have to set environment variables as follows:

```
$ export LC_ALL=en_US.UTF-8
$ export LANG=en_US.UTF-8
```

Issue the following command at the command line:

```
$ ipython profile create --parallel --profile=mpi
```

The preceding command will create a file in our home directory, which can be found at `.ipython/profile_mpi/iplogger_config.py`.

Add the following line in this file:

```
c.IPClusterEngines.engine_launcher_class = 'MPIEngineSetLauncher'
```

Start a cluster that uses the MPI profile as follows:

```
$ ipcluster start --profile=mpi --engines=MPI --debug
```

The preceding command specifies that we are using the `mpi` profile and MPI engine with debug-level logging. We can now interact with the cluster from an IPython Notebook. Start a notebook with plotting enabled and with NumPy, SciPy, and matplotlib automatically imported as follows:

```
$ ipython notebook --profile=mpi --log-level=DEBUG --pylab inline
```

The preceding command uses the `mpi` profile with debug log level. The notebook for this example is stored in the `IPythonParallel.ipynb` file in this book's code bundle. Import the IPython Parallel `Client` class and the `statsmodels.api` module as follows:

```
In [1]:from IPython.parallel import Client
import statsmodels.api as sm
```

Load the sunspots data and calculate the mean:

```
In [2]: data_loader = sm.datasets.sunspots.load_pandas()
vals = data_loader.data['SUNACTIVITY'].values
glob_mean = vals.mean()
glob_mean
```

The following will be output:

`Out [2]: 49.752103559870541`

Create a client as follows:

```
In [3]: c = Client(profile='mpi')
```

Create a view to the clients with the following line:

```
In [4]: view=c[:]
```

IPython has the concept of **magics**. These are special commands specific to IPython notebooks. Enable magics as follows:

```
In [5]: view.activate()
```

Load the `mpi_ipython.py` file in this book's code bundle:

```
from mpi4py import MPI
from numpy.random import random_integers
from numpy.random import randn
import numpy as np
import statsmodels.api as sm
import bottleneck as bn
import logging


def jackknife(a, parallel=True):
    data_loader = sm.datasets.sunspots.load_pandas()
    vals = data_loader.data['SUNACTIVITY'].values

    func, _ = bn.func.nanmean_selector(vals, axis=0)
    results = []

    for i in a:
        tmp = np.array(vals.tolist())
        tmp[i] = np.nan
        results.append(func(tmp))
```

```
        results = np.array(results)

    if parallel:
        comm = MPI.COMM_WORLD
        rcvBuf = np.zeros(0.0, 'd')
        comm.gather([results, MPI.DOUBLE], [rcvBuf, MPI.DOUBLE])

    return results

if __name__ == "__main__":
    skiplist = np.arange(39, dtype='int')
    print jackknife(skiplist, False)
```

The preceding program contains a function, which performs **jackknife resampling**. Jackknife resampling is a type of resampling where we omit one of the observations in the sample and then calculate the statistical estimator we are interested in. In this case, we are interested in the mean. We leave one observation out by setting it to NumPy NaN. Then, we call the Bottleneck nanmean() function on the new sample. The following is the load command:

```
In [6]: view.run('mpi_ipython.py')
```

Next, we split and spread an array with all the indices of the sunspots array:

```
In [7]: view.scatter('a',np.arange(len(vals),dtype='int'))
```

The a array can be displayed in the notebook as follows:

```
In [8]: view['a']
```

Here is the output of the preceding command:

```
Out[8]:[array([ 0,  1,  2,  3,  4,  5,  6,  7,  8,  9, 10, 11, 12,
13, 14, 15, 16,  17, 18, 19, 20, 21, 22, 23, 24, 25, 26, 27, 28, 29,
30, 31, 32, 33,  34, 35, 36, 37, 38]), ... TRUNCATED ...]
```

Call the jackknife() function on all the clients:

```
In [9]: %px means = jackknife(a)
```

Once all the worker processes are done, we can view the result:

```
In [10]: view['means']
```

The result is a list of as many processes as we started. Each process returns a NumPy array containing means calculated by jackknife resampling. This structure is not very useful, so transform it into a flat list:

```
In [11]: all_means = []

for v in view['means']:
    all_means.extend(v)

mean(all_means)
```

You will get the following output:

```
Out [11]: 49.752103559870577
```

We can also compute the standard deviation, but that is easy so we will skip it. It's much more interesting to plot a histogram of the jackknifed means:

```
In [13]: hist(all_means, bins=sqrt(len(all_means)))
```

Refer to the following plot for the end result:

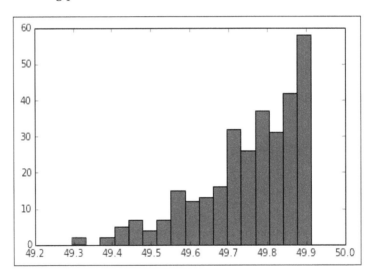

For troubleshooting, we can use the following line that displays error messages from the worker processes:

```
In [14]: [(k, c.metadata[k]['started'], c.metadata[k]['pyout'],
c.metadata[k]['pyerr']) for k in c.metadata.keys()]
```

Summary

In this chapter, we tuned the performance of the sentiment analysis script from *Chapter 9, Analyzing Textual Data and Social Media*. Using profiling, Cython, and various improvements, we doubled the execution speed of that example. We also used multiprocessing, Joblib, Jug, and MPI via IPython Parallel to take advantage of parallelization.

This was the last chapter of this book. After the appendices and the index, there is only the back cover. Of course, the learning process will not stop. Change the code to suit your needs. It's always nice to have a private data analysis project, even if it is just for practice. If you can't think of a project, join a competition on `http://www.kaggle.com/`. They have several competitions with nice prizes. If you are interested in NumPy, you can look forward to the second edition of *NumPy Cookbook, Ivan Idris, Packt Publishing*, which is planned for 2015.

A
Key Concepts

This appendix gives a brief overview and glossary of technical concepts used throughout the book.

Amdahl's law predicts the maximum possible speedup due to parallelization. The number of processes limits the absolute maximum speedup. Some parts of any given Python code might be impossible to parallelize. We also have to take into account overhead from parallelization setup and related interprocess communication. Amdahl's law states that there is a linear relationship between the inverse of the speedup, the inverse of the number of processes, and the portion of the code that cannot be parallelized.

ARMA models combine autoregressive and moving average models. They are used to forecast future values of time series.

Artificial Neural Networks (ANN) are models inspired by the animal brain. A neural network is a network of neurons — units with inputs and outputs. The output of a neuron can be passed to a neuron and so on, thus creating a multilayered network. Neural networks contain adaptive elements, making them suitable to deal with nonlinear models and pattern recognition problems.

Augmented Dickey Fuller (ADF) test is a statistical test related to cointegration.

Autocorrelation is the correlation within a dataset and can indicate a trend. For example, if we have a lag of one period, we can check whether the previous value influences the current value. For that to be true, the autocorrelation value has to be pretty high.

Autocorrelation plots graph **autocorrelations** of time series data for different lags. Autocorrelation is the correlation of a time series with the same lagged time series.

The **autoregressive model** is a model that uses (usually linear) regression to forecast future values of a time series using previous values. Autoregressive models are a special case of the ARMA models. They are equivalent to ARMA models with zero moving average components.

The **bag-of-words model** is a simplified model of text, in which the text is represented by a bag of words. In this representation, the order of the words is ignored. Typically, word counts or the presence of certain words are used as features in this model.

Bubble charts are an extension of the scatter plot. In a bubble chart, the value of a third variable is represented by the size of the bubble surrounding a data point.

Cassandra Query Language (**CQL**) is a query language for Apache Cassandra with a syntax similar to SQL.

Cointegration is similar to correlation and is a statistical characteristic of time series data. Cointegration is a measure of how synchronized two time series are.

Clustering aims to partition data into groups called clusters. Clustering is usually unsupervised in the sense that the training data is not labeled. Some clustering algorithms require a guess for the number of clusters, while other algorithms don't.

CSS (**Cascading Style Sheets**) is a language used to style elements of a web page. CSS is maintained and developed by the World Wide Web Consortium.

CSS selectors are rules used to select content in a web page.

Character codes are included in NumPy for backward compatibility with **Numeric**. Numeric is the predecessor of NumPy.

Data type objects are instances of the `numpy.dtype` class. They provide an object-oriented interface for manipulation of NumPy data types.

Eigenvalues are scalar solutions to the equation $Ax = ax$, where A is a two-dimensional matrix and x is a one-dimensional vector.

Eigenvectors are vectors corresponding to eigenvalues.

The **exponential moving average** is a type of moving average with exponentially decreasing weights with time.

Fast Fourier Transform (**FFT**) is a fast algorithm to compute the Fourier transform. FFT is O(N log N), which is a huge improvement over older algorithms.

Filtering is a type of signal-processing technique, which involves removing or suppressing part of the signal. Many filter types exist including the median and Wiener filter.

Fourier analysis is based on the **Fourier series** named after the mathematician Joseph Fourier. The Fourier series is a mathematical method to represent functions as an infinite series of sine and cosine terms. The functions in question can be real or complex valued.

Genetic algorithms are based on the biological theory of evolution. This type of algorithms is useful for searching and optimization.

Graphical Processor Units (GPUs) are specialized circuits used to display graphics efficiently. Recently, GPUs have been used to perform massively parallel computations (for instance, to train neural networks).

The **Hierarchical Data Format (HDF)** is a specification and technology for the storage of big numerical data. The HDF group maintains a related software library.

The **Hilbert-Huang transform** is a mathematical algorithm to decompose a signal. This method can be used to detect periodic cycles in time series data. It was used successfully to determine sunspot cycles.

HyperText Markup Language (HTML) is the fundamental technology used to create web pages. It defines tags for media, text, and hyperlinks.

The **Internet Engineering Task Force (IETF)** is an open group working on maintaining and developing the Internet. IETF is open in the sense that anybody can join in principle.

JavaScript Object Notation (JSON) is a data format. In this format, data is written down using JavaScript notation. JSON is more succinct than other data formats such as XML.

k-fold cross-validation is a form of cross-validation involving k (a small integer number) random data partitions called **folds**. In k iterations, each fold is used once for validation and the rest of the data is used for training. The results of the iterations can be combined at the end.

Kruskal-Wallis one-way analysis of variance is a statistical method that analyzes sample variance without making assumptions about their distributions.

The **lag plot** is a scatter plot for a time series and the same time series lagged. A lag plot shows autocorrelation within time series data for a certain lag.

The **learning curve** is a way to visualize the behavior of a learning algorithm. It is a plot of training and test scores for a range of train data sizes.

Logarithmic plots (or log plots) are plots that use a logarithmic scale. This type of plots is useful when the data varies a lot because they display orders of magnitude.

Logistic regression is a type of a classification algorithm. This algorithm can be used to predict probabilities associated with a class or an event occurring. Logistic regression is based on the **logistic function**, which has values in the range between zero and one, just like in probabilities. The logistic function can therefore be used to transform arbitrary values into probabilities.

MapReduce is a distributed algorithm used to process large datasets with a cluster of computers. The algorithm consists of **Map** and **Reduce** phases. During the Map phase, data is processed in parallel fashion. The data is split up in parts and on each part, filtering or other operations are performed. In the Reduce phase, the results from the Map phase are aggregated.

Moore's law is the observation that the number of transistors in a modern computer chip doubles every two years. This trend has continued since Moore's law formulation around 1970. There is also a second Moore's law, which is also known as Rock's law. This law states that the cost of R & D and manufacturing of integrated circuits increases exponentially.

Moving averages specify a window of previously seen data that is averaged each time the window slides forward by one period. The different types of moving average differ essentially in the weights used for averaging.

Naive Bayes classification is a probabilistic classification algorithm based on Bayes theorem from probability theory and statistics. It is called naive because of its strong independence assumptions.

Object-relational mapping (ORM) is a software architecture pattern for translation between database schemas and object-oriented programming languages.

Opinion mining or **sentiment analysis** is a research field with the goal of efficiently finding and evaluating opinions and sentiments in text.

Part of Speech (POS) tags are tags for each word in a sentence. These tags have a grammatical meaning such as a verb or noun.

REST (Representational State Transfer) is an architectural style for web services.

RSS (Really Simple Syndication) is a standard for the publication and retrieval of web feeds such as blogs.

The **scatter plot** is a two-dimensional plot showing the relationship between two variables in a Cartesian coordinate system. The values of one variable are represented on one axis and the values of the other variable are represented by the other axis. We can quickly visualize correlation this way.

Signal processing is a field of engineering and applied mathematics that handles the analysis of analog and digital signals, corresponding to variables that vary with time.

SQL is a specialized language for relational database querying and manipulation. This includes creating tables, inserting rows in tables, and deleting tables.

Stopwords are common words with low-information value. Stopwords are usually removed before analyzing text. Although filtering stopwords is a common practice, there is no standard definition for stopwords.

Supervised learning is a type of machine learning that requires labeled training data.

Support vector machines (**SVM**) can be used for regression (SVR) and classification (SVC). SVM maps the data points to points in a multidimensional space. The mapping is performed by a so-called **kernel function**. The kernel function can be linear or nonlinear.

Term frequency-inverse document frequency (**tf-idf**) is a metric measuring the importance of a word in a corpus. It is composed of a term frequency number and an inverse document frequency number. The term frequency counts the number of times a word occurs in a document. The inverse document frequency counts the number of documents in which the word occurs and takes the inverse of the number.

A **time series** is an ordered list of data points starting with the oldest measurements first. Usually, each data point has a related timestamp.

B
Useful Functions

This appendix lists useful functions organized by packages for matplotlib, NumPy, pandas, scikit-learn, and SciPy.

matplotlib

The following are useful matplotlib functions:

- `matplotlib.pyplot.axis(*v, **kwargs)`: This is the method to get or set axis properties. For example, `axis('off')` turns off the axis lines and labels.

- `matplotlib.pyplot.figure(num=None, figsize=None, dpi=None, facecolor=None, edgecolor=None, frameon=True, FigureClass=<class 'matplotlib.figure.Figure'>, **kwargs)`: This function creates a new figure.

- `matplotlib.pyplot.grid(b=None, which='major', axis='both', **kwargs)`: This function turns the plot grids on or off.

- `matplotlib.pyplot.hist(x, bins=10, range=None, normed=False, weights=None, cumulative=False, bottom=None, histtype='bar', align='mid', orientation='vertical', rwidth=None, log=False, color=None, label=None, stacked=False, hold=None, **kwargs)`: This function plots a histogram.

- `matplotlib.pyplot.imshow(X, cmap=None, norm=None, aspect=None, interpolation=None, alpha=None, vmin=None, vmax=None, origin=None, extent=None, shape=None, filternorm=1, filterrad=4.0, imlim=None, resample=None, url=None, hold=None, **kwargs)`: This function displays an image for array-like data.

- `matplotlib.pyplot.legend(*args, **kwargs)`: This function shows a legend at an optionally specified location (for instance, `plt.legend(loc='best')`).

- `matplotlib.pyplot.plot(*args, **kwargs)`: This function creates a two-dimensional plot with single or multiple (x, y) pairs and a corresponding optional format string.

- `matplotlib.pyplot.scatter(x, y, s=20, c='b', marker='o', cmap=None, norm=None, vmin=None, vmax=None, alpha=None, linewidths=None, verts=None, hold=None, **kwargs)`: This function creates a scatter plot of two arrays.

- `matplotlib.pyplot.show(*args, **kw)`: This function displays a plot.

- `matplotlib.pyplot.subplot(*args, **kwargs)`: This function creates subplots if the row number, column number, and index number of the plot are given. All these numbers start from one. For instance, `plt.subplot(221)` creates the first subplot in a two-by-two grid.

- `matplotlib.pyplot.title(s, *args, **kwargs)`: This function puts a title on the plot.

NumPy

The following are useful NumPy functions:

- `numpy.arange([start,] stop[, step,], dtype=None)`: This function creates a NumPy array with evenly spaced values within a specified range.

- `numpy.argsort(a, axis=-1, kind='quicksort', order=None)`: This function returns the indices that will sort the input array.

- `numpy.array(object, dtype=None, copy=True, order=None, subok=False, ndmin=0)`: This function creates a NumPy array from an array-like sequence such as a Python list.

- `numpy.dot(a, b, out=None)`: This function calculates the dot product of two arrays.

- `numpy.eye(N, M=None, k=0, dtype=<type 'float'>)`: This function returns the identity matrix.

- `numpy.load(file, mmap_mode=None)`: This function loads NumPy arrays or pickled objects from .npy, .npz, or pickles. A memory-mapped array is stored in the filesystem and doesn't have to be completely loaded in the memory. This is especially useful for large arrays.

- `numpy.loadtxt(fname, dtype=<type 'float'>, comments='#', delimiter=None, converters=None, skiprows=0, usecols=None, unpack=False, ndmin=0)`: This function loads data from a text file into a NumPy array.

- `numpy.mean(a, axis=None, dtype=None, out=None, keepdims=False)`: This function calculates the arithmetic mean along the given axis.

- `numpy.median(a, axis=None, out=None, overwrite_input=False)`: This function calculates the median along the given axis.

- `numpy.ones(shape, dtype=None, order='C')`: This function creates a NumPy array of a specified shape and data type, containing ones.

- `numpy.polyfit(x, y, deg, rcond=None, full=False, w=None, cov=False)`: This function performs a least squares polynomial fit.

- `numpy.reshape(a, newshape, order='C')`: This function changes the shape of a NumPy array.

- `numpy.save(file, arr)`: This function saves a NumPy array to a file in the NumPy `.npy` format.

- `numpy.savetxt(fname, X, fmt='%.18e', delimiter=' ', newline='\n', header='', footer='', comments='# ')`: This function saves a NumPy array to a text file.

- `numpy.std(a, axis=None, dtype=None, out=None, ddof=0, keepdims=False)`: This function returns the standard deviation along the given axis.

- `numpy.where(condition, [x, y])`: This function selects array elements from input arrays based on a Boolean condition.

- `numpy.zeros(shape, dtype=float, order='C')`: This function creates a NumPy array of a specified shape and data type, containing zeros.

pandas

The following are useful pandas functions:

- `pandas.date_range(start=None, end=None, periods=None, freq='D', tz=None, normalize=False, name=None, closed=None)`: This function creates a fixed frequency date-time index

- `pandas.isnull(obj)`: This function finds NaN and None values

- `pandas.merge(left, right, how='inner', on=None, left_on=None, right_on=None, left_index=False, right_index=False, sort=False, suffixes=('_x', '_y'), copy=True)`: This function merges the DataFrame objects with a database-like join on columns or indices

- `pandas.pivot_table(data, values=None, rows=None, cols=None, aggfunc='mean', fill_value=None, margins=False, dropna=True)`: This function creates a spreadsheet-like pivot table as a pandas DataFrame

- `pandas.read_csv(filepath_or_buffer, sep=',', dialect=None, compression=None, doublequote=True, escapechar=None, quotechar='"', quoting=0, skipinitialspace=False, lineterminator=None, header='infer', index_col=None, names=None, prefix=None, skiprows=None, skipfooter=None, skip_footer=0, na_values=None, na_fvalues=None, true_values=None, false_values=None, delimiter=None, converters=None, dtype=None, usecols=None, engine='c', delim_whitespace=False, as_recarray=False, na_filter=True, compact_ints=False, use_unsigned=False, low_memory=True, buffer_lines=None, warn_bad_lines=True, error_bad_lines=True, keep_default_na=True, thousands=Nment=None, decimal='.', parse_dates=False, keep_date_col=False, dayfirst=False, date_parser=None, memory_map=False, nrows=None, iterator=False, chunksize=None, verbose=False, encoding=None, squeeze=False, mangle_dupe_cols=True, tupleize_cols=False, infer_datetime_format=False):` This function creates a `DataFrame` from a CSV file

- `pandas.read_excel(io, sheetname, **kwds):` This function reads an Excel worksheet into a `DataFrame`

- `pandas.read_hdf(path_or_buf, key, **kwargs):` This function returns a pandas object from an HDF store

- `pandas.read_json(path_or_buf=None, orient=None, typ='frame', dtype=True, convert_axes=True, convert_dates=True, keep_default_dates=True, numpy=False, precise_float=False, date_unit=None):` This function creates a pandas object from a JSON string

- `pandas.to_datetime(arg, errors='ignore', dayfirst=False, utc=None, box=True, format=None, coerce=False, unit='ns', infer_datetime_format=False):` This function converts a string or list of strings to datetime

Scikit-learn

The following are useful scikit-learn functions:

- `sklearn.cross_validation.train_test_split(*arrays, **options):` This function splits arrays into random train and test sets

- `sklearn.metrics.accuracy_score(y_true, y_pred, normalize=True, sample_weight=None):` This function returns the accuracy classification score

- `sklearn.metrics.euclidean_distances (X, Y=None, Y_norm_squared=None, squared=False):` This function computes the distance matrix for the input data

SciPy

This section shows useful SciPy functions:

scipy.fftpack

- `fftshift(x, axes=None)`: This function shifts the zero-frequency component to the center of the spectrum

- `rfft(x, n=None, axis=-1, overwrite_x=0)`: This function performs a discrete Fourier transform of an array containing real values

scipy.signal

- `detrend(data, axis=-1, type='linear', bp=0)`: This function removes the linear trend or a constant from the data

- `medfilt(volume, kernel_size=None)`: This function applies a median filter on an array

- `wiener(im, mysize=None, noise=None)`: This function applies a Wiener filter on an array

scipy.stats

- `anderson(x, dist='norm')`: This function performs the Anderson-Darling test for data coming from a specified distribution

- `kruskal(*args)`: This function performs the Kruskal-Wallis H test for data

- `normaltest(a, axis=0)`: This function tests whether data complies to the normal distribution

- `scoreatpercentile(a, per, limit=(), interpolation_method='fraction')`: This function computes the score at a specified percentile of the input array

- `shapiro(x, a=None, reta=False)`: This function applies the Shapiro-Wilk test for normality

C
Online Resources

The following is a list of links to documentation, forums, articles, and other information:

- The Apache Cassandra database: `http://cassandra.apache.org`
- Beautiful Soup: `http://www.crummy.com/software/BeautifulSoup`
- The HDF Group website: `http://www.hdfgroup.org`
- A gallery of interesting IPython notebooks: `https://github.com/ipython/ipython/wiki/A-gallery-of-interesting-IPython-Notebooks`
- The Graphviz open source graph visualization software: `http://graphviz.org/`
- The IPython website: `http://ipython.org/`
- matplotlib (a Python plotting library): `http://matplotlib.org/`
- MongoDB (an open source document database): `http://www.mongodb.org`
- The mpi4py docs: `http://mpi4py.scipy.org/docs/usrman/index.html`
- NLTK (Natural Language Toolkit): `http://www.nltk.org/`
- NumPy and SciPy Documentation: `http://docs.scipy.org/doc/`
- NumPy and SciPy Mailing Lists: `http://www.scipy.org/Mailing_Lists`
- Open MPI (a high performance message passing library): `http://www.open-mpi.org`
- Packt Publishing help and support: `http://www.packtpub.com/support`
- The pandas home page: `http://pandas.pydata.org`
- Python performance tips: `https://wiki.python.org/moin/PythonSpeed/PerformanceTips`

- Redis (an open source, key-value store): `http://redis.io/`
- Scikit-learn (machine learning with Python):
  `http://scikit-learn.org/stable/`
- Scikit-learn performance tips:
  `http://scikit-learn.org/stable/developers/performance.html`
- SciPy performance tips: `http://wiki.scipy.org/PerformanceTips`
- SQLAlchemy (the Python SQL toolkit and Object Relational Mapper):
  `http://www.sqlalchemy.org`
- The Toolz utility functions documentation:
  `http://toolz.readthedocs.org/en/latest/`

Index

C

C 269
C++ 269
Cardinal Number (CD) tag 215
Cascading Style Sheets. *See* CSS
Cassandra
    key-value 208, 209
    references 207
    traditional relational databases 208, 209
Cassandra Query Language (CQL) 208, 306
C code
    calling 288-290
character codes 30, 306
classification
    performing, with logistic
        regression 238, 239
    performing, with support vector
        machines (SVM) 240, 241
cloud computing 263
clustering
    about 248, 306
    performing, with affinity
        propagation 248, 249
clusters 248
code
    profiling 280-283
coefficient of determination
    URL 242
cointegration
    about 170, 306
    defining 171-173
column families 207
column_stack function 38
column stacking 38
Command Line Interface (CLI) 21
Comma-separated Value (CSV) file 63
Comprehensive R Archive Network
    (CRAN) 265
concatenate() function 37
concat() function 104
corpora 211
correlate() function 174
crossover operator 253
CSS 138, 306

CSS selectors
    about 140, 306
    URL, for documentation 140
CSV files
    writing, with NumPy 120, 121
    writing, with pandas 120, 121
Cython
    installing 284, 287
cytoolz package 284

D

data
    querying, in pandas 94-96
    reading to Excel, with pandas 129, 130
    storing, in Redis 206
    storing, with PyTables 124-126
    writing to Excel, with pandas 129, 130
data aggregation 99-102
database
    accessing, from pandas 194, 195
    populating, with SQLAlchemy 198, 199
    querying, with SQLAlchemy 200
database cursor 192
DataFrame
    about 85-87
    appending 103, 104
    concatenating 103, 104
    creating 87-90
    data aggregation 99-102
    joining 105, 106
    pickling 122, 123
    reading, to HDF5 stores 126-128
    statistical methods 97, 98
    URL 87
    writing, to HDF5 stores 126-128
Data Science Toolbox
    URL 263
dataset 202, 203
datasets package 265
data structures, pandas
    DataFrame 85
    Series 85
data type objects 30, 306
dates
    dealing with 110-112

normality test, performing
    with SciPy 75-78
pseudo-random numbers 71
real random numbers 71
random_state parameter 239
rankdata() function 295
ravel function 34
read_sql() method 200
Really Simple Syndication. *See* RSS
real random numbers 71
Red Hat
    NumPy, installing on 12
Redis
    about 206
    data, storing in 206
    URL 206, 318
Reduce phase 296, 308
regression
    performing, with ElasticNetCV 242-244
reinforcement learning 234
relational database 191
remote data access 114-116
REmote DIctionary Server. *See* Redis
Representational State Transfer. *See* REST
reshape function 35
resize method 35
REST
    about 131, 308
    URL 131
REST web services
    using 131, 132
rfft() function 184
ridge method 242
rolling_mean() function 168
row_stack function 38
row stacking 38
rpy2
    installing 265
    reference link, for upgrading 265
R squared 242
RSS
    about 134, 308
    parsing 134, 135
    URL 134

S

scale() function 237
scatter plot
    about 148, 308
    creating 156, 157
scikit-learn
    about 235, 236
    functions 314
    references 318
SciPy
    about 9
    building, from source 14, 15
    git commands 15
    installing, with setup tools 15
    normality test, performing with 75-78
    references 23
    URL 11
scipy.constants module 265
scipy.fftpack
    functions 315
scipy.io.savemat() function 264
SciPy modules 59-61
scipy.optimize.leastsq() function 177
scipy.signal package
    about 187
    functions 315
scipy.stats
    functions 315
scipy.stats.kruskal() function 266
scipy.stats.rankdata() function 294
SciPy Superpack
    URL 13
score() method 239
semilogx() function 146
semilogy() function 146
sentiment analysis 222-224, 308
Series data structures
    about 85, 90
    creating 90-93
session, IPython shell
    saving 20
setup tools
    used, for installing IPython 15
    used, for installing matplotlib 15

W

Wakari
 URL 277
 working with 277, 278
WarGames
 reference link 234
Wiener filter
 about 187
 reference link 187
wiener() function 187
window function
 about 168
 reference link 168
Windows
 IPython, installing on 10, 11

word clouds
 creating 225-229
word frequencies
 analyzing 217, 218
Wordle
 about 225
 URL 225

Thank you for buying
Python Data Analysis

About Packt Publishing

Packt, pronounced 'packed', published its first book "*Mastering phpMyAdmin for Effective MySQL Management*" in April 2004 and subsequently continued to specialize in publishing highly focused books on specific technologies and solutions.

Our books and publications share the experiences of your fellow IT professionals in adapting and customizing today's systems, applications, and frameworks. Our solution based books give you the knowledge and power to customize the software and technologies you're using to get the job done. Packt books are more specific and less general than the IT books you have seen in the past. Our unique business model allows us to bring you more focused information, giving you more of what you need to know, and less of what you don't.

Packt is a modern, yet unique publishing company, which focuses on producing quality, cutting-edge books for communities of developers, administrators, and newbies alike. For more information, please visit our website: www.packtpub.com.

About Packt Open Source

In 2010, Packt launched two new brands, Packt Open Source and Packt Enterprise, in order to continue its focus on specialization. This book is part of the Packt Open Source brand, home to books published on software built around Open Source licenses, and offering information to anybody from advanced developers to budding web designers. The Open Source brand also runs Packt's Open Source Royalty Scheme, by which Packt gives a royalty to each Open Source project about whose software a book is sold.

Writing for Packt

We welcome all inquiries from people who are interested in authoring. Book proposals should be sent to author@packtpub.com. If your book idea is still at an early stage and you would like to discuss it first before writing a formal book proposal, contact us; one of our commissioning editors will get in touch with you.

We're not just looking for published authors; if you have strong technical skills but no writing experience, our experienced editors can help you develop a writing career, or simply get some additional reward for your expertise.

Parallel Programming with Python

ISBN: 978-1-78328-839-7   Paperback: 128 pages

Develop efficient parallel systems using the robust Python environment

1. Demonstrates the concepts of Python parallel programming.

2. Boosts your Python computing capabilities.

3. Contains easy-to-understand explanations and plenty of examples.

Building Probabilistic Graphical Models with Python

ISBN: 978-1-78328-900-4   Paperback: 172 pages

Solve machine learning problems using probabilistic graphical models implemented in Python with real-world applications

1. Stretch the limits of machine learning by learning how graphical models provide an insight on particular problems, especially in high dimension areas such as image processing and NLP.

2. Solve real-world problems using Python libraries to run inferences using graphical models.

3. A practical, step-by-step guide that introduces readers to representation, inference, and learning using Python libraries best suited to each task.

Please check **www.PacktPub.com** for information on our titles

Python Data Visualization Cookbook

ISBN: 978-1-78216-336-7   Paperback: 280 pages

Over 60 recipes that will enable you to learn how to create attractive visualizations using Python's most popular libraries

1. Learn how to set up an optimal Python environment for data visualization.

2. Understand the topics such as importing data for visualization and formatting data for visualization.

3. Understand the underlying data and how to use the right visualizations.

Building Machine Learning Systems with Python

ISBN: 978-1-78216-140-0   Paperback: 290 pages

Master the art of machine learning with Python and build effective machine learning systems with this intensive hands-on guide

1. Master machine learning using a broad set of Python libraries and start building your own Python-based ML systems.

2. Covers classification, regression, feature engineering, and much more guided by practical examples.

3. A scenario-based tutorial to get into the right mind-set of a machine learner (data exploration) and successfully implement this in your new or existing projects.

Please check **www.PacktPub.com** for information on our titles

www.ingramcontent.com/pod-product-compliance
Lightning Source LLC
Chambersburg PA
CBHW062056050326
40690CB00016B/3112